THE COMPLETE ANTIQUE SHOP DIRECTORY

FOR MICHIGAN

Listing Every Known Antique Shop and Mall in the State

Plus for Many Shops:

Days & Hours of Operation
Directions for Finding Shop & Malls
Detailed Maps Showing Locations
Size or Specialty of the Shop

Published by:

Downtown Research Company
Edward Lawrence
208 Fairhope Ave. Suite 6
Fairhope AL 36532

334-990-2489
AntiqueDir@aol.com
www.AntiqueShops.net

 Printed in the United States of America. ISBN Number 1-930042-01-9

THE 2001 COMPLETE ANTIQUE SHOP DIRECTORY FOR MICHIGAN

- - Table of Contents - -

-- Table of Contents, continued --

Index of Towns and Cities

City, County Sequence Number, County, Page

HOW THE BOOK IS ORGANIZED

Antique shops are listed geographically, starting with the southern-most tier of counties and working north. Within each tier, counties are listed from west to east. The First Chapter contains those counties in the southern tier, along the Indiana and Ohio border. The Second Chapter includes the counties in the next tier of counties to the north, etc.

Within each county shops are grouped by town or city, generally moving from north to south and west to east. Maps for each county, and many cities, show locations of antique shops contributing to the cost of printing the book.

Each county has an identification number. The number to the left of the decimal point is the Tier Number. The number to the right of the decimal point is the County Sequence Number within that Tier.

Efforts have been made to make this Directory as complete and accurate as possible. Antique shops do close and move, however, and new ones open. The Publisher cannot be responsible for erroneous or outdated information. Users of this Directory should be aware that hours indicated are "targets", and that sometimes antique dealers go to auctions or are gone on personal business, and may not be in at a time they are normally open. It is always best to call if you intend to drive out of your way to visit a shop. Please send or E-mail a note to the publisher with any additions or corrections.

Index of Counties

Tier & Sequence Number & County

Map of Michigan: Southern Portion of Lower Peninsula

5.4 Tier and County Sequence Number

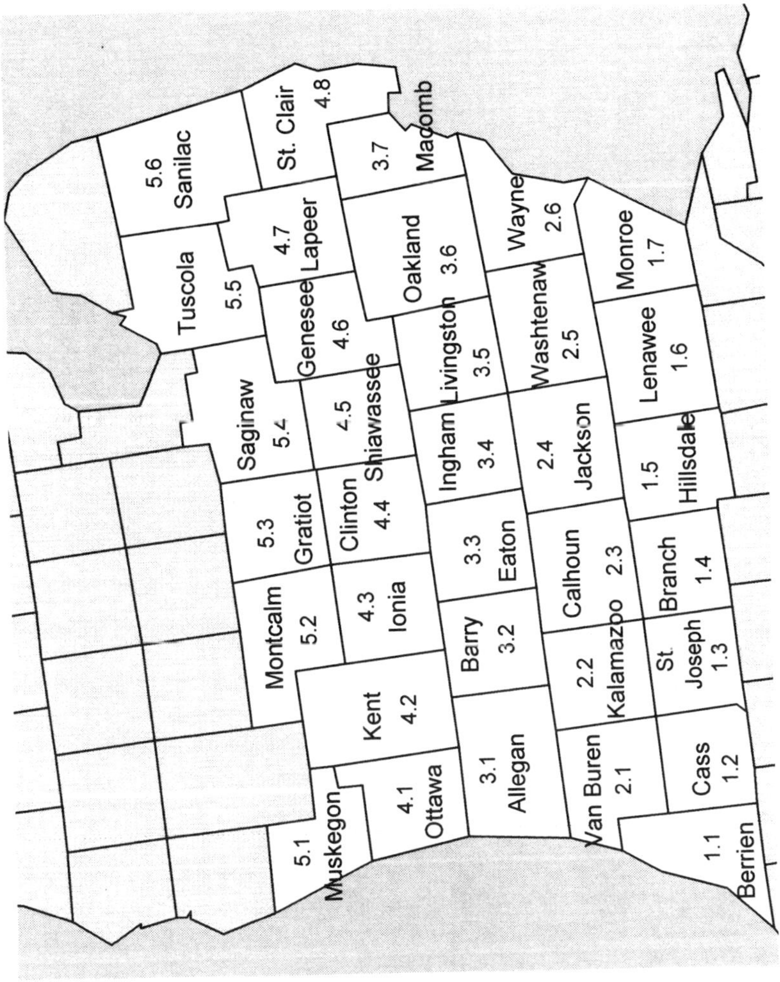

Tier 1 Along the Indiana & Ohio Border
Tier 2 The I-94 Route
Tier 3 Saugatuck-Lansing-Royal Oak
Tier 4 Grand Rapids-Flint-Port Huron
Tier 5 The M-46 Route

Map of Michigan:
Northern Portion of Lower Peninsula

9.4 Tier and County Sequence Number

Tier 6 The M-20 Route
Tier 7 Ludington-Gladwin-Standish
Tier 8 The M-55 Route
Tier 9 The M-72 Route
Tier 10 The M-32 Route
Tier 11 South of Mackinac

Map of Michigan, Upper Peninsula

12.03	Tier and County Sequence Number

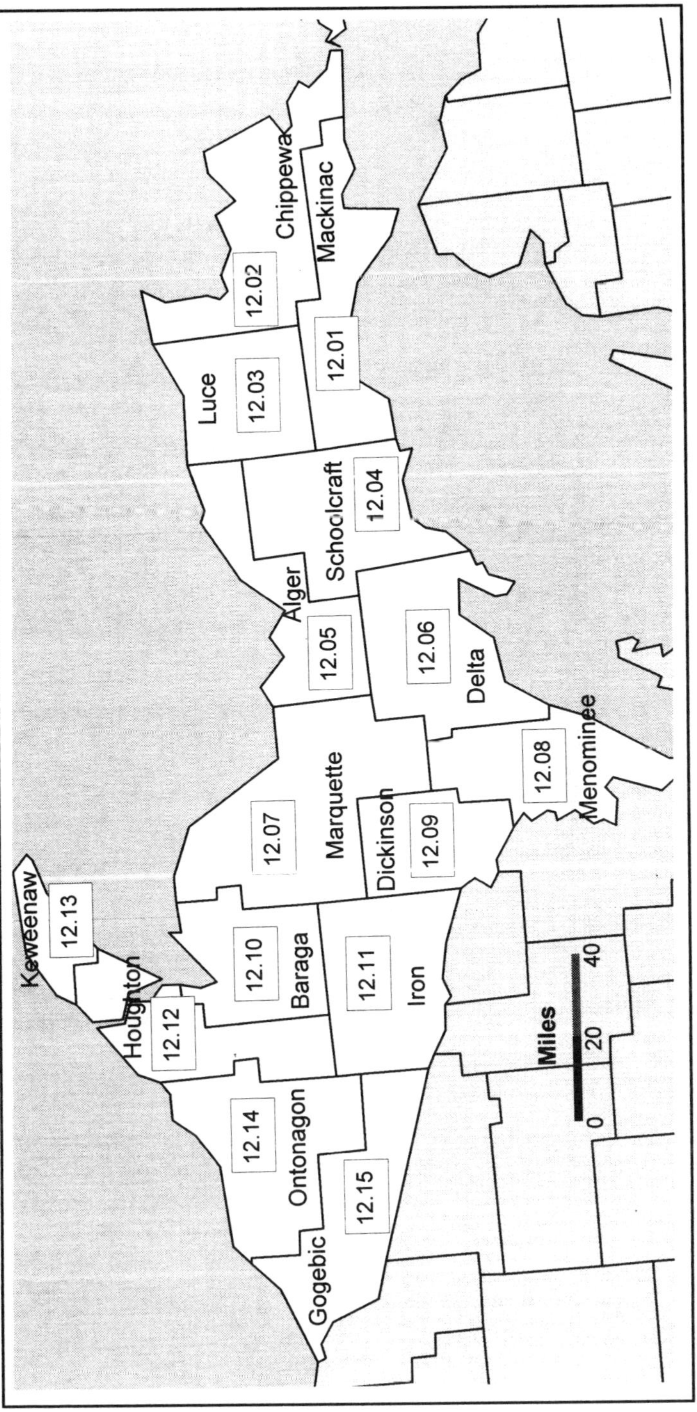

TIER 1:
ALONG THE INDIANA & OHIO BORDER

1.1 Berrien County

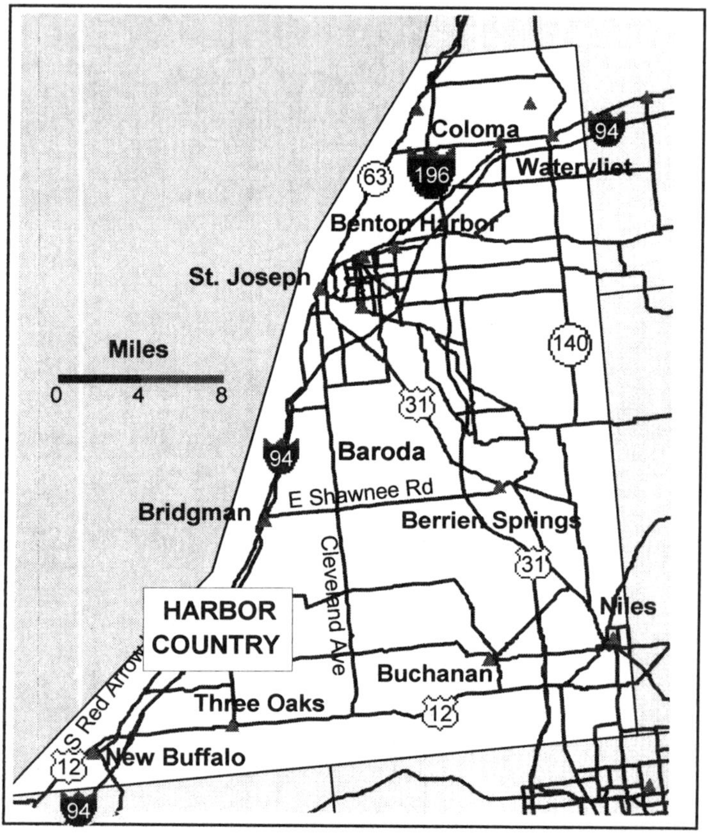

NEW BUFFALO

1 Rainbow's End Antiques
18712 LaPorte Road (Whittaker), New Buffalo MI 49117
616 469-2655
May to Oct.: Daily 10 to 6;
Nov. to April: Sat. & Sun. 10 to 5
I-94 Exit 1, west one block toward New Buffalo.
General line of furniture and other quality antiques.

New Buffalo, Union Pier, Lakeside:

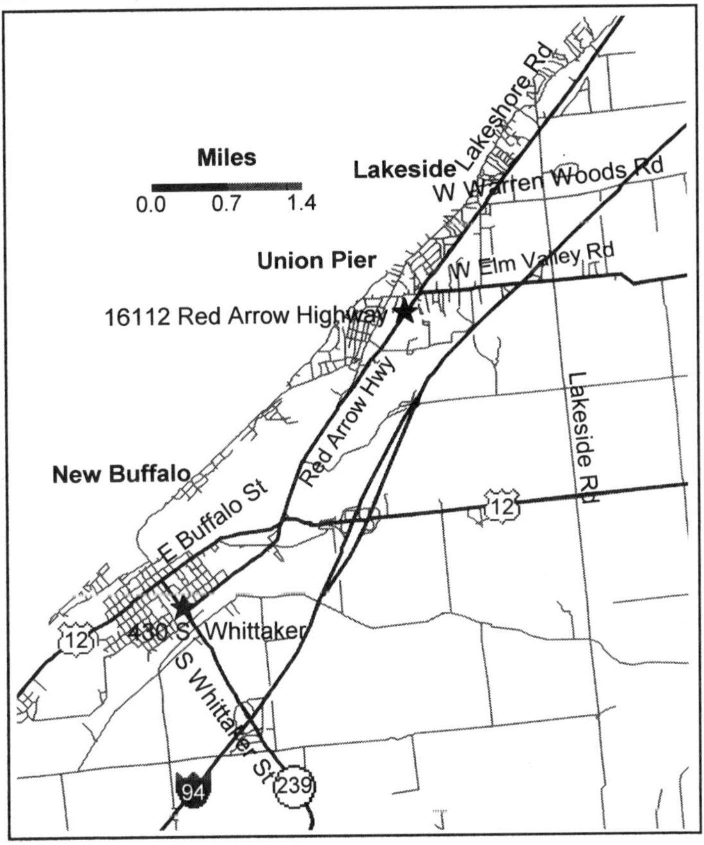

2 Classic Galleries
430 South Whittaker Street, New Buffalo MI 49117
616 469-6281; Fax: 616 469-6280
Daily 11 to 6
Midway between I-94 Exit 1 and downtown New Buffalo, west side of street.
European antiques, garden statuary, bronzes, marble, lighting, home furnishings. Auctions several times a year.

3 Da Barn Antiques
U.S. Highway 12, New Buffalo MI 49117
616 943-4456 Open weekends only.

UNION PIER

4 The Plum Tree
16337 Red Arrow Highway, Union Pier MI 49129
616 469-5980 Open weekends only.

5 K.L.M. Galleries
16142 Red Arrow Highway, Union Pier MI 49129
616 469-6957

6 Frog Forest Findings
16100 York Road, Union Pier MI 49129
616 469-7050
Fri. to Mon. 12 to 6; hours subject to change. Closed January.
West of I-94 Exit 6, south side of Union Pier Road.
Gas Station memorabilia, furniture, and new stuff.

7 Union Pier Antique Mall
9300 Union Pier Road, Union Pier MI 49129
616 469-2555 I-94 Exit 6

LAKESIDE

(Map on previous page.)

8 Fenway Gallery
14958 Lakeside Road, Lakeside MI 49116
616-469-2818 www.fenwaygallery.com
Art and some antiques.

9 Lakeside Antique Center
14876 Red Arrow Highway, Lakeside MI 49116
616 469-7717 lakeside_antiques@yahoo.com
www.lakesideantiques.com
May to Sept.: Daily 11 to 6;
Oct. to April: Fri. to Mon. 11 to 6
Five miles north of New Buffalo.
French, English & Americana.

10 Lakeside Antiques
14866 Red Arrow Highway, Lakeside MI 49116
616 469-4467 or 616 469-0341 for appointments

HARBERT

11 The Good The Bad & The Ugly
10385 Red Arrow Highway, Harbert MI 49115
616-469-7105

HARBOR COUNTRY: *The southwest corner of Berrien County including New Buffalo, Union Pier, Lakeside, Harbert, Sawyer, and Three Oaks.*

Harbert & Sawyer:

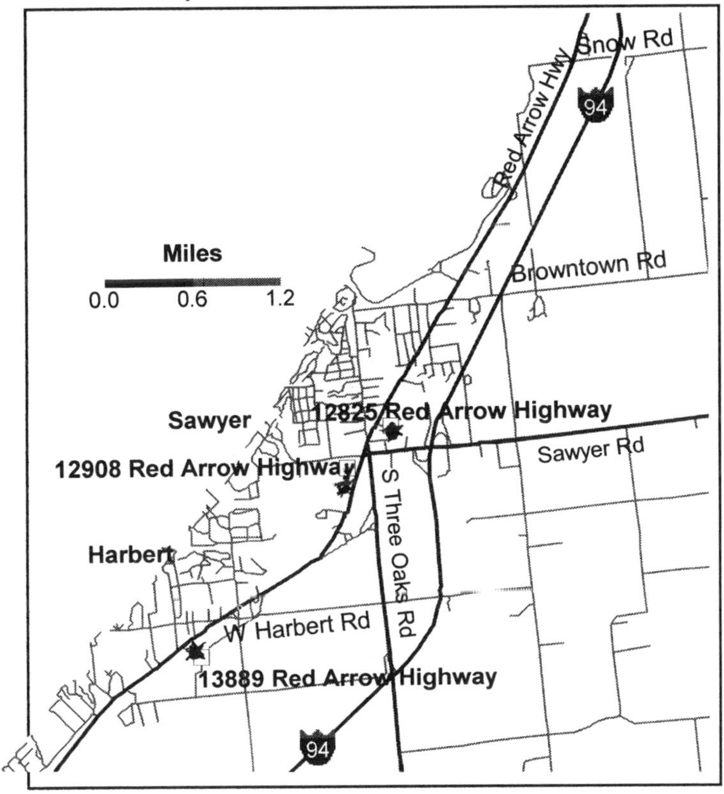

12 Harbert Antique Mall
13889 Red Arrow Highway, Harbert MI 49115
616 469-0977
Mon. to Fri. 10 to 6, Sat. 10 to 7, Sun. 12 to 7
Closed Wed. in winter.
East side of highway.
Featuring upholstered furniture, art, vintage chandeliers & lighting, fine glass, pottery, collectibles.
50 dealers.

13 Marco Polo Antiques
13630 Red Arrow Highway, P.O. Box 331, Harbert MI 49115
616 469-6272

14 Callas
13446 Red Arrow Highway, Harbert MI 49115
616 469-3674

SAWYER

(Map on previous page.)

15 Nestings
13025 Red Arrow Highway, Sawyer MI 49125
616 426-8109
Antiques, art, home accessories.

16 Jeff's Trading Post
13212 Red Arrow Highway, Sawyer MI 49125
616 426-3145
Hoosier Cabinets, glass & bottles, etc.

17 Timeless Treasures Antiques & Collectibles
12908 Red Arrow Highway, Sawyer MI 49127
616 426-3636
April to Nov.: Daily 10:30 to 5:30;
Dec. to March: Thurs. to Mon. 10:30 to 5:30
Southwest corner Red Arrow Highway & Sawyer Road.
General line of antiques & collectibles.

18 Dunes Antique Center, Inc.
12825 Red Arrow Highway, Sawyer MI 49125
Phone: 616 426-4043; Fax: 616 426-8238;
www.dunesantiques.com
Mon. to Sat. 10 to 6, Sun. 11 to 6, closed Tues.
I-94 Exit 12, then 300 yards west; east side of Red Arrow Highway, just north of Sawyer Road.
Over 70 dealers; art, pottery, furniture, glass, etc.

19 Tara Hill Antique Mall
12816 Red Arrow Highway, Sawyer MI 49125
616 426-8673

20 Stewart James Antiques Galleria
12619 Red Arrow Highway, Sawyer MI 49125
616-426-3133

20.5 Rabbit Run Art & Antiques
12274 Red Arrow Highway, Sawyer MI 49125
616-426-6017
Recently moved from Douglas.

THREE OAKS

Three Oaks:

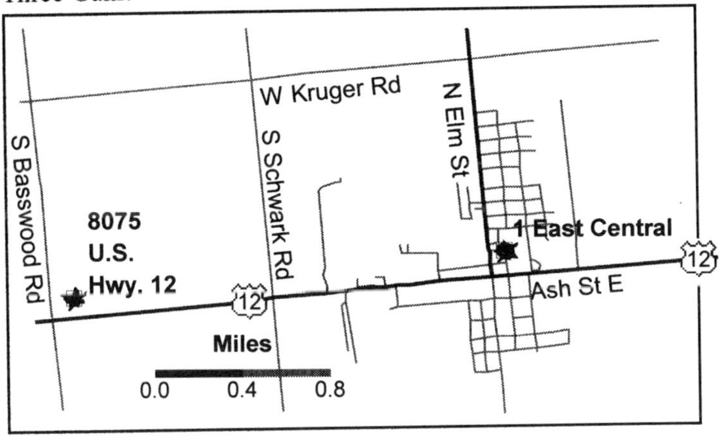

21 Hank's Ole School House
8075 U.S. Highway 12 West, Three Oaks MI
(P.O. Box 383 Union Pier MI 49129)
616 469-4015; Res. & fax: 773-721-6086
Memorial Day to Labor Day: Sat. 10 to 5, Sun. 10 to 4;
Labor Day to Nov.: Weekends by chance.
Half way between New Buffalo and Three Oaks, north side of highway, at Basswood Road.
Collectibles, antiques, resale.

22 Springdale
17 South Elm Street, Three Oaks MI 49129
(P.O. Box 34, Hartford MI 49057)
Phone & fax: 616 621-3642
Springdale is currently located at Lakeside Antiques, in Lakeside. The shop will be relocating to this location in 2001.

23 Jenney's Antiques
9 North Elm Street, Three Oaks MI 49128
616 756-7219 Closed Christmas until March or April.

24 The Heartworks Antiques & Collectibles
1 East Central Drive, Three Oaks MI 49128
616 756-9800 hrtwrks@triton.net
Memorial Day to end of Sept.: Thurs. thru Sun. 11 to 5:30;
Winter: Fri. thru Sun. 11 to 5:30
Half block east of downtown, just north of the tracks.
"Antiques & collectibles to warm the heart."

BRIDGMAN

Bridgman & Baroda:

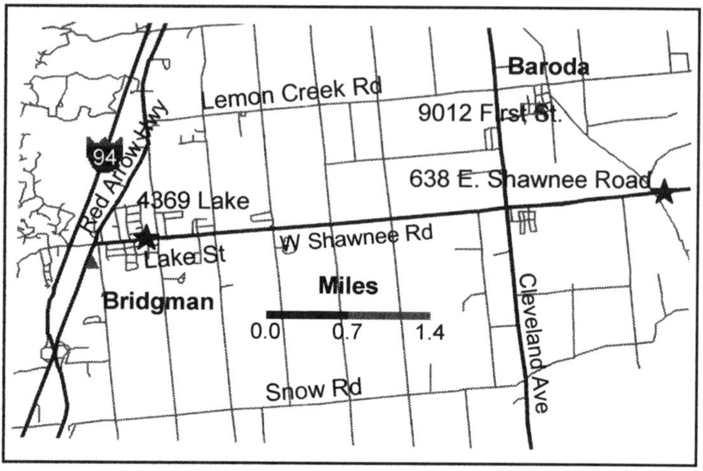

25 Rideout Antiques
4369 Lake Street, Bridgman MI 49106
616 465-6855
Mon. to Fri. 10 to 5; Sun. 1 to 6;
Closed Centerville Sundays and April 1 to 18.
Red Arrow Highway to stoplight, east on Lake St. (Shawnee Road); tan & tiel stucco 2 story building on left.
Glass, china, silverplate, vintage, & unusual small items.

BARODA

26 Shawnee Road Antiques
638 East Shawnee Road, Baroda MI 49101
616 422-1382
April to Dec. 1: Every day 1 to 5.
Winter: by chance or appointment.
Midway between Berrien Springs and Bridgman, south side of road.
Furniture, quality smalls and collectibles.

27 Homeless Treasures
9012 First Street, P.O. Box 342 , Baroda MI 49101
616 422-6110; Fax: 616-422-6129 homtr@aol.com
Every day 10:30 to 6
Two blocks south of intersection of Stevensville-Baroda Road and Lemon Creek Road.
Wide assortment of antiques and furniture. Also custom furniture refinishing & repair; furniture is hand stripped.

28 Classics
9004 First Street, P.O. Box 155, Baroda MI 49101
616 422-1991 Floral shop, gifts, and antiques.

STEVENSVILLE

29 Bill's Real Antiques
7566 Red Arrow Highway, Stevensville MI 49127
616 465-3246

30 J's Bit of Everything
4173 Red Arrow Highway, Stevensville MI 49127
616-429-1577

NILES

Niles:

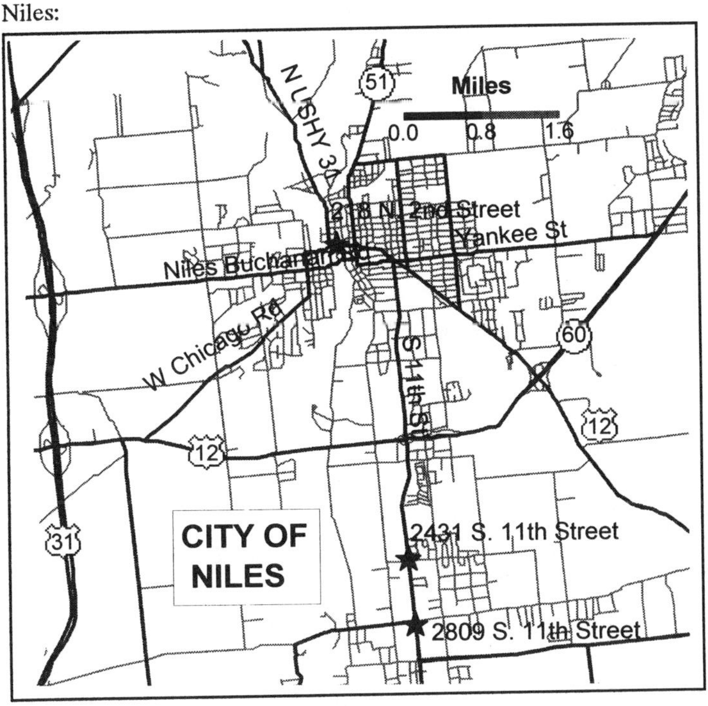

31 Michiana Antique Mall
2423 South 11th St. (Bus. U.S. 31/M 51), Niles MI 49120
616 684-7001; 800 559-4694
E-mail: michianaantiquemall@compuserve.com
Web-site: www.michianaantiquemall.com
7 days, 10 to 6 (Closed four major holidays.)
East side of highway, between Niles and South Bend.
94 dealers, 27,000 square feet; air conditioned.

32 Picker's Paradise Antique Mall
2809 South 11th Street (Highway M-51), Niles MI 49120
616 683-6644
7 days, 10 to 6
East side of highway, between Niles and South Bend.
107 dealers, 30,000 square feet.

33 Oak Street Antiques & Collectibles
1008 Oak Street, Niles MI 49120
No telephone listed.

34 Yankee Heirloom
211 North 2nd Street, Niles MI 49120
616-684-0462; 616-684-3588 Open by appointment only.

35 Four Flags Antique Mall
218 North 2nd Street, Niles MI 49120
616 683-6681
Summer: Mon. to Sat. 10 to 6, Sun. 12 to 6;
Winter: Mon. to Fri. 10 to 5, Sat. 10 to 6, Sun. 12 to 6
Downtown Historic Niles, a block north of the main street.
22,000 square feet, 60 dealers.

36 Niles Antique Mall
220 North Front Street, Niles MI 49120
616 683-6652 Antiques, decoys, used furniture, etc.

37 B & B Carriage Trade Antiques
305 East Main, Niles MI 49120
616-684-0756

Note: a shop with a Niles address is located in 1.2, Cass County.

BUCHANAN

38 Millrace Antiques & Collectibles
122 East Front Street, Buchanan MI 49107
616 695-2005

SODUS

39 Virgo Antiques
4106 River Road, P.O. Box 2, Sodus MI 49126
616 927-3880
Sat. & Sun. 12 to 5, or by chance. Closed Jan. 1 to May 1.
From Exit 29 of I-94 go south on Pipestone Road, left at stop sign, right on River Road.
Primitives, cut glass, etc.

Sodus Area:

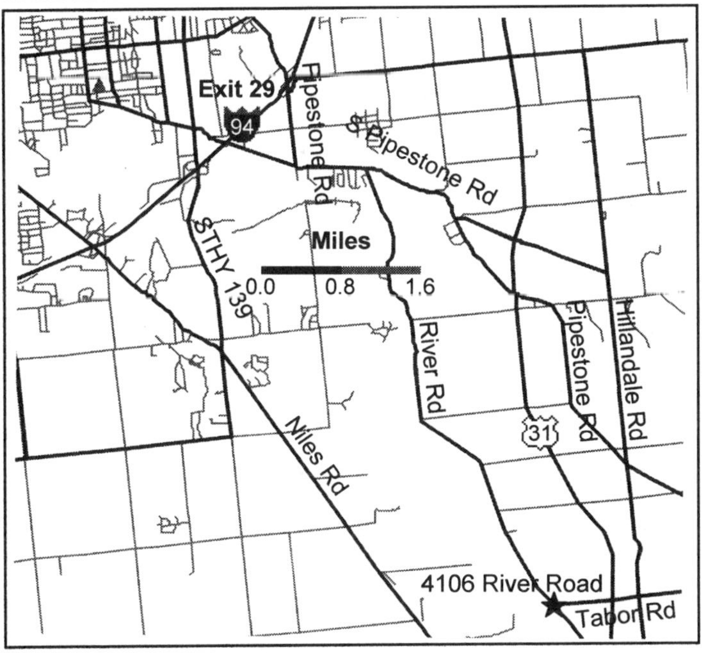

BERRIEN SPRINGS

40 More & More Antiques & Collectibles
6659 U.S. 31 & 33, Berrien Springs MI 49103
616 428-9084
A block south of Rocky Weed Road.

ST. JOSEPH

St. Joseph & Benton Harbor:

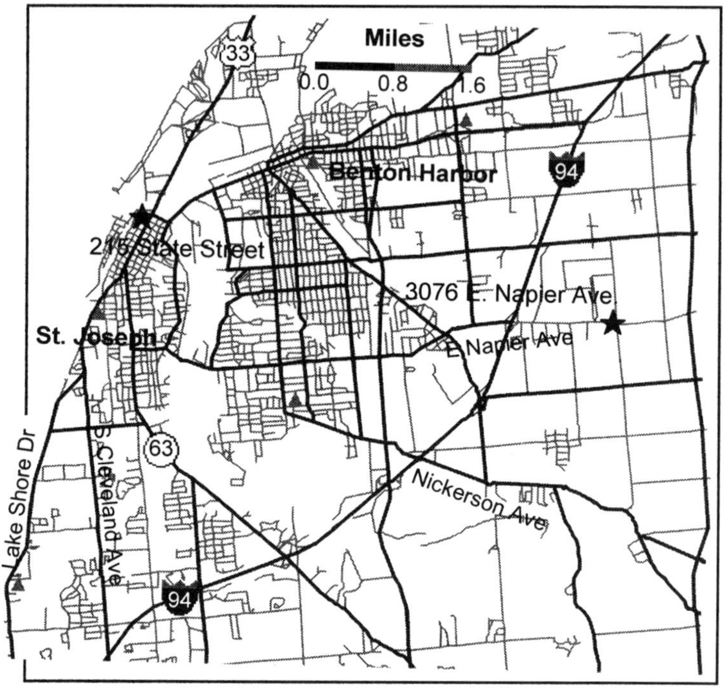

41 Anvil Antiques
3439 Hollywood Road, St. Joseph MI 49085
616 429-5132 East from I-94 Exit 27 on M-63 1 block, south on Hollywood one block.

42 Miller's Antiques & Collectibles
719 Gard Avenue, St. Joseph MI 49085
616 983-2900; Fax: 616 983-2940

43 Days of Yore
215 State Street, St. Joseph MI 49085
616 983-4144
cbyore@cpuinc.net
April thru Dec.: Mon. to Sat. 10 to 5, Sun. 12 to 5
Closed major holidays.
Downtown, east side of the street, a block west of Bus. 94.
Furniture, 50's items, jewelry, china, glass, misc.

44 Upper Crust Giftware & Antiques
312 State Street - Suite A, Saint Joseph MI 49085
(616) 983-7766

BENTON HARBOR

45 Good Old Times Antiques
3076 East Napier Avenue, Benton Harbor MI 49022
616 925-8422
Most days: 1 to 4 by chance or appointment.
1 mile east of I-94 Exit 30, south side of road.
Large selection of quality furniture and accessories.

COLOMA

Coloma & Watervliet:

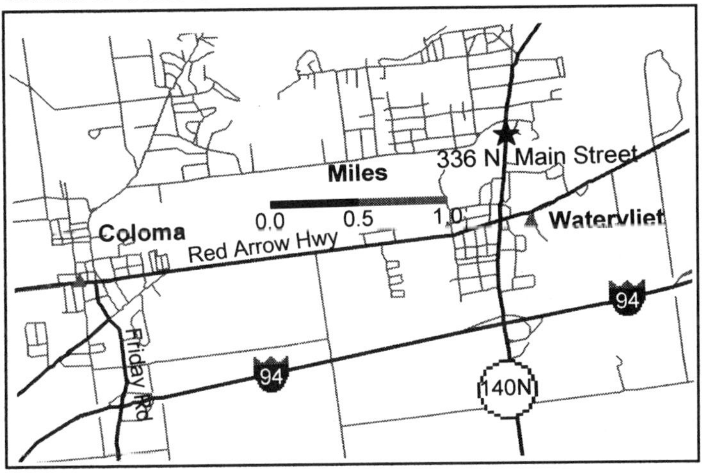

46 Linda's Antiques & Crafts
120 N. Church Street, P.O. Box 70, Coloma MI 49038
616 468-7917

47 The Millstone Shop
6162 Martin Road, Coloma MI 49038
616 468-6667
East from I-96 (Exit 7) on Hagar Shore 3/4 mile, south on Martin, first building on the west side.

48 Myrt's Antiques & Collectibles
82331 45th Avenue, Coloma MI 49038
616 849-0536
Summer: Every day 9 to 7;
Winter: Every day 10 to 4, but call first.
From I-196 take Exit 7 west to the Blue Star Highway, then go north 2.5 miles to 145th Street and go right; shop is in the rear of the first house to the right.
Furniture, glassware, collectibles, etc.

WATERVLIET

(Map on previous page.)

49 Trade Winds Antiques
336 North Main Street, Watervliet MI 49098
616 463-8281 twlarry@cybersol.com
Every Day 10 to 5; Sun. 12 to 5
I-94 Exit 41, north to Downtown.
Collectibles, glass, postcards, and general line.
Also: full service bead store.

50 Z's Antiques
7579 Red Arrow Highway West, P.O. Box 345, Watervliet MI 49098
616 463-5487

Note: All Military Antiques has moved to Bloomingdale in Van Buren County.

Eastern Niles area:

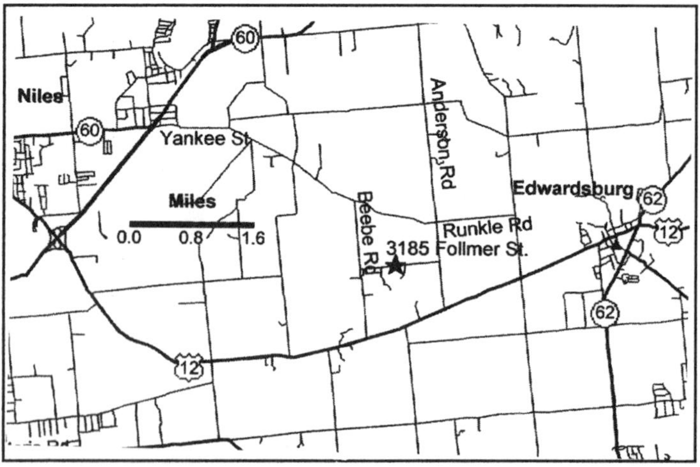

1.2 Cass County

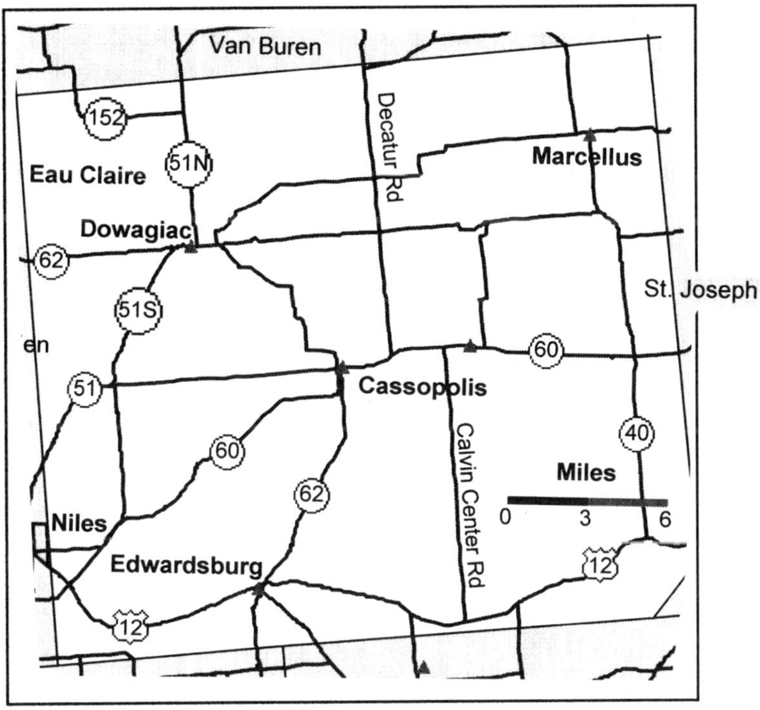

EDWARDSBURG

1 Argus Antiques
26878 West Main Street (U.S. 12), P. O. Box 416,
Edwardsburg MI 49112 616-663-2883

2 Peddler's Antiques
26828 West Main Street, Edwardsburg MI 49112
616-663-8305

NILES

Note: The main part of Niles is in Berrien County, Section 1.1.

3 B. & J. Antiques
3185 Follmer Street, Niles MI 49120
616-663-8354
Tues. to Sat. 12 to 5:30, Sun. by Chance.
8 miles east of Niles, north of U.S. 12 between Anderson & Bebee Streets.
General line. *(See map on opposite page.)*

EAU CLAIRE

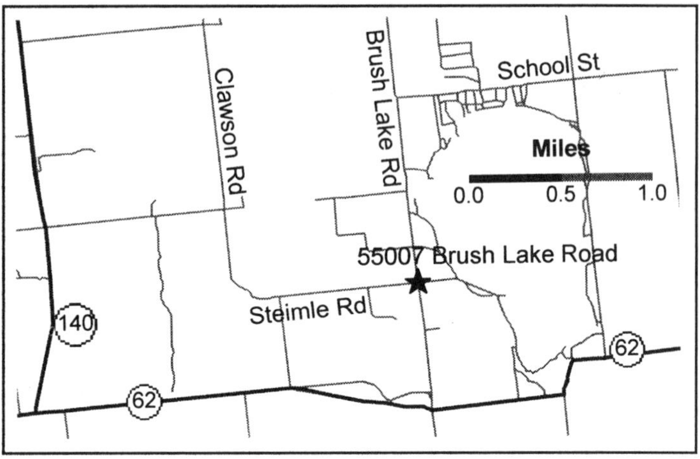

4 Oak Hill Antiques
6520 Brush Lake Road (at Eureka), Eau Claire MI 49098
616-782-9292

5 Walmar Antiques
55007 Brush Lake Road, Eau Claire MI 49111
616-782-2315
Open by appointment or chance. It's the Huff residence, so they are there most of the time.
Corner of Brush Lake & Eureka Roads, a quarter mile north of Indian Lake Golf Course.
Furniture, glass, pottery, & primitives

DOWAGIAC

6 Galeria Dowagiac
202 South Front Street, Dowagiac MI 49047
616-782-1160
Mon. to Sat. 10 to 5, or by appointment
June 1 thru Labor Day: Also Thurs. to 9 & Sun 11 to 4
Downtown, corner of Front and Commercial.
Antiques, art, gifts and accessories.
Also Custom framing.

Dowagiac:

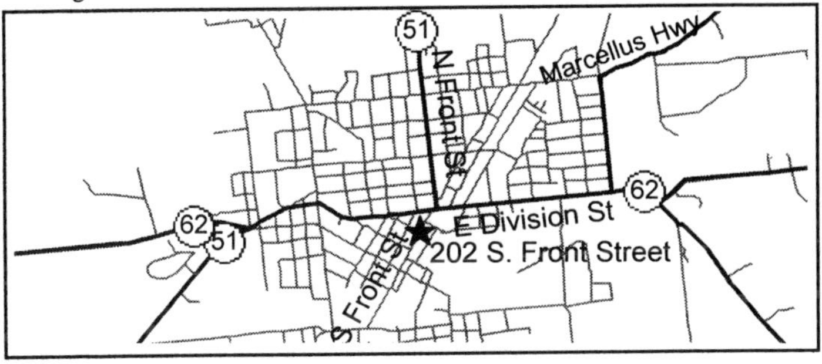

7 Golden Arrow Antiques
200 S. Front Street, Dowagiac MI 49047

8 Hairitage
123 S. Front Street, Dowagiac MI 49047 616-782-3693

CASSOPOLIS

9 Antique Haven
637 S. O'Keefe Street, Cassopolis MI 49031
616-445-3671 antiquehaven@aol.com
www.rubylane.com\shops\ayne-tique
www.rubylane.com\shops\annietiques
Most days 9 to 5, Sun. 12 to 5, closed Wed.; call ahead.
South of downtown, east side of the street.
Fine country antiques and smalls.
Antique & household appraisals by Jayme-Ayne Peregrine.

1.3 St. Joseph County

CONSTANTINE

1 J & K Floral & Country Cupboard
145 South Washington, Constantine MI 49042
616-435-2175
Flowers, gifts, and some antiques.

2 Antique Stoppe
63941 U.S. 131 North, Constantine MI 49042
616-244-5596

THREE RIVERS

3 Nettie Dee's Antiques
25 North Main Street, Three Rivers MI 49093
616-273-9579
Tues. to Sat. 10:30 to 5:00; Sun. & Mon. by chance.
Downtown
Dolls, Carnival Glass, furniture, quality dishes, etc.

Three Rivers:

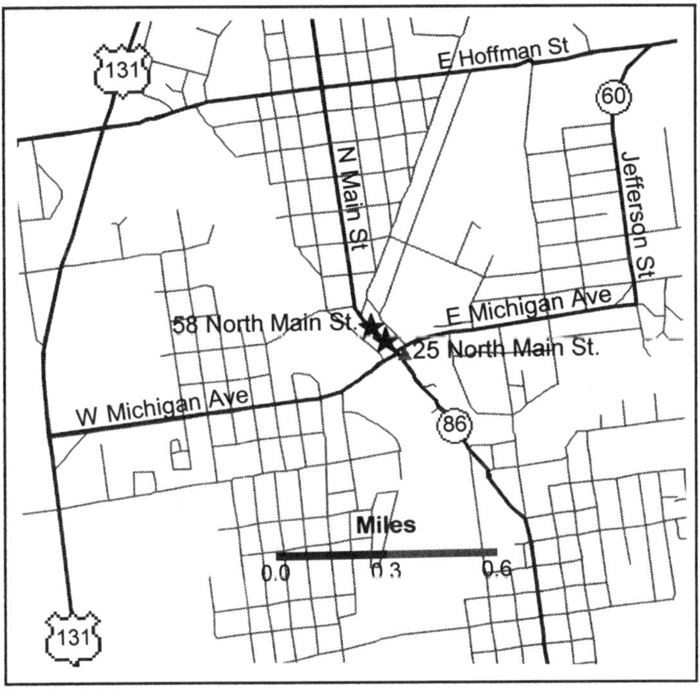

4 Antoinettes Antiques
51 North Main Street, Three Rivers MI 49093
616-273-3333
Hunting, fishing, sporting antiques.

5 Olde Town Antiques
58 North Main Street, Three Rivers MI 49093
616-273-2596
Daily 10 to 5, Sun. 12 to 5, closed Tues.
Downtown, west side of street.
Furniture and a general line of antiques.

6 Links to the Past
52631 U.S. 131, Three Rivers MI 49093
616-279-7310
Mon. to Sat. 10 to 5, Sun. 11 to 5, closed Wed.
Mid-way between Three Rivers & Schoolcraft, east side of highway U.S. 131 (20 minutes from the Indiana State line).
Antiques, books, collectibles; 3,000 square feet.

7 Rust & Dust
52601 U.S. 131 North, Three Rivers MI 49093
616-273-3288 rustanddust@earthlink.net

STURGIS

8 The Collectors' Place
208 East Chicago Road (U.S. 12), Sturgis MI 49091
616-659-6066

9 Antiques
1904 East Chicago , Sturgis MI 49091
616-651-6455
Garage on the side of the house.

10 Jan Douglas Antiques
30205 East Fawn River Road, Sturgis MI 49091
616-651-7471
Fawn River Road is 1.5 miles south of East U.S. 12.

LEONIDAS

11 Remember When Antique Mall
100 M-60, P.O. Box 24, Leonidas MI
616-496-3595

Branch County:

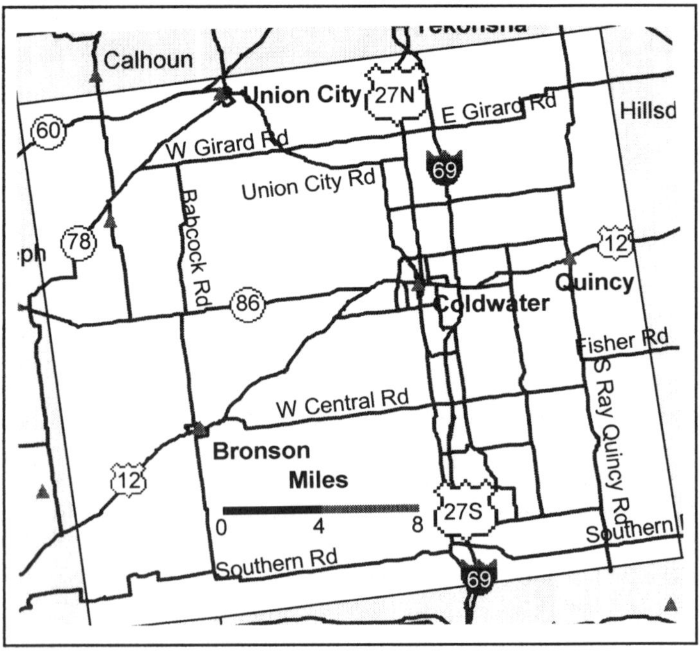

1.4 Branch County

(Map on previous page.)

BRONSON

1 Shackleton's Antiques
103 East Chicago, Bronson MI 49028

QUINCY

2 Collector's Paradise Antique Mall
47 East Chicago Road (U.S. 12), Quincy MI 49082
No telephone listed.

3 Mel's Antique Emporium
929 U.S. Highway 12, Quincy MI 49082
517-639-5803

4 The Old Granary
128 E. Chicago Street (U.S. 12), Quincy MI 49082
517-639-8485

5 Quincy House Antiques
851 East Chicago Street, Quincy MI 49036
517-278-7727; 517-639-9527

UNION CITY

(Map on following page.)

6 Raymond's Country Barn Antiques
950 Union City Road, Union City MI 49094
517 279-9370

7 19th Century Lighting Co.
601 N. Broadway Street, Union City MI 49094
800-348-4552
lampman@19thcenturylighting.com
www.19thcenturylighting.com
Wed. to Sat. by chance or appointment.
Located at the Victorian Villa Bed & Breakfast Inn.
Quality Victorian Art Glass Chamber Lighting.

Union City:

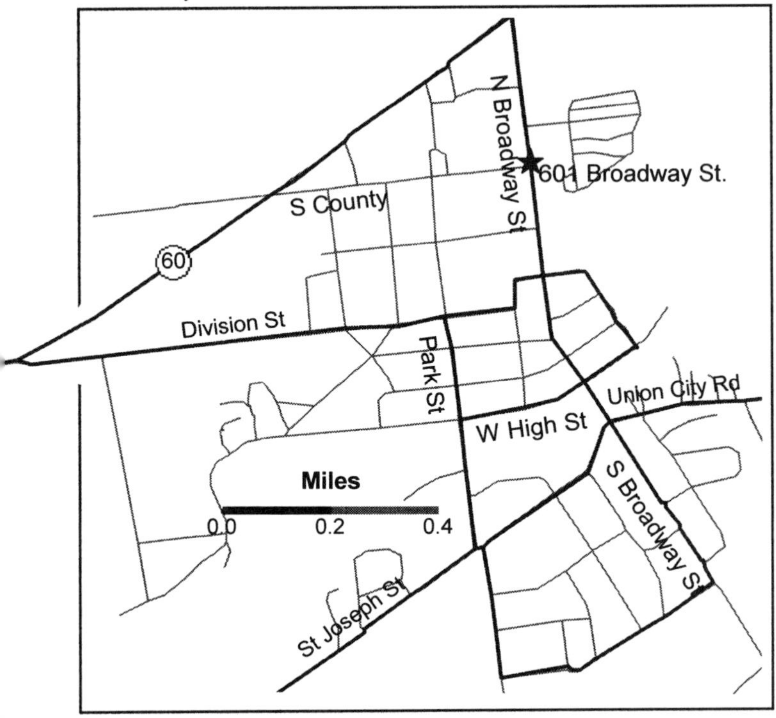

1.5 Hillsdale County

(Map on following page.)

ALLEN

1 Brown's Antiques & Refinishing
9260 West Chicago Road, Allen MI 49227
517 869-6969

2 Capital Antiques Mall
9115 West Chicago Road (U.S. 12)
517 869-2055

3 Allen Antique Mall
9011 West Chicago Road, P.O. Box 35, Allen MI 49227
517 869-2788

Hillsdale County:

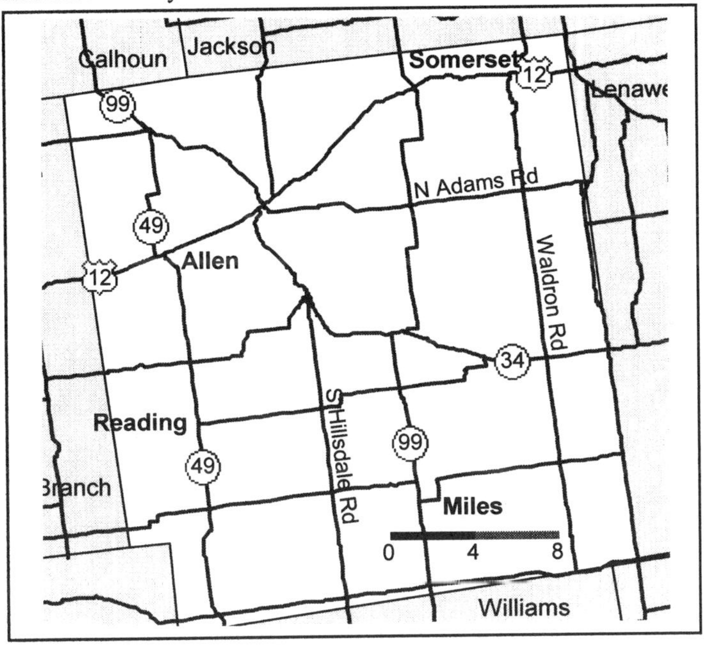

4 Peddlers Alley
162 West Chicago Road, Allen MI 49227
517 869-2280 shop; 517 523-3741 home

5 160 W. Chicago Antiques
160 West Chicago Road, Allen MI 49227
517 869-2929

6 Antique Mall
Proposed at the site of the former Andy's Antique Shop.
118 W. Chicago Road, Allen MI 49227

7 Old Allen Township Hall Shops
114 West Chicago Road, P.O. Box 7, Allen MI 49227
517 869-2575
postmaster@allsystemsgallery.com
www.allsystemsgallery.com/ethnoart
Every day 10 to 5
Downtown, north side of street.
Cowboy & Indian folk & tribal art; vintage clothing; Heisey Glass.

8 Simple Pleasures
109 West Chicago Road, P.O. Box 134, Allen MI 49227
517 869-2875

9 Hand & Hearts Antiques & Folk Carvings
109 West Chicago Road, Allen MI 49068
517 869-2553

10 Michiana Antiques
100-104 West Chicago Road, Allen MI 49227
517 869-2132

READING

11 The Finer Things
112 East Michigan Street, Reading MI 49274
517 283-2451

SOMERSET CENTER

12 Bob's Antiques
12611 Chicago Rd. (U.S. 12), Somerset Center MI 49282
517 688-3596

SOMERSET

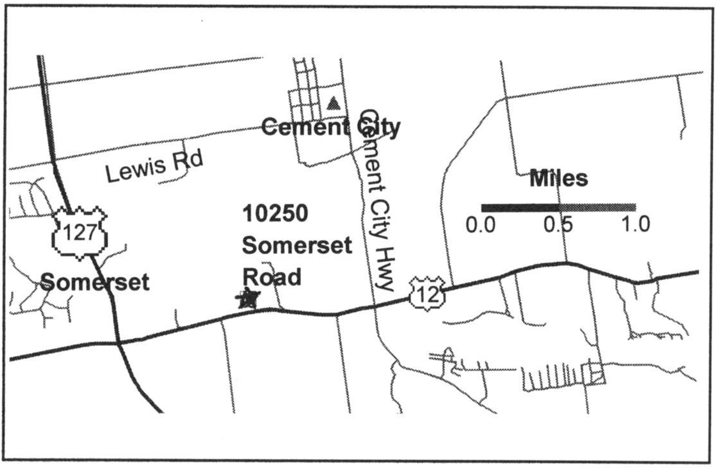

13 Oak Hill Antiques
10250 Somerset Road (U.S. 12), P.O. Box 171, Somerset MI 49281
517 547-4195
Daily: 10 to 6:30, Sun. 12 to 5, closed Tues.
One mile west of U.S. 12 & 127, north side of the highway.
Fine furniture & collectibles, lamp restoration (oil & electric), lamp shades, furniture repair, picture frame restoration & framing

1.6 Lenawee County

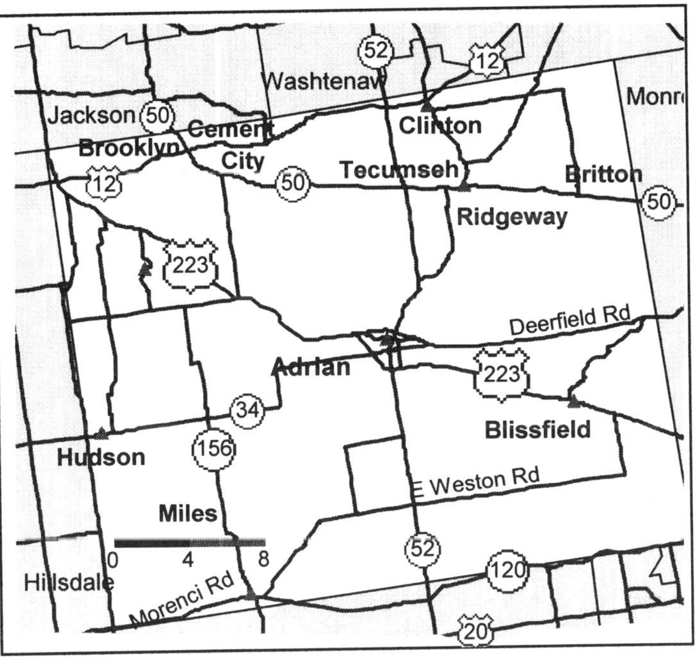

CEMENT CITY

1 Artesian Wells Antique Mall
U.S. Highways 12 & 127, Cement City MI 49233
517 547-7422

BROOKLYN

NOTE: The main part of Brooklyn, with three antique shops, is located in Jackson County.

2 The Enchanted Schoolhouse
14012 U.S. Highway 12 , Brooklyn MI 49230
517 592-4365; Fax: 517 467-2259

3 Muggsie's Antiques and Collectibles
13982 West U.S. Highway 12, Brooklyn MI 49230
517 592-2659

4 Brick Walker Tavern Antiques
11705 U.S. Highway 12, Brooklyn MI 49230
517 467-6961

5 Irish Hills Antiques
10600 U.S. Highway 12, Brooklyn MI 49230
517 467-4646

ONSTED

6 Bahlau's Trading Post
8410 US Highway 12, Onsted MI 49265
517-467-7277

ADRIAN

7 Marsh's Antique Mall
136 South Winter Street, Adrian MI 49221
517 263-8826

8 Birdsall Depot
4106 North Adrian (M-52 North), Adrian MI 49221
517 265-7107

BLISSFIELD

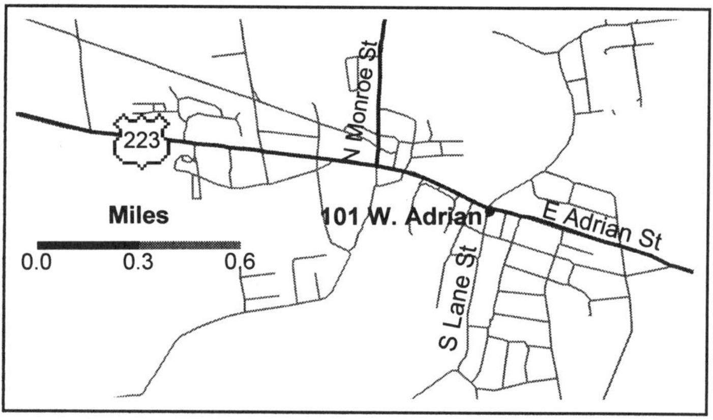

9 J & B Antiques Mall
109 West Adrian Street (U.S. 223), Blissfield MI 49228
517 486-3544

10 Blissfield Antique Mall
101 West Adrian Street, P.O. Box 114, Blissfield MI 49228
517 486-2236
Mon. to Sat. 10 to 5:30; Sun. 12 to 5
8 miles west of U.S. 23.
50 dealers

11 Williams Crossroads
10003 Adrian Street (U.S. 223 East), Blissfield MI 49228
517 486-3315

12 Memories on Lane Street
104 South Lane Street, Blissfield MI 49228
517 486-2327
Weekends

13 Blissfield General Store
105 South Lane, Blissfield MI 49228
517 486-5060
Antiques, gifts, sundries.

14 Green's Gallery Of Antiques
115 South Lane Street, Blissfield MI 49228
Days: 517 486-3080; Eves: 517 486-3025
Weekends by chance or by appointment.

TECUMSEH

Tecumseh, Ridgeway & Britton:

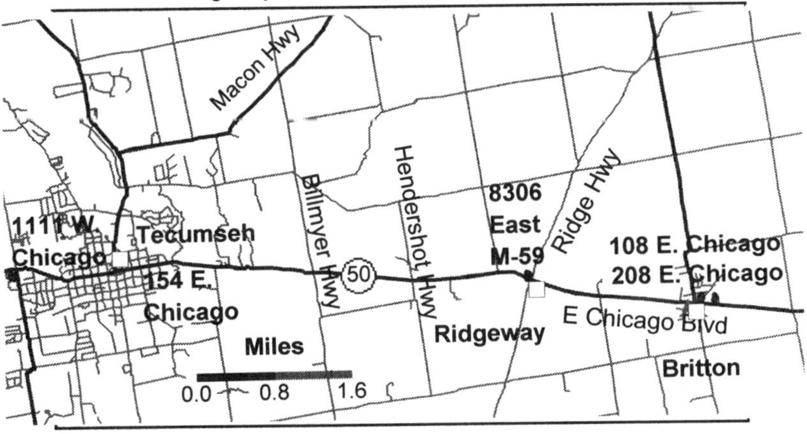

15 Hitching Post Antique Mall
1322 East Monroe Road, Tecumseh MI 49286
517 423-8277

16 Tecumseh Antique Mall
1111 West Chicago Blvd. (M-50), Tecumseh MI 49286
517 423-6082
Mon. to Sat. 10 to 5; Sun 12 to 5
North side of M-50, west end of town.
Large good quality mall. Over 100 dealers.

17 Great Ideas / Harold Robert Antiques
154 East Chicago Blvd. (M-50), Tecumseh MI 49286
517 423-6094
Mon. to Fri. 9 to 6:00, Sat. 9 to 5; Sun. 12 to 5
East end of downtown, south side of the street.
Fine furniture.

18 Walden Hidden Treasures
2389 East Monroe Road, Tecumseh MI 49286
517-424-4331

RIDGEWAY

(Map on previous page.)

19 Ridgeway Home Center
8304 East M-50, Ridgeway MI 49229
517 451-8232
E-Mail: fogelson@lni.net
Mon. to Sat. 9 to 5
North side of the highway.
Amish furniture, custom quilting and antiques.

BRITTON

(Map on previous page.)

20 YesterYears Antiques and Estate Sales
208 East Chicago (M-50), Britton MI 49229
517 451-8600
Thurs. to St. 11 to 5:30, many times till 7; other days by chance or appointment.
Five miles east of Tecumseh, eight miles west of Dundee.
Quality antiques - truly old items.

21 McKinney's Collectibles
108 East Chicago (M-50), P.O. Box 408, Britton MI 49229
517 451-2155
Mon. to Fri. 2 to 6; Sat. 10 to 5, or by appointment.
Eight miles west of U.S. 23, south side of the highway.
Complete line of comics and collectible cards. Beer signs, and the world's largest beer can store.

CLINTON

22 Old Homestead Antiques
2519 West U.S. 12 , Clinton MI 49236
517 456-4352

Clinton:

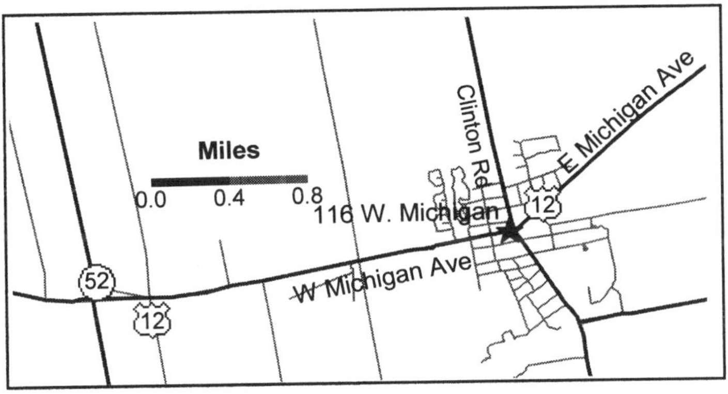

23 The Rose Patch
162 West Michigan, Clinton MI 49236
517 456-6473

24 Turn of the Century Lighting
116 West Michigan, P. O. Box 440, Clinton MI 49236
517 456-6019 turncent@lni.net
By chance or appointment.
Downtown
Hundreds of antique lighting fixtures in stock.

25 Oak City Antiques
1101 East U.S. 12, Clinton MI 49236
517 456-4444

1.7 Monroe County

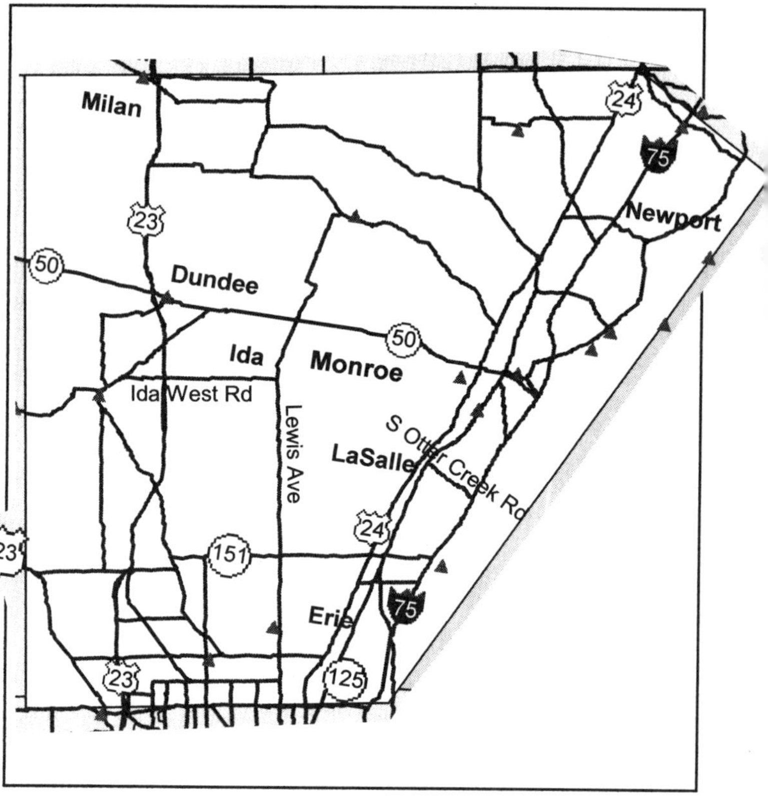

LaSALLE

1 American Heritage Antique Mall
5228 South Otter Creek Road, LaSalle MI 48145
734 242-3430; Fax: 734 242-3436

ERIE

2 Gedert's A Touch of the Past
7442 South Dixie , Erie MI 48133
734 848-8731 Open by chance.

MONROE

3 Sundance Enterprise
15074 South Telegraph Road, Monroe MI 48161
734-243-5156

City of Monroe:

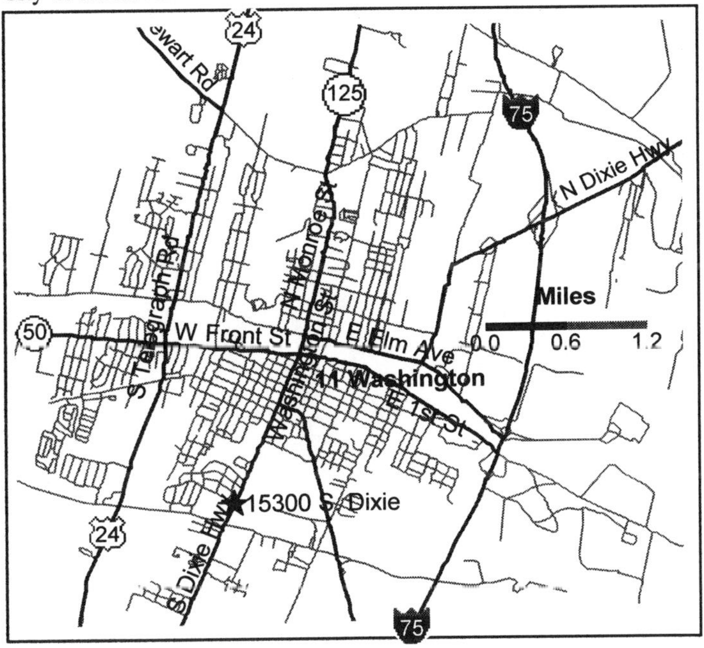

4 Sauer Furniture & Antiques
15300 South Dixie Highway (M-125), Monroe MI 48161
734 242-6284; storm@tdi.net
Tues. to Fri. 10 to 6, Sat. 10 to 5; Sundays before Christmas.
I-75 to Exit 11, west one mile to Dunbar, left one mile to M-125, left one quarter mile.
15,000 square feet, single owner; used furniture, antiques and collectibles.

5 Spainhower's Antiques
315 South Monroe, Monroe MI 48161
734 242-5411 Auctions, with some antiques for sale.

6 Take a Gander
20 South Monroe Street, Monroe MI 48161
734-384-1012

7 Critter Creek Antiques & Collectibles
11 Washington Street, Monroe MI 48161
734-457-5713
Mon. to Fri. 9 to 6, Sat. 11 to 4
Downtown, between Front & First Streets.
Located within Leski office supplies.
General line of antiques & collectibles, and memorabilia.

NEWPORT

Newport:

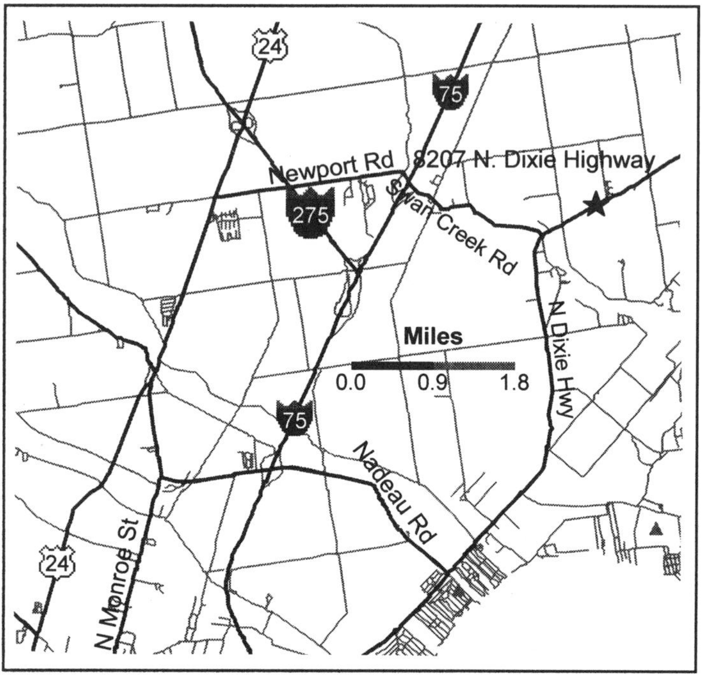

8 The Grainery
9093 Armstrong Road, Newport MI 48166
734 586-8252 Antique and new furniture; housewares.

9 J & L Antiques and Country
8207 North Dixie Highway , Newport MI 48166
734 586-8506
www.jlantiques.com E-Mail: info@jlantiques.com
Thurs. to Sat. 10 to 5, or by appointment.
I-75 to Exit 21, then east; left on Dixie highway one block, next to St. Charles Cemetery. Less than 2 miles from freeway.
Located in a circa 1887 brick farmhouse filled with antique oak furniture. Affordable antiques & collectibles. Custom made country pine furnishings.

DUNDEE

10 Dundee Antique Shoppe
141 Riley Street, Dundee MI 48131
734 529-9007

11. Swan Creek Candle Co.
129 Riley Street, Dundee MI 48131
734-529-7174

IDA

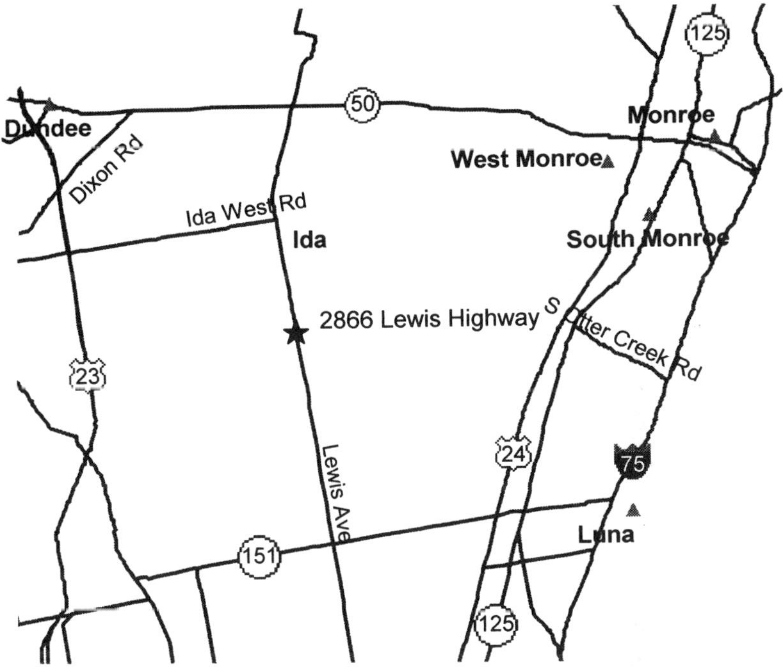

12 Derrys of Ida
2866 Lewis Avenue, P.O. Box 296, Ida MI 48140
734 269-2480
Tues. & Thurs. 10 to 5, Wed. 10 to 4:30, Fri. 10 to 6, Sat. 10 to 3:30
Near the downtown Ida area.
Antiques & handcrafted items.

MILAN

13 Tussing's Resale Shop
45 East Main Street, Milan MI 48160
734-439-7757

14 Exciting Treasures
31 East Main Street, Milan MI 48160
734-439-2800

TIER 2:
THE I-94 ROUTE

2.1 Van Buren County

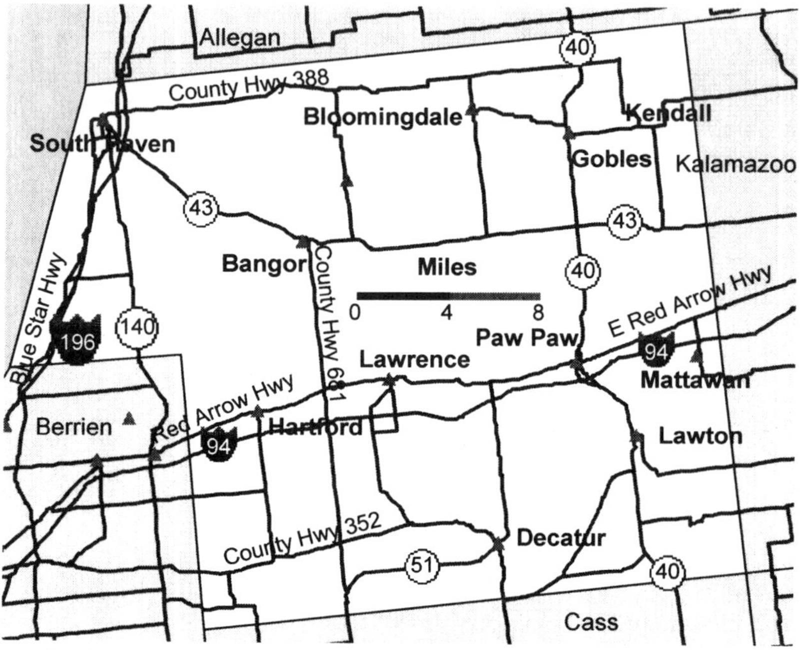

SOUTH HAVEN

1 Murphy's Mall
321 Center Street, South Haven MI 49090
616 639-1662

2 Cheyenne's Closet Vintage Shop
206 Center Street, South Haven MI 49090
616 637-2955

3 Carrousel Mini-Mall
330 South Kalamazoo Street, South Haven MI 49090
616 639-1501
Thurs. to Mon. 10:30 to 5:30
South of Phoenix, west side of the street.
Antiques and collectibles.

South Haven:

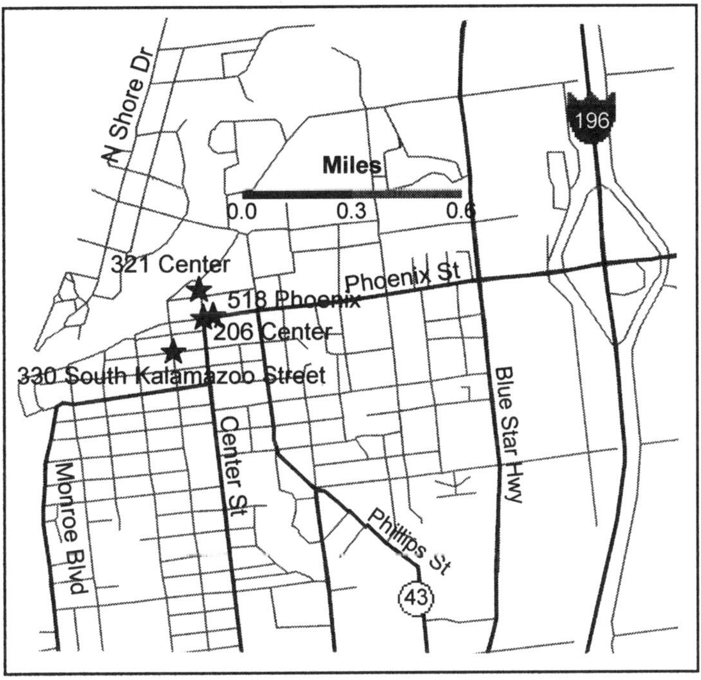

4 Hidden Room Book Shoppe
518 Phoenix Street, South Haven MI 49090
616 637-7222
Antiques and used books.

5 Anchor Antiques Ltd.
527 Phoenix Street, South Haven MI 49090
616 637-1500
June to Aug.: Mon. through Sat. 10 to 5;
Sept. to Dec.: Fri. Sat. & Sun. 10 to 5;
Closed Jan. Feb. & Mar.;
April & May: Thurs. to Sun. 10 to 5
I-96 Exit 20, at the Welcome Island; west on Phoenix Street to downtown; north side of the street.
Quality antiques, designer costume jewelry, period furniture and collectibles, specializing in elegant glass.

6 Sunset Junque Antiques
856 Blue Star Highway, South Haven MI 49090
616 637-5777

BANGOR

7 Don Cleveland Auto Museum, Country Store & Antique Shop
65215 M-43 West, Bangor MI 49013
616 427-8754

8 Bangor Antique Mall
215 West Monroe (M-43), Bangor MI 49013
616 427-8557

LAWRENCE

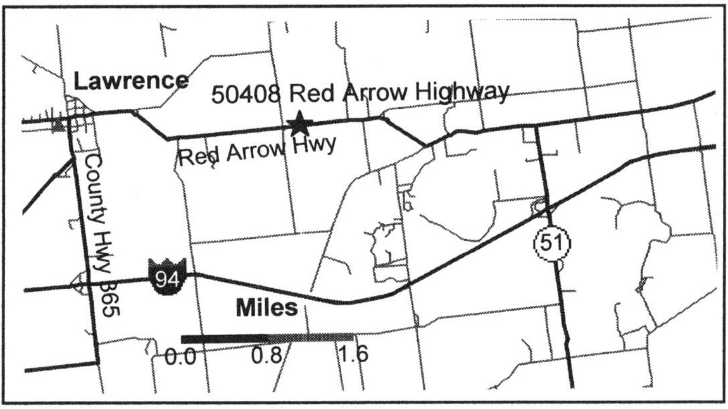

9 L & R Antiques
50408 Red Arrow Highway, P.O. Box 142, Lawrence MI 49064
616 674-8562
Sat. & Sun. 10 to 5
1 mile east of Lawrence, north side of road.
Books, art glass, furniture and general line.

PAW PAW

10 Antiques & Etc.
237 East Michigan, Paw Paw MI 49079
616 657-4640

11 Country Classics
34026 M-43, Paw Paw MI 49079
616 628-0043

MATTAWAN

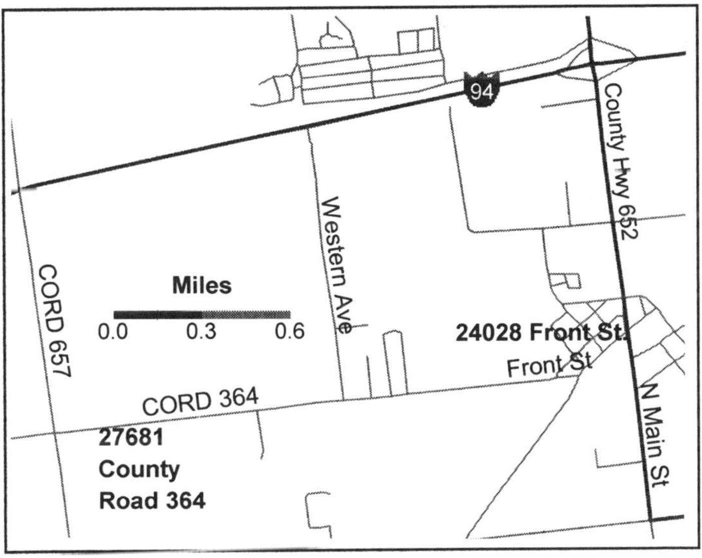

12 Witte's Antiques
27681 County Road 364 (Front Ave. West), P.O. Box 399, Mattawan MI 49071
616 668-4161
Fax: 616 668-5363
Closed Sunday; open year round. Appointment suggested.
Two miles west of downtown, south side of road.
Specializing in antique tools, primitives and tool auctions.

13 Meadowland Garden Gallery
57636 Murray St., Mattawan MI 49071
616 668-5404
Picture frames, gifts, a few antiques.

14 The Livery
57620 Murray Street, Mattawan MI 49071
616 668-3016 Antiques & gifts.

15 Halsey Dean Gallery
24028 Front Street, P.O. Box 617, Mattawan MI 49071
616 668-3510
Wed. to Sun. 12 to 5
Downtown, a half mile south of I-94 Exit 66.
Quality furniture and accessories.

16 William Lesterhouse Antiques
24020 Front Street, Mattawan MI 49071
616 668-3229

KENDALL

17 Kendall Antiques
26947 County Road 388 ("D" Avenue), Kendall MI 49002
616 628-5754

GOBLES

18 Country & More Antiques
21300 Highway M-40, Gobles MI 49055
616-628-4566
Only open April thru Sept. the last weekend of the month 9 a.m. to 6 p.m. (Allegan show weekends) and open Thurs. night prior to the weekend 6 p.m. to 9 p.m.
Dec. open the first weekend on the month 10 a.m. to 5 p.m. and Thurs. before 6 p.m to 9 p.m.
One mile south of Gobles.
Three dealers with a good selection of furniture & smalls. "We do not do shows."

BLOOMINGDALE

19 All Military Antiques
45624 County Road 380, Bloomingdale MI 49026
616-521-3890
Moved from Watervliet.

2.2 Kalamazoo County

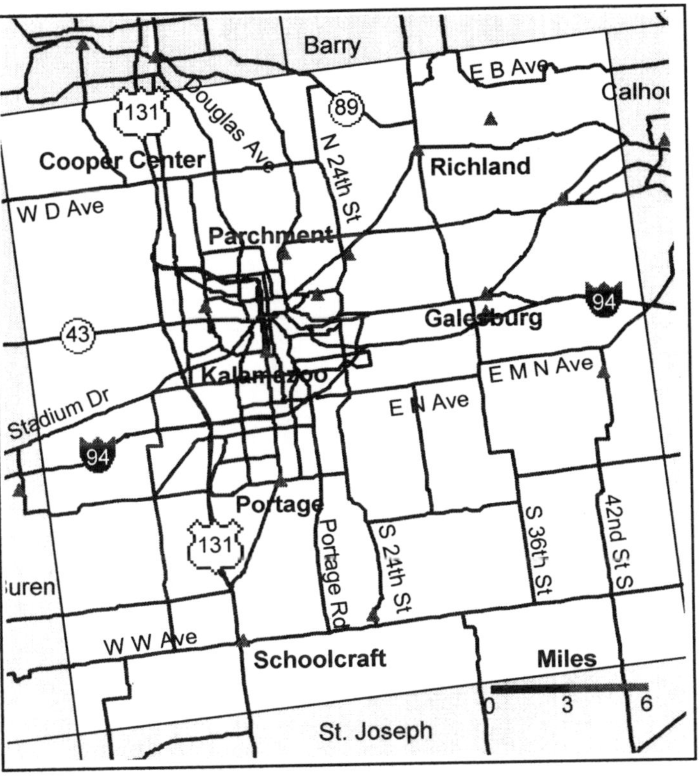

SCHOOLCRAFT

1 The Antique Gallery
113 North Grand (U.S. 131), Schoolcraft MI 49087
616 679-4018
Tues. to Sat. 10 to 5, Sun. 12 to 5
Downtown, west side of the street.

2 Ron's Grand Street Antiques & Mom's Memories
205 North Grand, Schoolcraft MI 49087
616 679-4774; E-Mail: grandst@net-link.net
Tues. to Sat. 10 to 5; Sun. 12 to 5
Downtown, west side of the street.
General line; emphasis on quality, with a sprinkling of unusual and hard-to-find items.

3 Schoolcraft Antique Mall
209 North Grand, P.O. Box 643, Schoolcraft MI 49087
616 679-5282

Schoolcraft:

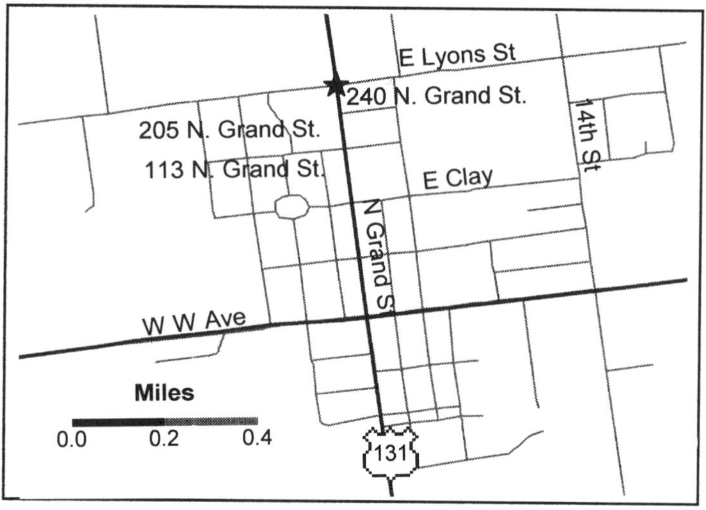

4 Norma's Antiques & Collectibles
231 North Grand, Schoolcraft MI 49087
616 679-4030

5 Prairie Home Antiques
240 North Grand (U.S. 131), Schoolcraft MI 49087
616 679-2062 or 877 679-2062
Mon. to Sat. 11 to 5, Sun. 12 to 5, closed some Wed.
Downtown, east side of the street.
Antique sewing tools, furniture, rugs, pottery, linens, garden antiques.

PORTAGE

6 Airport Antiques & Collectibles
5252 Portage Road, Portage MI 49002
616-385-3278

KALAMAZOO

7 Attic Trash & Treasures
1301 South Westnedge, Kalamazoo MI 49008
616 344-2189
Used furniture and antiques.

Central Kalamazoo:

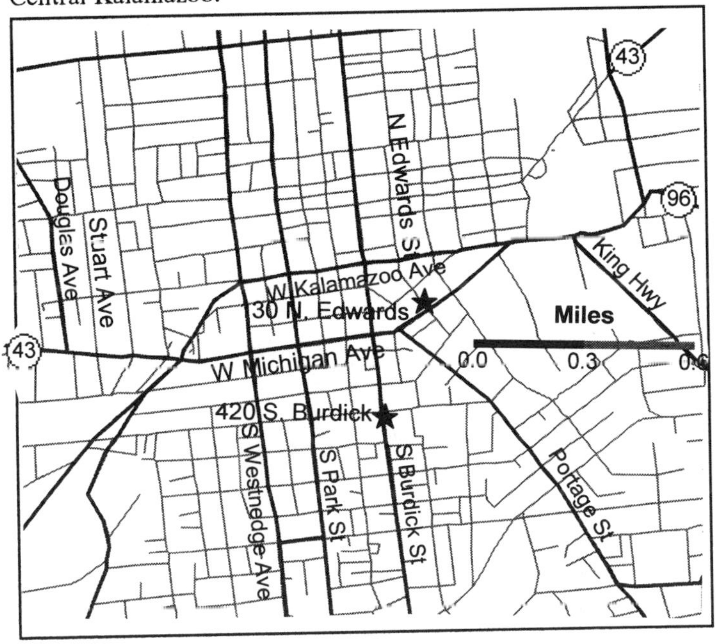

8 Pennyrose
906 South Westnedge, Kalamazoo MI 49008
616 381-8747
Art and a few antiques.

9 Lade Das
426 South Burdick, Kalamazoo MI 49008
616 342-6759
Vintage clothing.

10 JP's Coins & Collectibles
420 South Burdick, Kalamazoo MI 49007
616 383-2200 jpsconis@mei.net
Mon. to Sat. 10 to 5
Downtown, west side of the street, one block south of the State Theater.
Coins, collectibles, antiques, fashion jewelry.

11 The Emporium
313 East Kalamazoo Avenue, Kalamazoo MI 49007
616 381-0998
Mon. to Fri. 7 p.m. to 9 p.m., Sat. & Sun. 2 to 6
Downtown; northeast corner Kalamazoo & Pitcher.
18,000 square feet of furniture, 1,000 pieces on hand.

12 Kalamazoo Antiques Market
130 North Edwards Street, Kalamazoo MI 49007

616 226-9788

Mon. - Fri. 11 - 6,
Sat. 10 to 6,
Sun. 1 to 5

U.S. 131 Exit 36 east to downtown; I-94 Exit 78 north to downtown; Michigan Ave. to Edwards (Behind Wendy's).

A multi-dealer market in the heart of downtown Kalamazoo, displaying a wide variety of fine quality antiques, from primitives to Victorian to fifties.

Kalamazoo
Antiques Market

130 NORTH EDWARDS STREET
KALAMAZOO, MI 49007 616-226-9788

Multi-dealer market in the heart of downtown Kalamazoo, offers a broad variety of fine quality antiques: Primatives to Victorian to Fifties

HOURS: MON.-FRI. 11 AM-6PM
SAT. 10 AM-6PM, SUN. 1PM-5PM

Directions: From US 131: Exit 36 East to downtown. From I-94: Exit 78 N. to downtown Michigan Ave. to Edwards (behind Wendy's)

13 Heritage Architectural Salvage
150 North Edwards, Kalamazoo MI 49000
616 385-1004

14 Brook Farm General Market
3006 Douglas, Kalamazoo MI 49004
616 342-6551
Antiques and new & used furniture.

15 Red Wagon Antiques
5348 North Riverview, Kalamazoo MI 49004
616 382-5461

16 Alamo Depot Antique Mall
6187 West "D" Avenue, Kalamazoo MI 49009
616 373-3885; Fax: 616 373-7048
Mon. to Sat.: 10 to 6, Sun. 12 to 6
South side of road, 1/2 mile west of U.S. 131 Exit 44. Quality oak furniture, glassware and accessories. 9,600 square foot multi-dealer mall, credit cards accepted. Visit the Club Car Restaurant and Alamo Depot Craft Mall right next door.

Northwestern Kalamazoo Area:

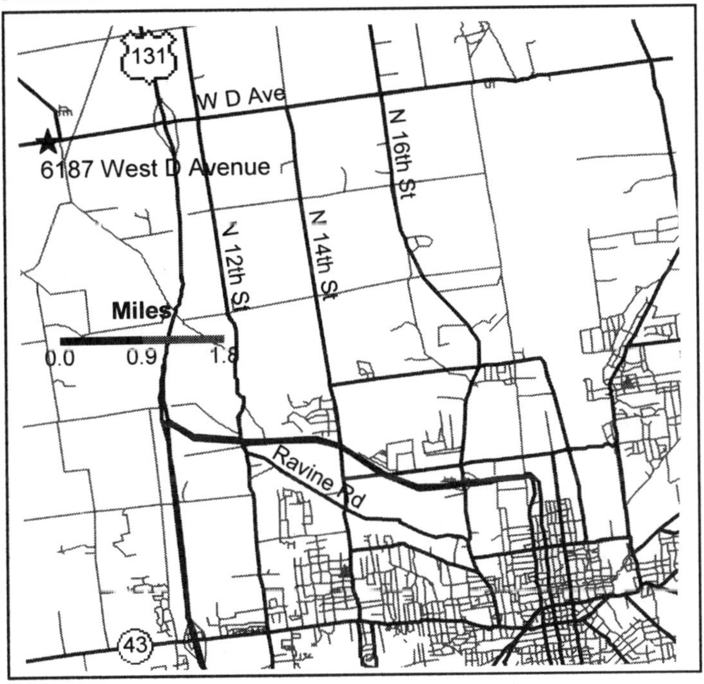

PARACHMENT

17 Welborn Antiques
6300 North Riverview, Parchment MI 49004
616 345-3665

RICHLAND

18 Gull Lake Galleries
8988 West D Avenue, P.O. Box 588, Richland MI 49009
616-629-3133
Mostly art; some antiques.

GALESBURG

19 Grant's Antique Market
33 West Battle Creek Street, Galesburg MI 49053
616 665-4300

2.3 Calhoun County

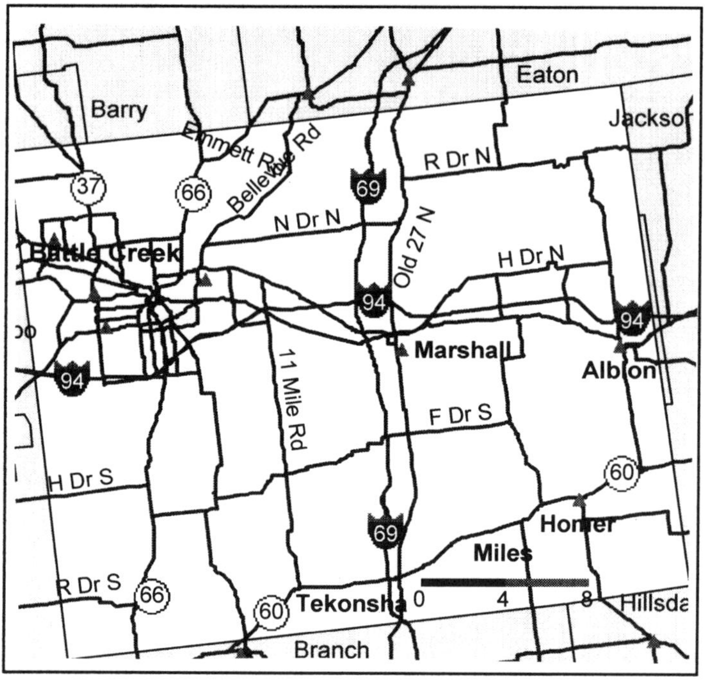

BATTLE CREEK

1 Karen's Keepsakes Antique Mall
4359 Capitol Avenue, Battle Creek MI 49015
616 979-1800
www.AmericanAntiquities.com
Mon. to Sat. 10 to 5
1.6 miles south of I-94, east side of road. Park and enter in the rear.
Gifts, primitives, Steiff bears, Victorian, jewelry, quilts, furniture, glassware, new Fenton Art Glass, and Kellogg memorabilia.

2 Old Beckley School Antiques
3019 Beckley Road, Battle Creek MI 49015
616-979-1842 or 616-964-2682

3 Mini Antique & Variety Mall
22 South 20th Street, Battle Creek MI 49015
616-963-7603
Mostly collectibles; few antiques.

Battle Creek:

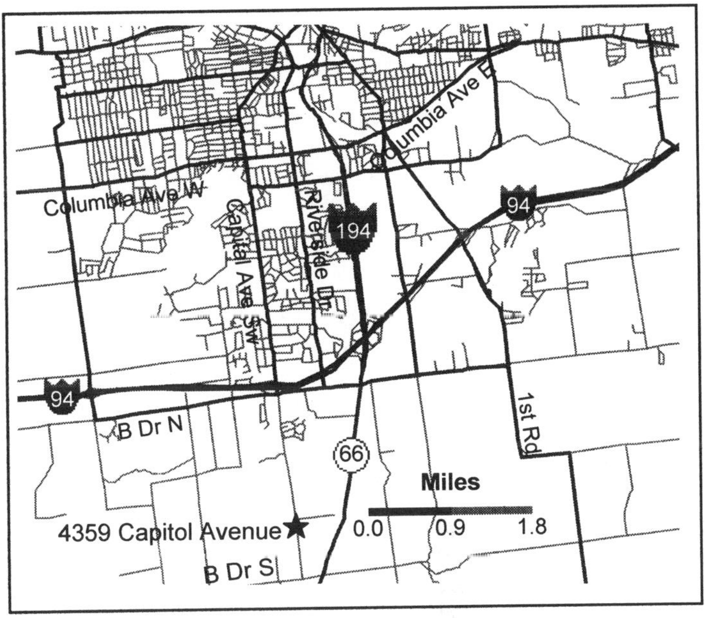

4 Timeless Treasures
548 Capital Ave. S.W., Battle Creek MI 49015
616 964-6341
Used furniture, collectibles, some antiques.

MARSHALL

5 Little Toy Drum Antiques
135 West Michigan Avenue, Marshall MI 49068
616 781-9644
Gifts and antiques.

6 Finders Keepers
125 1/2 West Michigan Avenue, Marshall MI 49068
616 789-1611

7 J.H. Cronin Antique Center
101 West Michigan Avenue, Marshall MI 49068
616 789-0077
Mon. to Sat. 10 to 6 (Jan. & Feb. until 5); Sun. 12 to 5
Downtown Marshall, which is the city where I-94 and I-69 intersect. Located in National Historic Landmark District. Toys, banks, advertising, furniture, glass, etc. All items guaranteed - no reproductions. "Always buying antiques."

Marshall:

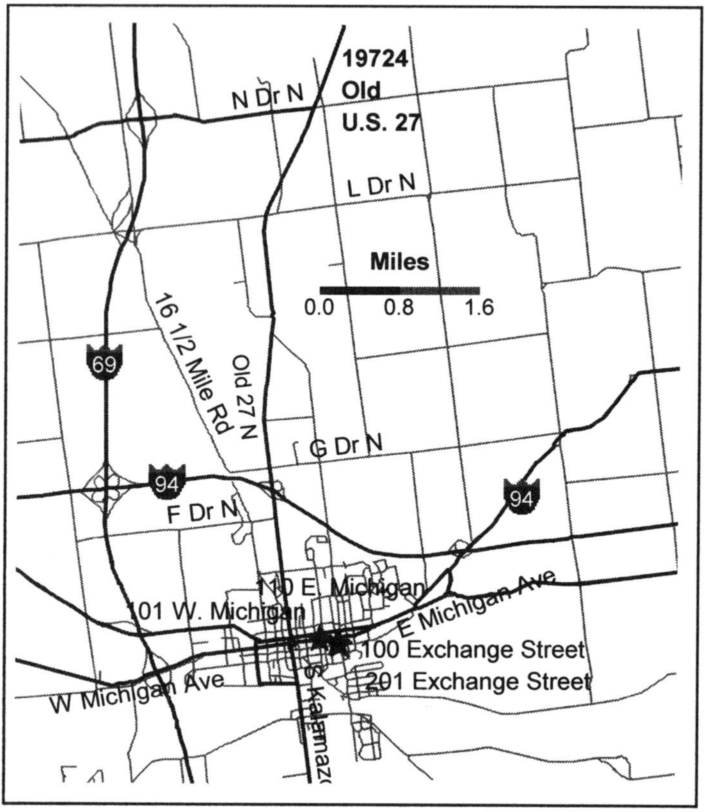

8 Keystone Antiques
110 East Michigan Avenue, Marshall MI 49068
616 789-1355.
Wed. to Fri. 1 to 5, Sat. 10 to 5, Sun. 1 to 5
Downtown
Architectural and general antiques, and new & old concrete garden statuary.

9 Smithfield Banques
117 East Michigan Avenue, Marshall MI 49201
616 781-6969

10 McKee Monument & Mercantile
201 Exchange Street, Marshall MI 49068
616 781-8921 merkantile@voyager.net
Daily 11 to 5:30, Sun. 12 to 5:30, closed Wed. & Thurs.
Downtown at East Green & Exchange Streets, a block south of Michigan Ave.
Country store setting; advertising, toys, dolls, books, & vintage clothing.

11 Marshall House Antique Centre
100 Exchange Street, Marshall MI 49068
616 781-7841 www.marshalltoday.com
Mon. to Sat. 11 to 5, Sun. 12 to 5
Just off the main street next to a little park, east edge of downtown, in a beautiful old mansion.
14 dealers. Quality Victorian antiques, specializing in walnut; also Haviland China, primitives, etc.

12 Country House Antiques
19724 North Old U.S. 27, Marshall MI 49068
616 781-2046 Call first, or by chance.
6 miles north of Marshall on Old U.S. 27, east side of road just north of "N" Drive.
Country furniture, finished & in the rough, & country accessories; also herbs & dried flowers.

13 Bushong's Antiques
18600 16 Mile Road, (Turkeyville) Marshall MI 49068
616 781-5832

TEKONSHA

14 Kempton's Country Classics
1129 Marshall Road South (Old U.S. 27), Tekonsha MI 49092 517 279-8130

HOMER

15 Bailey's Antiques
102 East Main Street, Homer MI 49245, 517 568-4014

2.4 Jackson County

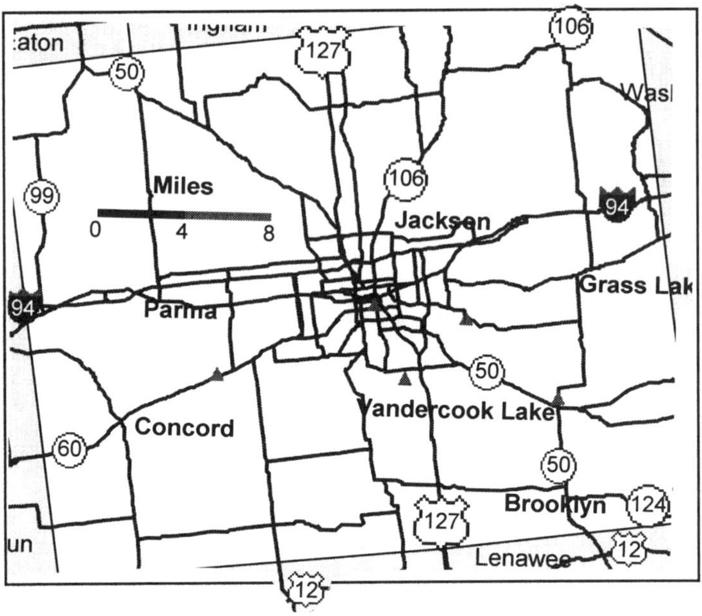

CONCORD

(Map on following page.)

1 Fuzzy's Old Toys
12123 Spring Arbor Road (M-60 East), Concord MI 49237
517 524-9027

2 King Road Granary
12700 King Road, Concord MI 49237
517 524-6006
May to Nov. 15: Daily 10 to 6
South from I-94 Exit 127 on West Concord Road 3.5 miles to King Road, west 1/2 mile; north side of road.
General line of antiques, plus ethnic dolls and Indian items.

PARMA

Concord & Parma:

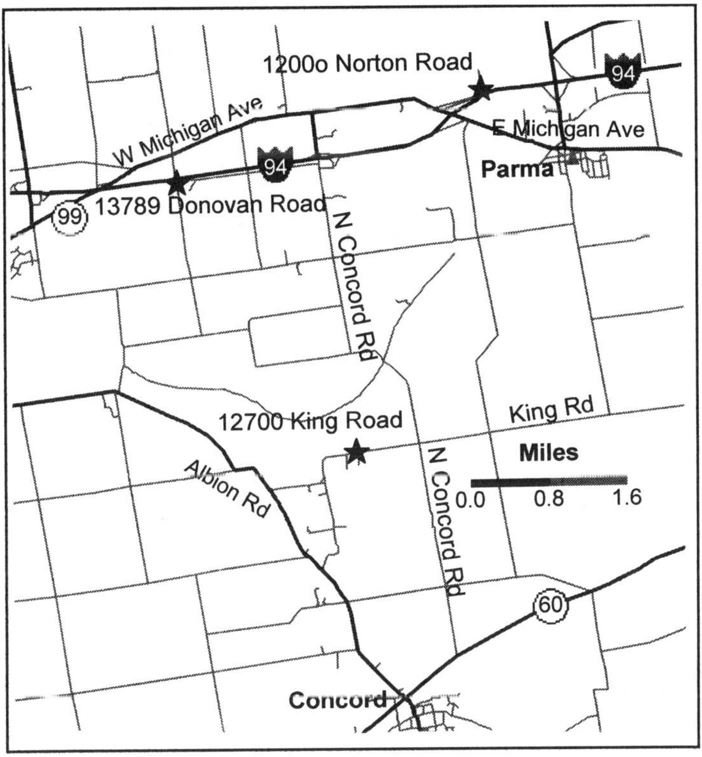

3 Cracker Hill Antique Mall
12000 Norton Road, Parma MI 49269
517 531-4200
Mon. to Sat. 10 to 6; Sun. 12 to 6
Exit 128, north side of I-94.
40 + dealers. Tin & cast iron toys, and a large variety of general items. In business since 1984.

4 Harley's Antique Mall
13789 Donovan Road, Parma MI 49224
517 531-5300 alexcornwall@hotmail.com
Open 10 to 8 364 Days a Year.
I-94 Exit 127, southwest corner.
Michigan's most friendly mall! Open until 8 p.m. 364 days a year! Save up to 40% at the on-site bookstore, offering Michigan's widest selection of antique price guides, historical Dover Reprints, history of fashion and architecture books. European specialty food store on site, too.

JACKSON

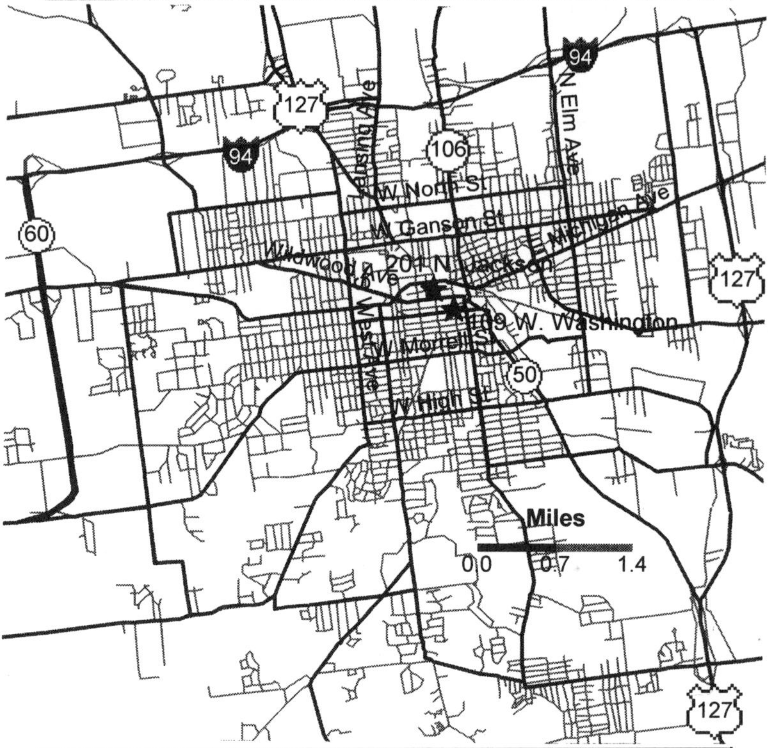

5 The Jackson Antique Mall
201 North Jackson Street, Jackson MI 49201
517 784-3333
Mon. to Sat.: 10 to 6, Sun. 12 to 5
Northeast corner Pearl & Jackson Streets, downtown.
40 dealers.

6 The Camp Gallery
109 West Washington, Jackson MI 49201
517 780-0606; 800 962-5038
Mon. to Fri. 9 to 6; Sat. 9 to 5, Sun. call ahead; closed Holidays.
Downtown, on east-bound Business Route 94.
15,000 square feet; antiques, collectibles, crafts.

7 Ann's Copper Brass & Glass
218 South Mechanic, Jackson MI 49201
517 782-8817

8 Second Hand Rose
129 East Michigan Avenue, Jackson MI 49201
517 789-8239

9 Larry's Antiques & Treasures
6780 Brooklyn Road, Jackson MI 49201
517-536-8515

GRASS LAKE

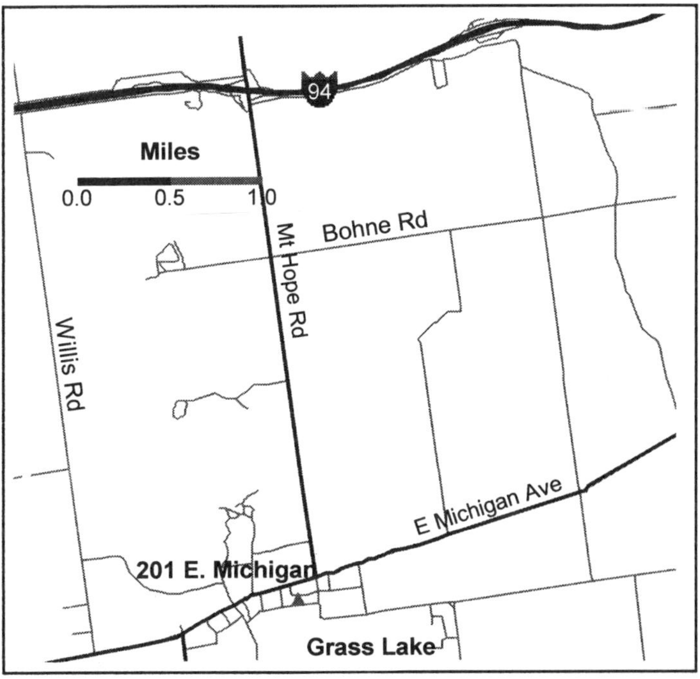

10 Grand Illusion Gallery & Architectural Salvage

201 East & 103 West Michigan, P. O. Box 220, Grass Lake MI 48240
517 522-8715
Summer: Mon. to Sat. 10 to 4, Sun. 12 to 4;
Winter by chance or appointment. Call first.
I-94 Exit 150 south 3.1 miles. Downtown, south side of street.
Architectural salvage, art, jewelry.

BROOKLYN

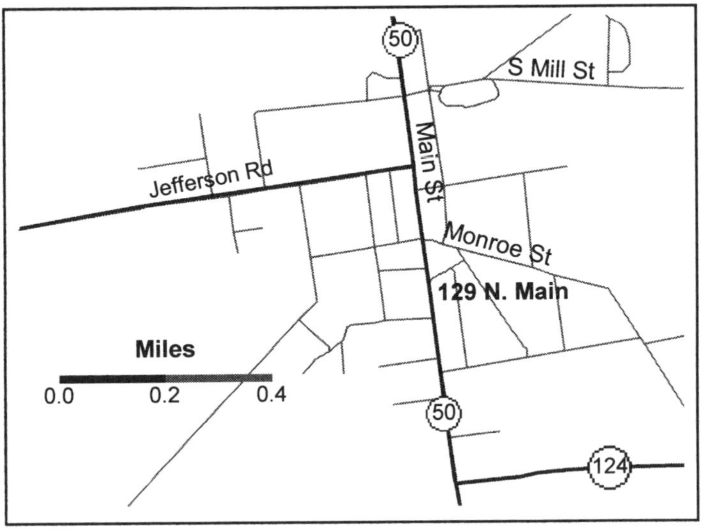

11 Brooklyn Depot / Brosamer's Bells
207 Irwin Street, Brooklyn MI 49230
517 592-6885
Office furniture and bells.

12 Memory Lane Antiques
12939 South M-50, Brooklyn MI 49230
517 592-4218

13 Pinetree Centre Antique Mall

129 North Main Street, P.O. Box 605, Brooklyn MI 49230
517 592-3808
Daily 10 to 5; Sun. 12 to 5
Downtown, east side of the Square.
Good line of furniture and primitives.

2.5 Washtenaw County

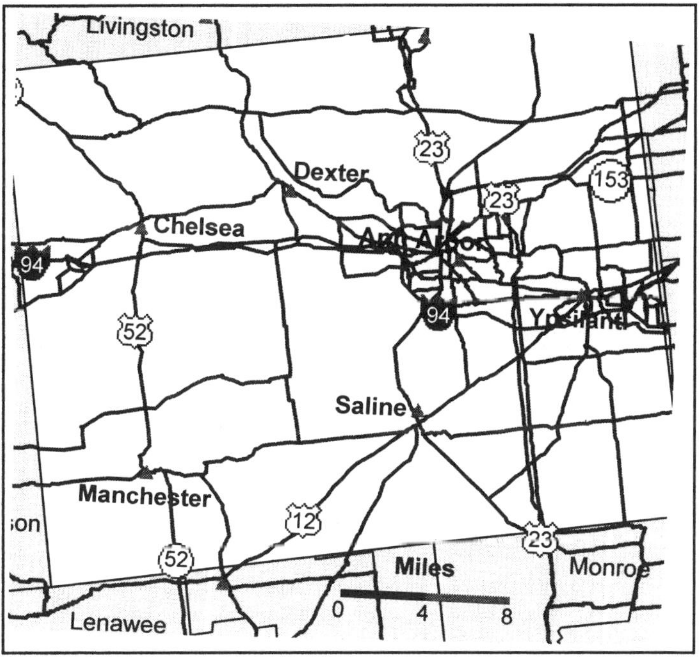

MANCHESTER

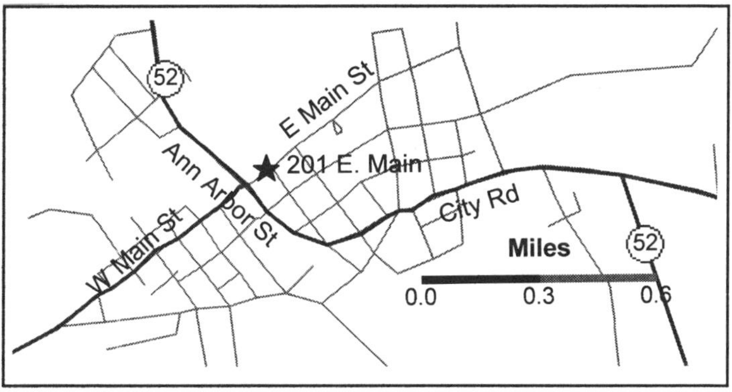

1 Limpert Antiques
201 East Main Street, P.O. Box 524, Manchester MI 48158
734-428-7400 (Leave message)
delimpert@netzero.net
Tues. 12 to 4, Fri. to Sun. 12 to 4:30
First level of Manchester Mill.
Civil War, advertising, primitives etc.

2 Manchester Antique Mall
116 East Main Street, Manchester MI 48158
734-428-9357

3 The 18th Century Shoppe
122 East Main Street, P.O. Box 557, Manchester MI 48158
734-428-7759 Country wares, herbs, gifts; a few antiques.

4 Raisin Valley Antiques
201 East Main Street, Manchester MI 48158
734-428-7766; res. 734-428-8518

CHELSEA

5 Darwin's Studio
9080 Beeman Road, Chelsea MI 48118
734-475-9730
Tues. through Thursday 9 to 5, or by chance or appointment.
I-94 Exit 159, north on Main Street, left on Waterloo, right on Beeman.
Stained Glass, and Antique Slot Machines.

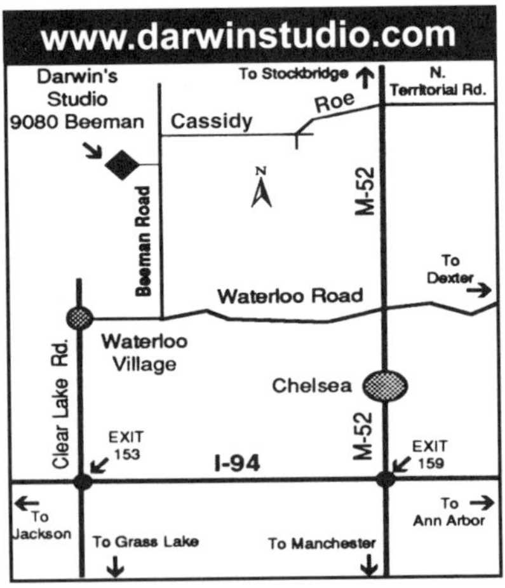

6 Uptown Antiques & Littlewares
Sylvan Building, 114 North Main Street, Chelsea MI 48118
734-475-6940

7 The Chelsea Collection
112 West Middle St., Chelsea MI 48118
734-433-3300

8 Chelsea Woodwork & Antiques
407 North Main Street, Chelsea MI 48118
734-475-8020

DEXTER

9 Johnson's Antique Shop
11511 Jackson Road, Dexter MI 48130
734-475-1902; 734-769-3848

10 Glenbrier Antiques
351 North Dancer Road, Dexter MI 48130
734-475-2961 (or 475-6780)

11 Designer's Cove
3127 Baker Road, Dexter MI 48130
734-426-2688 Upholstery shop with some antiques.

ANN ARBOR

12 Past Presence Antiques
303 South Division, Ann Arbor MI 48104
734-663-2352

Chelsea:

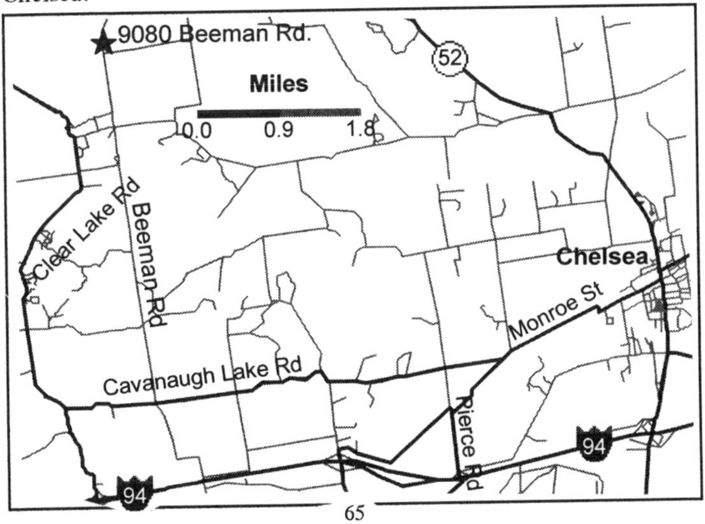

Ann Arbor:

13 The Lotus Gallery
1570 Covington Drive, Ann Arbor MI 48103
734-665-6322
By appointment at your convenience.
South on Main to Pioneer High School, west on Sciochurch to Covington, then right on Covington.. Oriental antiques, ceramics, jade, ivory, etc. from Han to 19th Century. Southwestern American Indian art, ceramics Navaho Rugs, baskets from archaic to modern.

14 Kaleidoscope Books & Collectibles
217 South State Street, Ann Arbor MI 48104
734-995-9887
Collectibles, some antiques.

15 Arcadian Too
118 South Main Street, Ann Arbor MI 48104
734-994-8856 TAntiquesh@aol.com
Mon. to Thurs. 11 to 6, Fri. & Sat. 11 to 9, Sun. 12 to 6
Downtown, west side the street, south of Washington. Antique furniture, depression glass, sterling, flo blue, jewelry. Good quality shop.

16 Arcadian Antiques & Collectibles
13-15 Nickels Arcade, Ann Arbor MI 48104
734-994-3433 Fax: 734-994-5714
TAntiquesh@aol.com wwwArcadianAntiques.com
Mon. to Sat. 10 to 5, Sun. 12 to 5
The historic Arcade is located on the east side of Maynard Street between William and Liberty Streets.
Antique purses, cameos, pocket watches, antique jewelry, furniture, Depression Glassware, quilts.

17 Barclay Gallery
218 South Main, Ann Arbor MI 48104
734-663-2900

Downtown Ann Arbor:

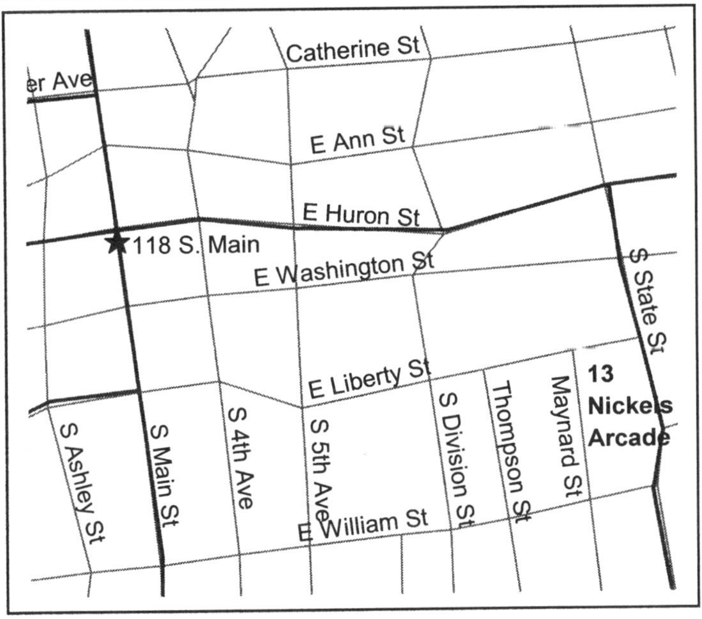

18 The Treasure Mart
529 Detroit Street, Ann Arbor MI 48104
734-662-9887
Household goods and antiques on consignment.

19 MacGregor's Outdoors, Inc.
803 North Main, P.O. Box 7888, Ann Arbor MI 48107
734-761-9200; Fax: 734-761-9204
In addition to antique furniture, MacGregor's is a full-line Orvis fly fishing dealer.

20 Antiques Mall of Ann Arbor
2739 Plymouth Road, Ann Arbor MI 48105
734-663-8200

21 Garage Sale Gallery
5060 Jackson Road, Ann Arbor MI 48103
734-665-9454
Collectibles, junk, stuff, and some antiques.

SALINE

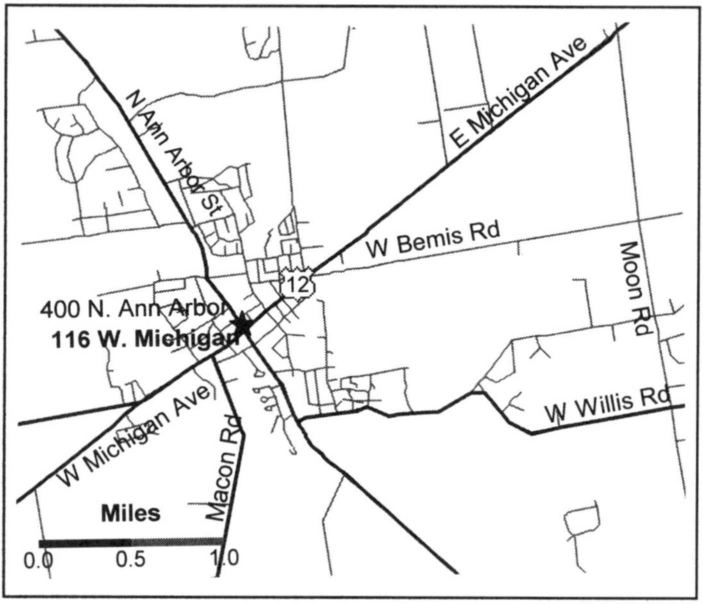

22 Antique International Interiors
405 North Ann Arbor Street, Saline MI 48176
734-944-3500
Interiors; only a few antiques.

23 The Drowsy Parrot
105 North Ann Arbor, Saline MI 48176
734-429-8595
Restaurant with a few antiques.

24 Pineapple House Interiors
101 East Michigan, Saline MI 48176
734-429-1174
Interior design, decorative items, furniture, some antiques.

25 Salt City Antiques
116 West Michigan Ave. (U.S. 12), Saline MI 48176
734-429-3997 www.saltcityantiqueshop.com
Mon. to Sat. 10 to 5, Sun. 11 to 5
Downtown, north side of street.
17 dealers. Furniture, glassware, pottery, vintage clothing, 50's collectibles, Victorian items, primitives, etc.
Collection of Blue Ridge dinnerware, and Hall China, Roseville, Gouda, Weller, Watt, and other pottery. Clocks & watches.
New owners: Carol McEachran and son Steven Hudock.

26 The Weinhardt Collection
400 N. Ann Arbor Street, Saline MI 48176
734-429-4005 weinhardt1@aol.com
www.tias.com/stores/weinhardt1
Daily 10 to 8
One block north of Michigan Avenue, downtown Saline.
Glassware, furniture, coins, pottery. Internet auction service. Cases & spaces for rent.

27 Attic Treasures Antiques
10360 Moon Road, Saline MI 48176
734-429-4242

YPSILANTI

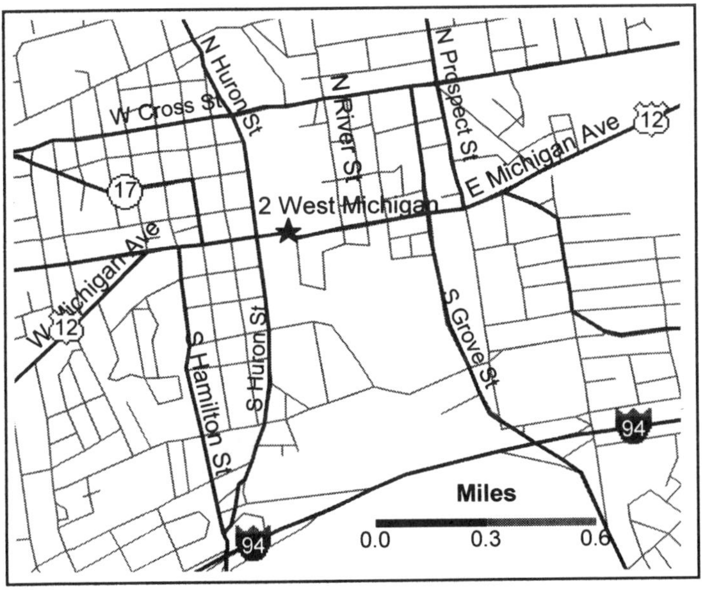

28 Schmidt's Antiques
5138 West Michigan, Ypsilanti MI 48197
734-434-2660

29 Materials Unlimited
2 West Michigan Avenue, Ypsilanti MI 48197
800-299-9462; Fax 734-482-3636
www.materialsunlimited.com
Mon. to Sat. 10 to 5
Downtown, north side of street just east of Huron Street. 15,000 square feet of antiques and architecturals. Lighting, mantels, furniture, glass and more.

30 Silver Spoon Antiques
27 and 32 East Cross, Ypsilanti MI 48197
734-484-9960

31 Jim MacDonald's Antiques & Apple Annies Vintage Clothing
29 East Cross Street, Ypsilanti MI 48198
734-481-0555

32 McFarlane Antiques
10970 Ford Road (M-153), Ypsilanti MI 48197
734-482-1307

SALEM

33 Pegasus Antiques
7700 Currie Road, Salem
248 348-6652

Belleville:

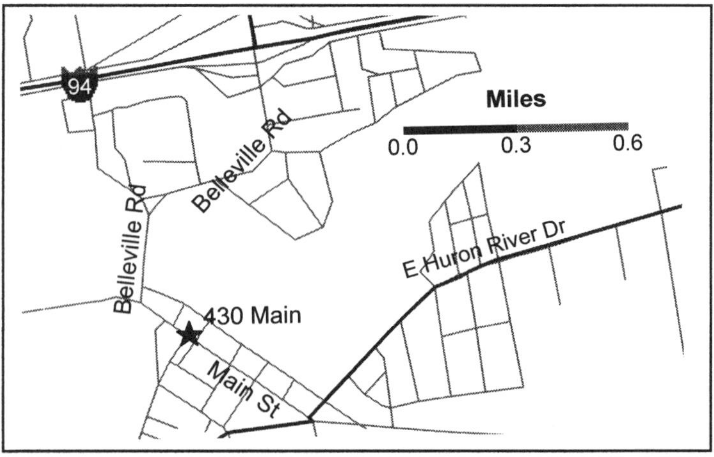

2.6 Wayne County

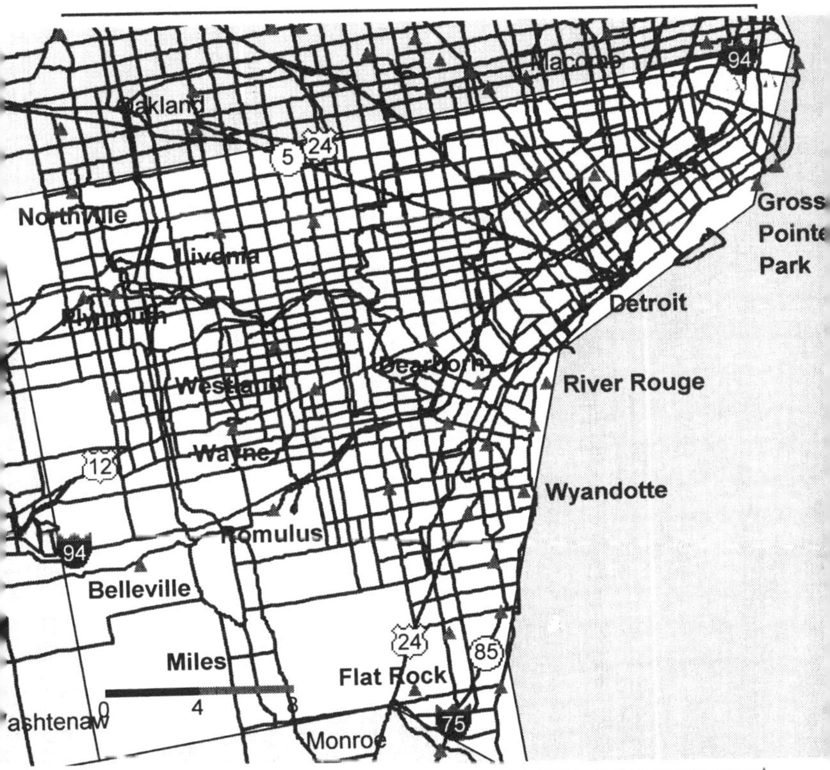

BELLEVILLE

(Map on previous page.)

1 Antiques on Main
430 Main Street, Belleville MI 48111
734-699-8285
Mon. to Sat. 10 to 5, Sun. 1 to 5
Exit 190 from I-94, south 1/2 mile in downtown Belleville. East side of the street.
General line antiques, primitives, furniture, china, pottery, books.

ROMULUS

2 Udders Nostalgia Shop
36628 Goddard Road, Romulus MI 48174
734-941-1465 No antique furniture.

WAYNE

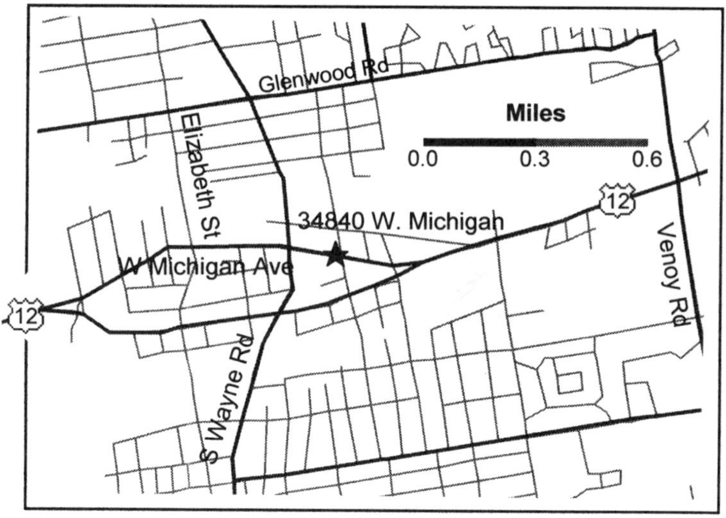

3 Sanders Antiques
35118 West Michigan (West-bound lanes.), Wayne MI
48184 734-721-3029
Moving to a new location in mid 2000.

4 Blue Willow Antiques Inc.
34840 West Michigan (West-bound lanes.), Wayne MI 48184
734-729-4910
Mon. to Sat. 11 to 6
North side of street, 1 block east of Wayne Road.
Pottery and a general line of antiques.

5 Heritage Colonial Upholstering & Antiques
32224 Michigan Avenue, Wayne MI 48184
734-722-2332

GARDEN CITY

6 Craftique Craft & Antiques Mall
5846 Middlebelt , Garden City MI 48135
734-525-9900 www.craftique.com

7 Desirable Disks I
29478 Ford Road, Garden City MI 48135
734-522-2460 Vintage records.

WESTLAND

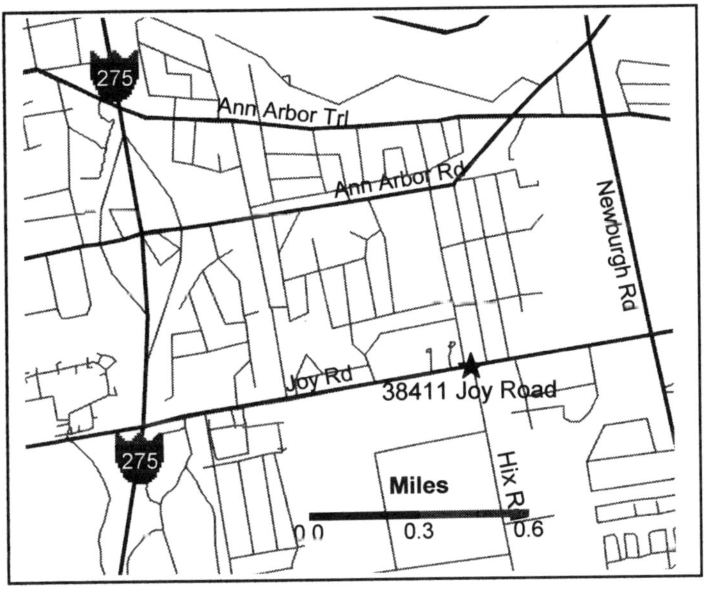

8 Antiques & Collectibles
38411 Joy Road, Westland MI 48185
734-254-9581
www.newfcomputers.com/a&c
Mon. to Sat. 11 to 7; Thanksgiving to Christmas: call for hours.
Closed holidays.
Joy-Hix Shopping Plaza, east of I-275.
"Primitives to the present. Buy, Sell, Trade." Beanie babies, sports, dolls, glassware, Pokemon, Princess Di collectibles.

PLYMOUTH

9 Looking Glass Antiques
580 Forest, Unit 1, Plymouth MI 48170
734-451-0021
Mon. to Thurs. 11 to 5, Fri. 11 to 8, Sat. 10 to 5
At corner of Wing, south of Ann Arbor Trail and west of Main Street.
"From crystal to crocks...we've got it!"

10 Decades
8070 North Territorial Road, Plymouth MI 48170
734-354-0142

Plymouth:

11 Jack's Corner Bookstore
583 West Ann Arbor Trail, Plymouth MI 48170
734-455-2373

12 Bellerose
689 North Mill Street, Plymouth MI 48170
734-454-5510
Bellerose7@aol.com
Tues. to Sat. 11 to 5
Three blocks north of Plymouth Road.
Antiques, architectural elements, and vintage textiles.

13 Kalik's Antiques
198 West Liberty, Plymouth MI 48170
734-455-5595; Fax: 734-455-3805

14 In My Attic
157 West Liberty Street, Plymouth MI 48170
734-455-8970

15 Upstairs, Downstairs Antiques
149 West Liberty, Plymouth MI 48170
734-459-6450

NORTHVILLE

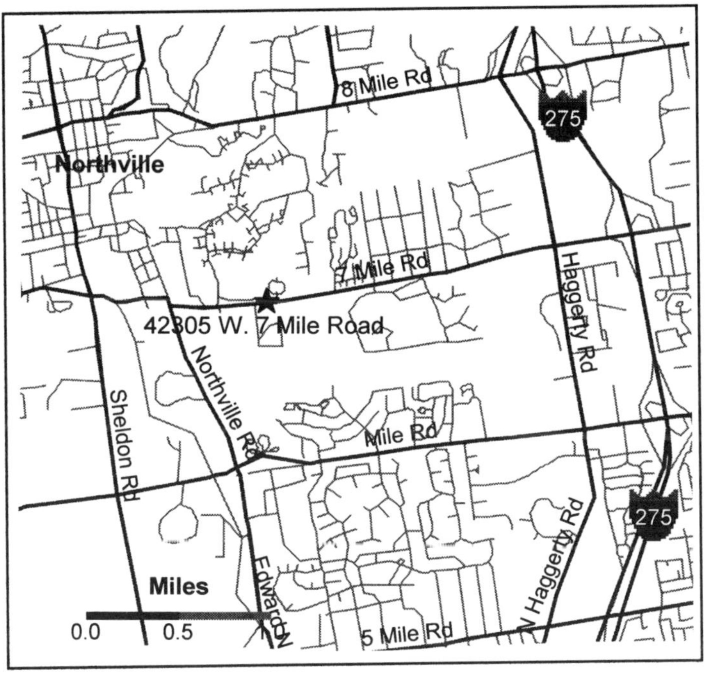

16 The Barn Antiques
48120 West 8 Mile Road, Northville MI 48167
248 349-0117

17 Knightsbridge Antique Mall
42305 West 7 Mile Road, Northville MI 48167
248 344-7200
Daily 11 to 6, Wed. to 8
Two miles west of I-275, in strip mall, south side of road. Furniture, pottery, paintings, etc. High quality mall; 26,000 sq. ft., 200 dealers.

18 Morrison's Antiques
105 East Main Street, Northville MI 48167
248 348-8898

19 McGuires Fine Art Gallery
341 East Main Street, Northville MI 48167
248-348-5550

20 Sweet Dreams of Northville
124 East Main Street, Northville MI 48167
248-305-7222

LIVONIA

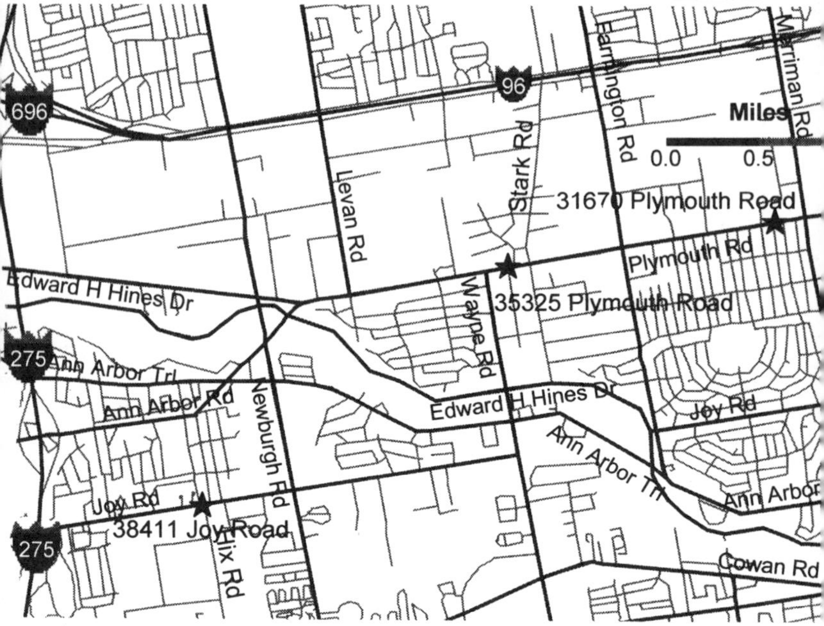

21 Town Peddler Craft & Antique Mall
35323 Plymouth Road, Livonia MI 48150
734-513-2577 www.townpeddler.com
Mon. to Sat. 10 to 8, Sun. 11 to 6
East of Levan, W of Wayne Road.
One of two locations of Town Peddler Mall.

22 Town & Country Antiques Mall
31630 Plymouth Road, Livonia MI 48150
734-425-4344
Mon. Tues. Wed. & Sun. 11 to 6, Thurs. to Sat. 11 to 8
1 block west of Merriman Road, 1 mile south of I-96, behind East Side Mario's Restaurant.
55 dealers. Depression Glass, furniture, sports memorabilia, jewelry, etc.

23 Dora's Place (Now 'N' Then)
33200 Seven Mile Road, Livonia MI 48152
248 476-0055
Tue. to Sat. 11 to 5, Sun. 12 to 4
North side of the Street, 2 blocks east of Farmington Road.
Gifts, jewelry, collectibles, antiques.

24 Saddle Grove Antiques
35800 Ann Arbor Trail, Livonia MI 48150
734-422-4488

TRENTON

25 Don's Antiques & Collectibles
2857 West Jefferson, Trenton MI 48183
734-676-0622

WYANDOTTE

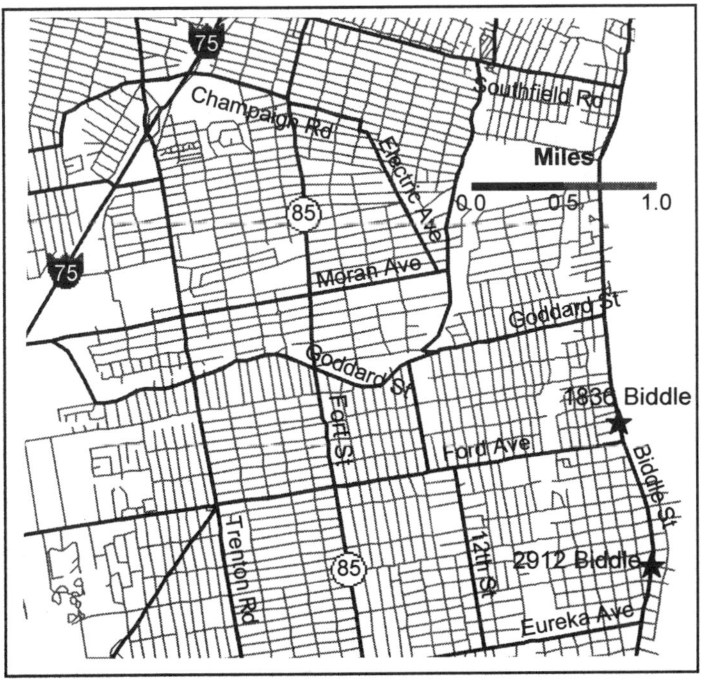

26 Red Robin Antiques & Resale
2721 10th Street, Wyandotte MI 48192
734-283-0312

27 Tony's Junk Shop
1325 Fort , Wyandotte MI 48192
734-283-2160 Pawn shop with antiques and collectibles.

28 Almost Antique
1728 Eureka Road, Wyandotte MI 48192
734-285-0477

29 Raggedy Dan's
1842 Biddle, Wyandotte MI 48192
734-283-3370

30 Affordable Antiques & Resale
1836 Biddle , Wyandotte MI 48192
734-282-1852
Tues. thru Sat. 10 to 6
West side of highway, north of North Line Road.
Collectibles, pottery, dolls, designer clothing, & much more - new items weekly.

31 Old Gray House Antiques
303 Oak Street, Wyandotte MI 48192
734-285-2555

32 Yesterday's Treasures
258 Elm Street, Wyandotte MI 48192 734-283-5232

33 Armstrong's Antiques & Collectibles
2912 Biddle Street, Wyandotte MI 48192
734-282-3072
Mon. to Fri. 11 to 6, Sat. 10 to 5, closed Sun.
Downtown, southwest corner Oak & Biddle.
String instruments, Barbies/dolls, glassware, sports/fishing, furniture, toys/games, linens, fine collectibles.

LINCOLN PARK

34 Mr. Robinson's Resale
4145 Dix Highway, Lincoln Park MI 48146 313-382-1600

FLAT ROCK

35 Motor City Antique Gallery
13431 Telegraph, Flat Rock MI 48134
734-782-4018
Tues. to Sun. 10 to 6
North of I-275 five miles on Telegraph Road, 1 3/4 miles north of Flat Rock.

(See Display Ad on the following page.)

DEARBORN

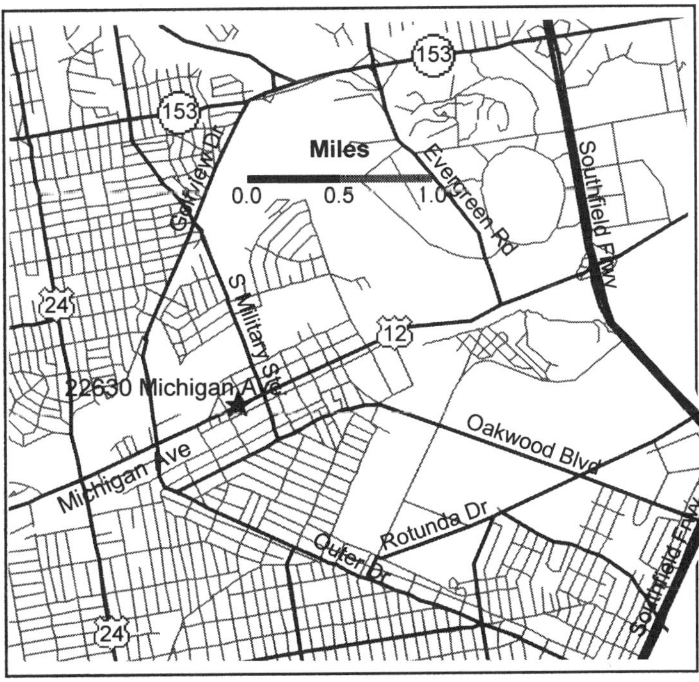

36 Comer-Copia
21903 Michigan Avenue, Dearborn MI 48124
313-565-0875

37 Retro Image
14246 Michigan Avenue, Dearborn MI 48126
313-582-3074

38 Desirable Discs II
13357 Michigan Avenue, Dearborn MI 48126
313-581-1767 Vintage records, posters, books, etc.

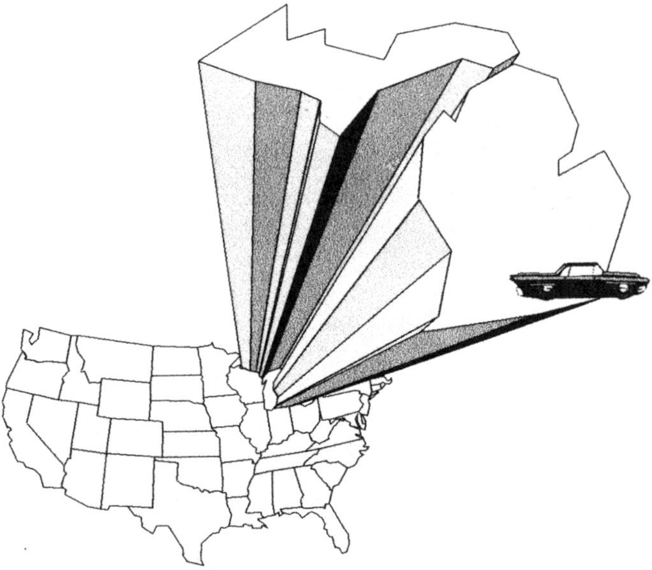

Motor City Antique Gallery

13431 Telegraph Rd.
Flat Rock MI 48134
(734) 782-4018
(734) 782-4910 Fax
WWW.motorcityantiques.com

17,000 Sq. Ft.
About 100 Dealers
Located 1 ¾ miles south of Flat Rock
or
5 miles north of I-275 on Telegraph Rd.
Open 6 Days a week
Tues. – Sun. 10:00 AM – 6:00 PM
Closed Mondays

39 Village Antique Mall
22630 Michigan Avenue, Dearborn MI 48124

313-563-1230

Mon. to Sat. 10:30 to 5:30; Sun. 12 to 5; Thurs. to 7:30
Closed major holidays.

Between Telegraph Road (U.S. 24) and Southfield Freeway.

Antiques, collectibles, jewelry, advertising, military, furniture.

5,000 square feet.

40 A & D Antiques
13354 Michigan Avenue, Dearborn MI 48126
313-581-6183

DETROIT

41 New World Antique Gallery
12101 Grand River, Detroit MI 48204
313-834-7008

42 The Junque Shop Antiques
7807 Michigan Avenue, Detroit MI 48210
313-945-1870

43 Michigan Avenue Antiques
7105 Michigan Avenue, Detroit MI 48210
313-554-1012

44 Gilbert's Antiques & Fine Furniture
19150 Livernois Ave., Detroit MI 48221
313-340-1611

West Side Detroit:

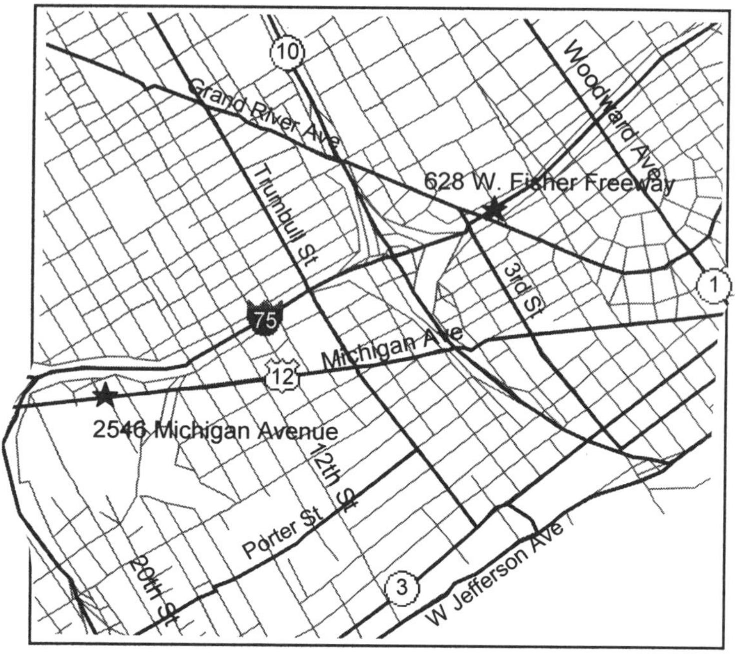

45 Xavier's
2546 Michigan Avenue, Detroit MI 48216
313-964-1222
Wed. to Fri. 11 to 5, Sat. 10 to 6
6 blocks west of Tiger Stadium.
Mission, Art Deco & Moderne furniture and Accessories.

46 Detroit Antique Mall & Senate Resale
828 West Fisher Freeway , Detroit MI 48201
313-963-5252
Tues. to Sat. 11 to 6
Northwest of downtown. North side of entrance ramp to Fisher Freeway, just west of Grand River Avenue. (There is a street to avoid entering freeway after leaving the mall.) Large selection of architectural items, old lighting, art deco, modern, and much much more.

47 DuMouchelle Art Gallery
409 East Jefferson, Detroit MI 48226
313-963-6255

48 Dell Pryor Galleries
1452 Randolph, Detroit MI 48226
313-963-5977 Contemporary art and antiques.

Downtown Detroit:

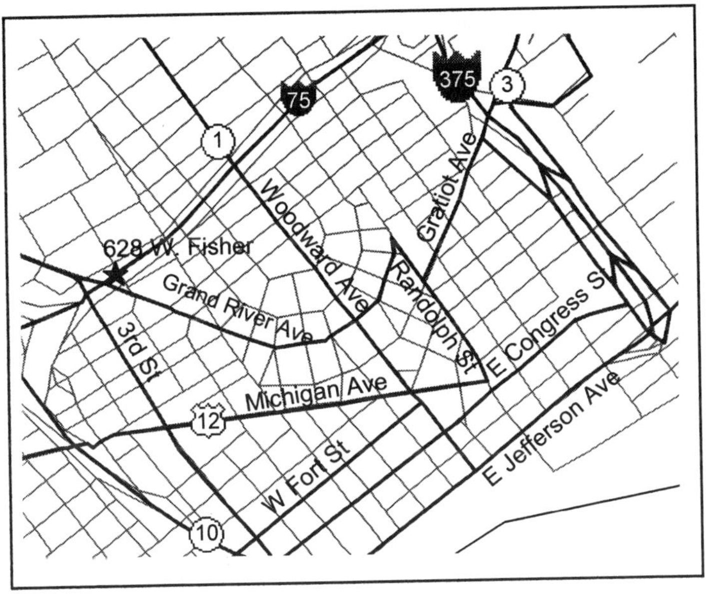

49 Marketplace Antiques
2047 Gratiot, Detroit MI 48207
313-567-8250
May be moving in late 2000.

50 Villa Domain Antiques & Collectibles
8469 East Jefferson, Detroit MI 48214
313-824-4600

51 William Charles Gallery
8025 East Agnes, Detroit MI 48214
313-823-0324

52 A-1 Good Used Furniture
13906 Mack Avenue, Detroit MI 48215
313-823-4888

53 London Gallery
16231 Mack Avenue, Detroit MI 48224
313-882-4776

54 Mike's Antiques
11109 Morang, Detroit MI 48224
313-881-9500

East Side Detroit:

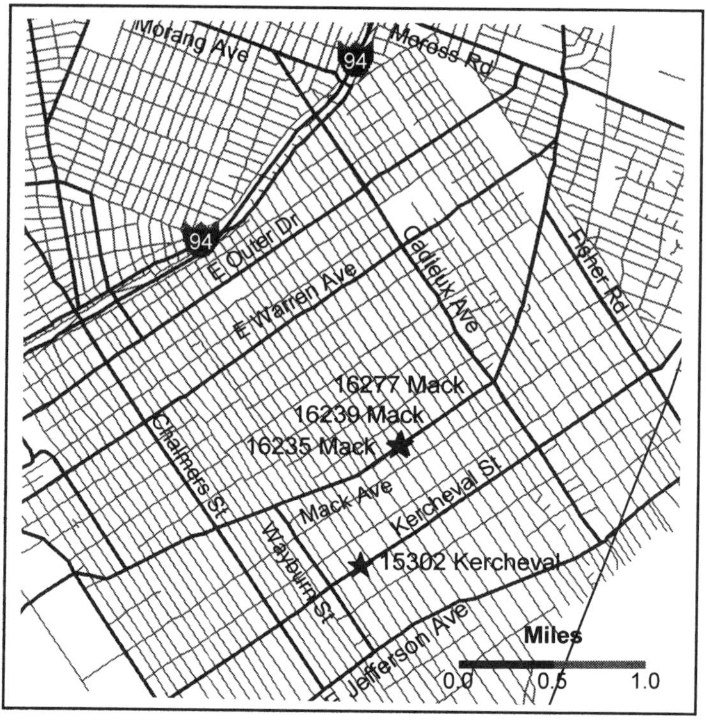

55 Park Antiques

16235 Mack Avenue, Detroit MI 48224
313-884-7652
Wed. to Sat. 12 to 5, Sun. 12 to 4
North side of street, west of Three Mile Road.
General line of quality antiques.

56 Another Time

16239 Mack Avenue, Detroit MI 48224
313-886-0830
Wed. to Sat. 11 to 6, Sun. 12 to 5
North side of street, west of Three Mile Road.
Lighting fixtures, mahogany furniture, expert lamp repair & restoration, etc.

GROSSE POINTE PARK

57 Lloyd David Antiques
15302 Kercheval, Grosse Pointe Park MI 48230
313-822-3452
Mon. & Wed. to Sat. 11 to 6
One mile west of Cadieux, south side of street.
Antique furniture, American art pottery, fine used furniture, and collectibles

TIER 3: SAUGATUCK-LANSING-ROYAL OAK

3.1 Allegan County

GLENN

1 Helen's Antiques
1662 Adams Road (Blue Star Highway), P.O. Box 56,
Glenn MI 49416
616-227-3211

2 Willow Bend Antiques
1671 Blue Star Highway, Glenn MI 49408
616-227-3200

DOUGLAS

3 White Birch Trading
2788 Blue Star Highway, Box 10, Douglas MI 49453
616-857-7474 Antiques, reproductions, garden collectibles.

Saugatuck - Douglas area:

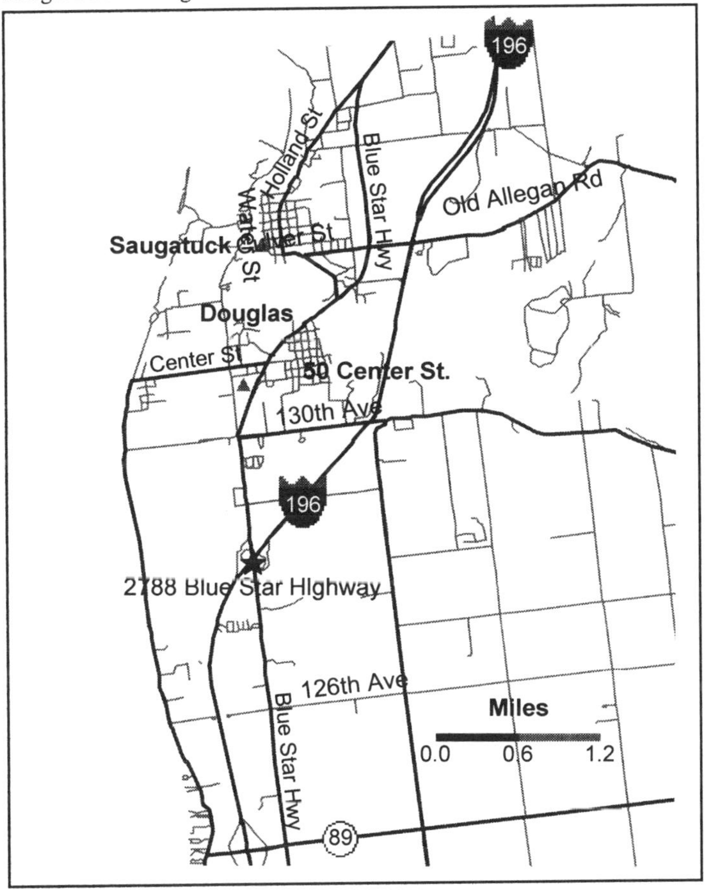

4 Bird Cage Antiques

Blue Star Highway & M-89., Douglas Area MI 49408
616-543-4732
Summer: Open Daily 12 to 6
Spring: Fri. thru Mon. 12 to 5
I-196 Exit 34, east a block to blinker light, then south at Shell Station one block; west side of street.
Large warehouse full of dining room sets, European furniture, etc. Large selection of chandeliers.

5 Bentleys Antiques

50 Center Street, Douglas MI 49406
616-857-3339
Hours vary by the season.
Downtown
Vintage posters, antiques, and art from Europe.

6 Olde House Antiques
112 Center Street, Douglas MI 49406
616-857-1623

7 Edwards Limited
36 Center Street, P.O. Box 601, Douglas MI 49406
616-857-1977

8 Rabbit Run Art & Antiques
Recently moved to Sawyer Michigan.
See page 16.

SAUGATUCK

9 Country Store Antiques
120 Butler Street, Saugatuck MI 49453
616-857-8601; if no answer call 616-396-1841

10 Swell Times
421 Water Street, P.O. Box 1163, Saugatuck MI 49453
616-857-8320

11 Andy's Antiques
3400 block Blue Star Highway, Saugatuck MI 49403

HOLLAND

12 Nob Hill Antique Mall
1261 Graafschap Rd., Holland MI 49423
616-392-1424
Mon. to Sat. 10 to 5:30
One mile south of 32nd Street.
Thirty dealers, 130 year old building.
Note: other shops & malls with a Holland address are located in Ottawa County, Section 4.1.

Note: Most shops in Holland are in Ottawa County, Section 4.1.

FENNVILLE

13 Anderson School House Gallery
5229 124th Avenue (M-89), Fennville MI 49408
616-561-2604
Mon. to Fri. 4:30 to 7, Sat. & Sun. 9 to 7
U.S. 31 to M-89 West; I-96 to M-89 East; two miles east of Fennville.

ALLEGAN

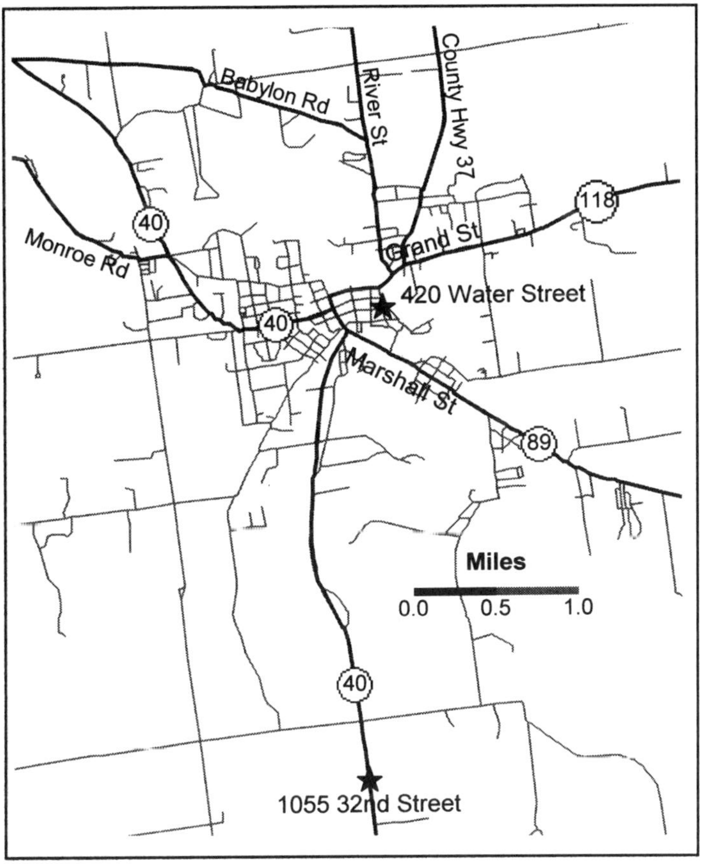

14 Water Street Place Mall Antiques Etc.
420 Water Street, Allegan MI 49010
616-673-5841
Mon. to Sat. 10 to 5, Sun. 12 to 5
Extended hours Allegan Show Weekends.
North end of beautiful historic Downtown Allegan.
Primitives to 50's: glassware, furniture, books, linens, jewelry, toys, dolls, and a Christmas Closet.
"We buy & sell Antiques."

15 B & C Emporium
204 Trowbridge Street, Allegan MI 49010
616-673-2815

16 Dawn's Antique Barn
1259 Williams Bridge Road, Allegan MI 49010
616-673-2253, 616-521-7529

17 Iron Horse Antiques
1055 32nd Street (M-40 South), Allegan MI 49055
616-673-2674 or 616-673-9417
May to Oct.: Thurs. to Sun. 12 to 7
East side of the highway.
Antiques, collectibles, and used horse tack.

OTSEGO

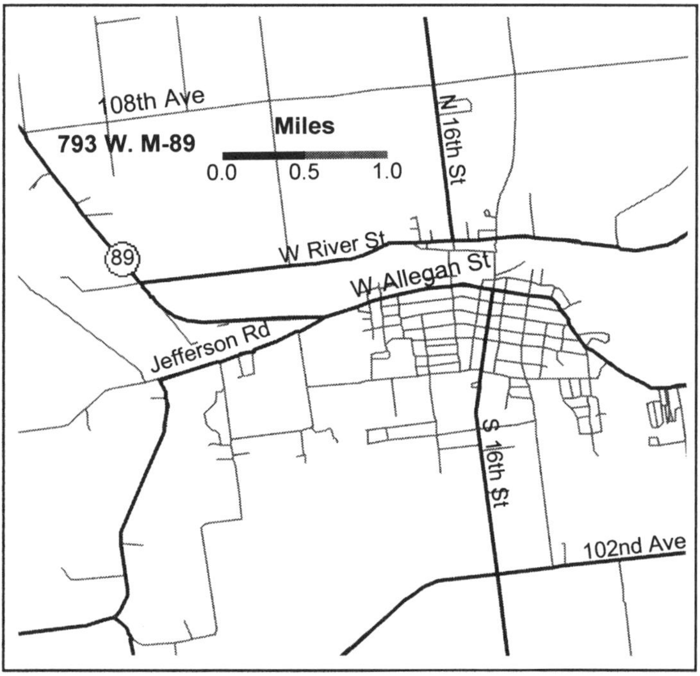

18 Little Red School House
793 West M-89, Otsego MI 49078
616-692-3833
Sat. & Sun. 11 to 5, or by appointment. Closed Jan.-March.
2 miles west of Otsego, northeast corner M-89 & 108th Avenue.
Antiques and collectibles.

19 Rustic Ranch
106th & M-89, Otsego MI 49078
616-694-9320

20 The Mercantile
506 West M-89, Otsego MI 49078
616-692-3630

21 Otsego Antiques Mall
114 West Allegan Street (M-89), Otsego MI 49078
616-694-6440

22 Harry J's & Missy
123 West Allegan, Otsego MI 49078
616-694-4318

PLAINWELL

23 Plainwell Antiques
220 South Main, Plainwell MI 49080
616 685-9030

24 Granny's Nook & Cranny
112 North Main Street, Plainwell MI 49080
616 685-4183

25 Junk'n Stuff'n Things
633 East Miller Road, Plainwell MI 49080
616 685-5755

DOOR

26 Back Door Antiques & Gifts
4219 18th Street, P.O. Box 42, Dorr MI 49323
616 681-9415

WAYLAND

(Map on following page.)

27 Duck Soup Antiques
578 132nd Avenue, Wayland MI 49348
616-792-1488, or 888-du1-soup
ducksoup@triton.net
BY appointment.
From U.S. 131 Wayland Exit: east to the light, go south about 2.5 miles; just past the cemetery go left on 132nd Avenue. The shop is next to the house 2.5 miles down on the right side.
Pottery, glassware, specializing in Roseville.

Wayland:

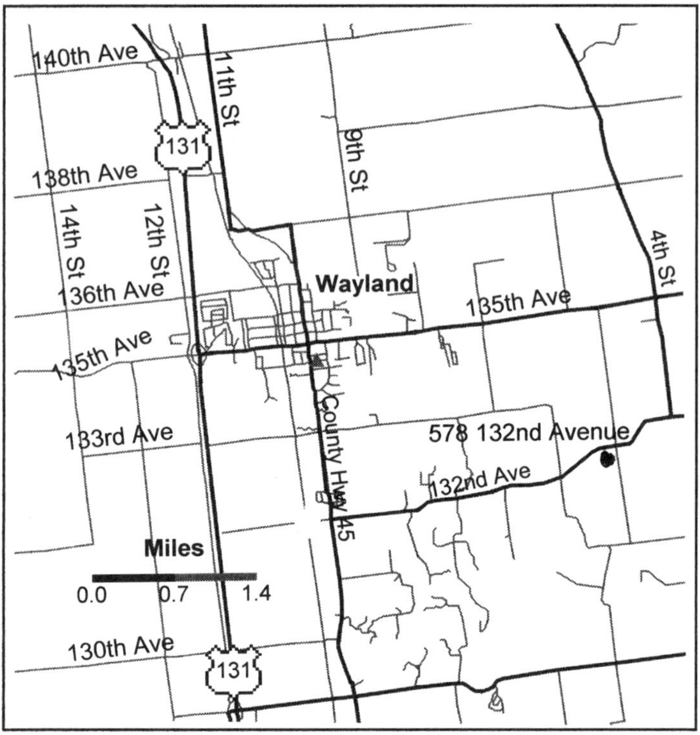

Hastings:

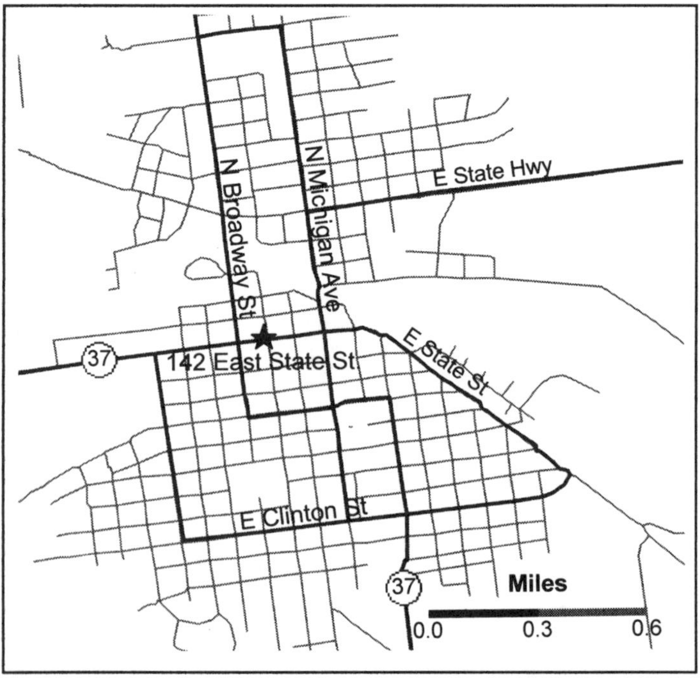

3.2 Barry County

HICKORY CORNERS

1 Hickory Hollow Antiques
14560 South Kellogg School Road, P.O. Box 121, Hickory Corners MI 49060 616 671-4222

HASTINGS

(Map on preceding page.)

2 Hastings Antique Mall
142 East State Street, Hastings MI 49058
616 948-9644
Tue. to Sat. 10 to 6, Sun. Mon. by chance.
Downtown, south side of the street.
2,200 square feet.
Spinners & weavers gallery on 2nd floor.

3 Daval's Used Furniture & Antiques
2020 Gun Lake Road (M-37/M-43), Hastings MI 49058
616 948-2463

4 Belles Antiques and Collectibles
2701 Lawrence Road, Hastings MI 49058
616-945-3797

DOSTER

5 The Elevator
12911 South Doster Road , Doster MI 49080
616 664-4676

DELTON

6 Aunt Ellen's Attic
117 South Grove Street (M-43), Delton MI 49046
616 623-8900

GUN LAKE

7 Park Place Antiques
11344 M-179 Highway, Gun Lake MI 49333
616-795-9208
www.homestead.com/parkplacegallery/home.html
U.S. 131 Bradley exit, east four miles.

NASHVILLE

8 Mar-Jay Collectibles
232 N. Main (M-66), Nashville MI 49058
616 945-5965

9 The Pig in the Poke
301 S. Main Street, Nashville MI 49058
616-758-3028

Eaton Rapids:

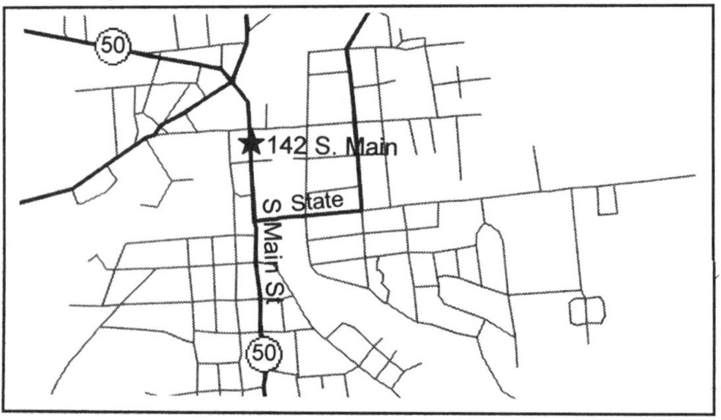

3.3 Eaton County

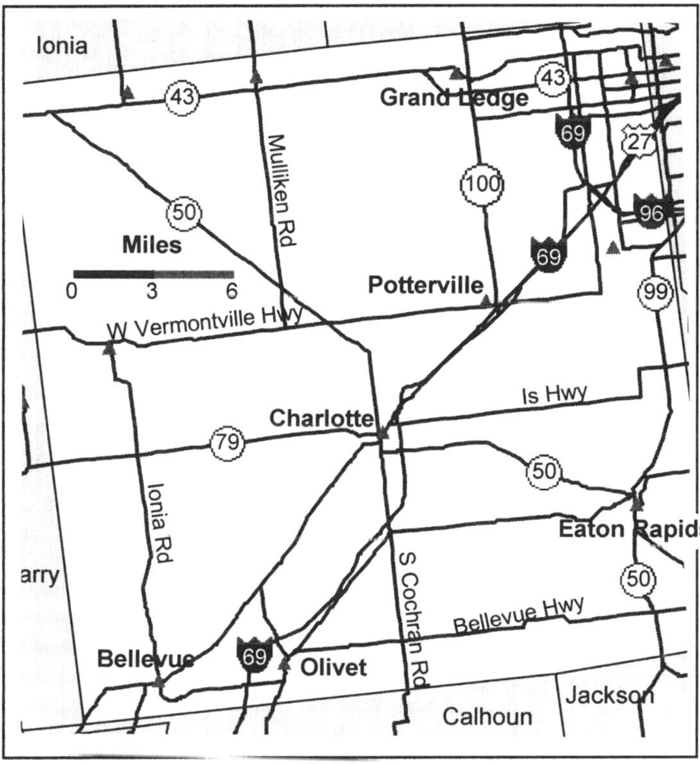

EATON RAPIDS

1 The Basket Case Antiques 'n Stuff
217 South Main Street, Eaton Rapids MI 48827
517 663-6100

2 Lita's Antiques & Treasures
142 South Main Street, Eaton Rapids MI 48827
517 663-7373

CHARLOTTE

3 The Doll Shop
116 S. Cochran, Charlotte MI 48813
517-543-7288

4 The Scottish Thistle
127 South Cochran, Charlotte MI 48813
517 541-1491

Charlotte:

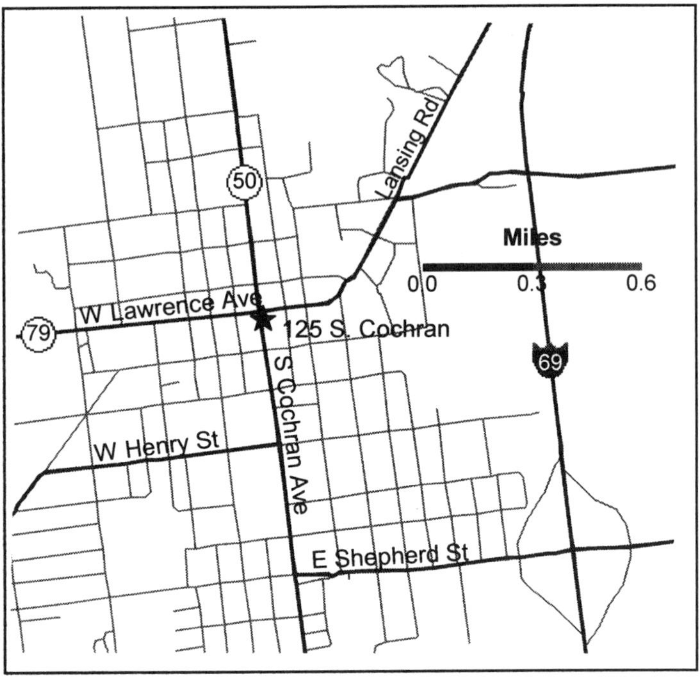

5 The Love Bug
111 W. Lawrence Avenue, Charlotte MI 48813
517-541-1113

6 Windwalker Antiques & Fine Art Gallery
125 South Cochran, Charlotte MI 48813
517 543-9933
Tues. to Fri. 10 to 5, Sat. 10 to 4, Sun. 12 to 5
Just down from the Old Court House.
"Unusual objects for the discerning collector."

POTTERVILLE

7 Main Street Estate Shop
200 West Main Street, P.O. Box 114, Potterville MI 48876
517 645-2909
Tues. to Fri. 10 to 4, Thurs. to 7
Downtown. Main Street is the northern-most street in town; downtown is 3 blocks west of M-100.
General line of antiques & collectibles; authorized Fenton dealer.
"Buy & sell daily."

Potterville:

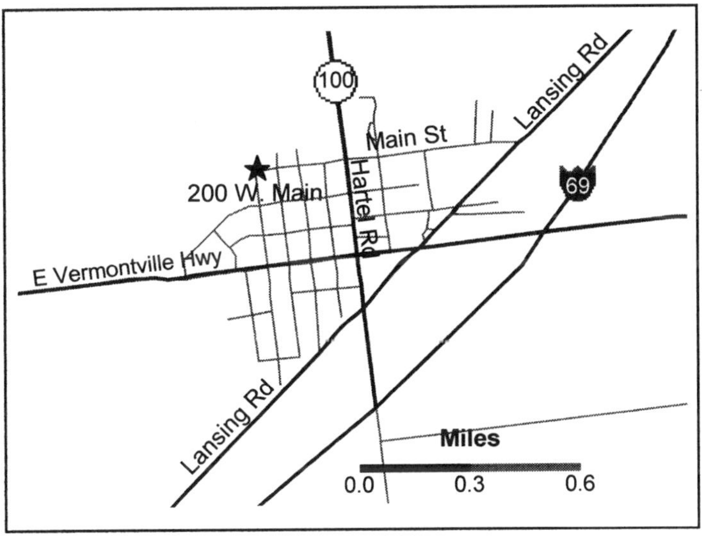

8 Mike Hager Antiques
216 Main Street, Potterville MI 48876
No telephone listed.

9 Ken's Antiques
112 West Main Street, Potterville MI 48876
No telephone listed.

GRAND LEDGE

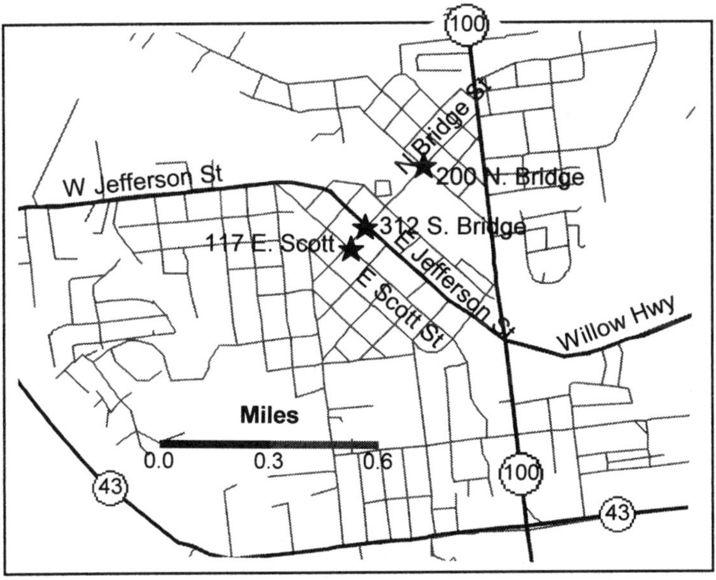

10 Bridge Street Church Antique Mall
200 North Bridge Street, Grand Ledge MI 48837
517 627-8637
Wed. to Sat. 10 to 5; Sun. 12 to 5
Downtown, northeast of the river.
2 floors, antiques & collectibles.

11 Grace Antiques and Fine Art
312 South Bridge Street, Grand Ledge MI 48837
517 622-1524
Mon. & Wed. to Sat. 10 to 7, Sun. 12 to 5
Downtown, next to Sun Theater.
Furniture, art pottery, art.

12 The Cat's Meow
117 East Scott Street, Grand Ledge MI 48837
517 622-3414 NBLOCKGLM@AOL
Mon. to Sat. 10 to 5:30
In the story book cottage off the Scott St. Parking Lot.
Antique & collectible glassware, dishes, 20's & 30's pieces, linens, jewelry, prints, etc

Leslie:

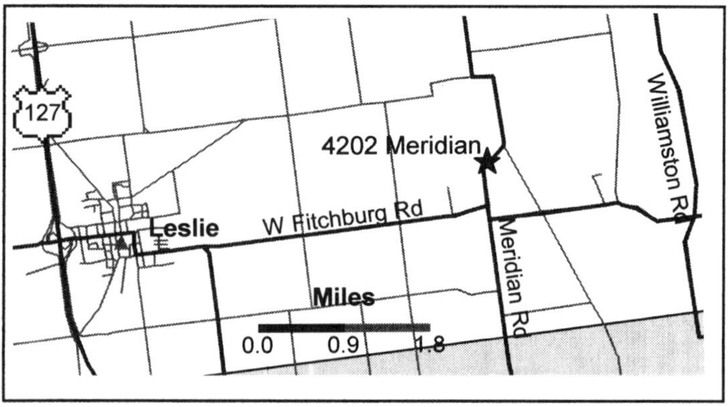

3.4 Ingham County

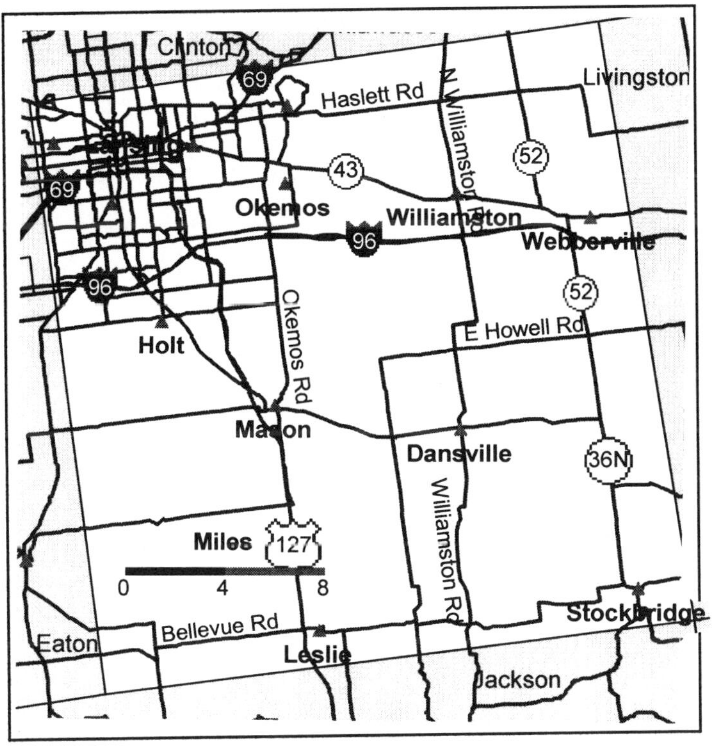

LESLIE

(Map on preceding page.)

1 Anns'tiques
4202 Meridian Road, Leslie MI 49251
517-589-9225
Wed., Sat. & Sun. 10 to 5
West side of road between Kinneville and Fitchburg Roads. 4 1/2 miles east of U.S. 127.
General line: furniture, pottery, collectibles, glass.

2 Leslie Antique Mall
149 South Main Street, P.O. Box 554, Leslie MI 49251
517-589-9430

MASON

3 Heard It Thru The Grapevine
4504 West Columbia Road, Mason MI 48854
517-676-2110

Mason:

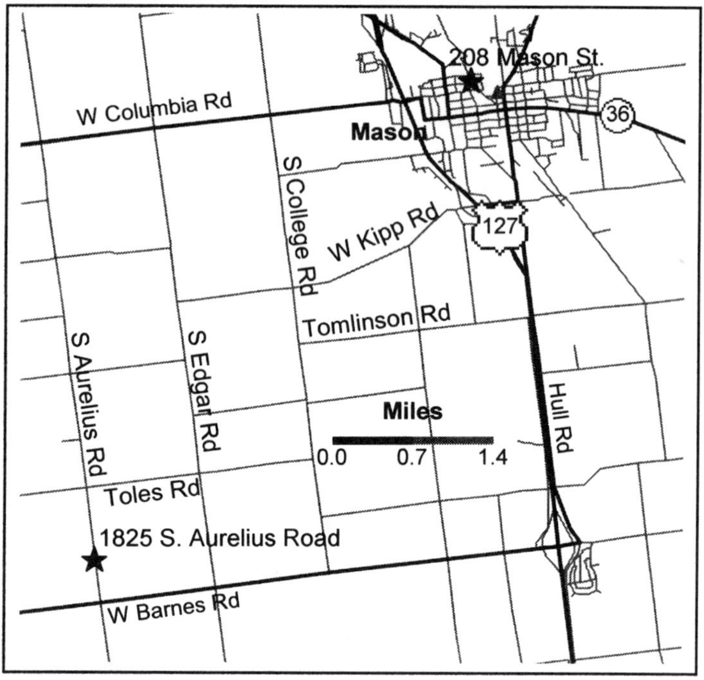

4 Art & Shirley's Antiques
1825 South Aurelius Road, Mason MI 48854
517-628-2065
Mon. to Sat. 11 to 5. If nobody is in the shop, knock on the door of the house in back.
From Route 127: West on Barnes Road 4 miles , then north a quarter mile on Aurelius.
From Holt: 7.5 miles south on Aurelius.
Caning, restoring, refinishing, and furniture in the rough.

5 Wood n' Glass Antiques
3154 Holt Road, Mason MI 48854
517-694-0120
rwtgreen@aol.com

6 Mason Antiques District
208 Mason Street, Mason MI 48854
517-676-9753
Web page: www.antiquedist.com
Every day 10 to 6
Two blocks east of Cedar Street, a mile east of U.S. 127. Mason Antiques District has 12 buildings and over 45 dealers. Shops listed on follwing page.

Included in the Mason Antiques District are the following:

6.1 1. Mason Antiques Market
111 Mason Street, Mason MI 48854
517-676-9753

6.2 2. Flamingo Road
Mason Street, Mason MI 48854
517-676-9753

6.3 3. The Carriage Shop
208 Mason Street, Mason MI 48854
517-676-1530

6.4 4. Peddlar's Row
208 Mason Street, Mason MI 48854
517-676-6388

6.5 5. Front Porch Antiques Mall
208 Mason Street, Mason MI 48854
517-676-6388

6.6 6. The Loft Antiques Co-Op
208 Mason Street, Mason MI 48854
517-676-0400

6.7 7. Old Mill Antiques Mall
207 Mason Street, Mason MI 48854
517-676-1270

6.8 8. Rusty Nail Warehouse
208 Mason Street, Mason MI 48854
517-676-1270

OKEMOS

7 Farm Village Antique Mall
3448 South Hagadorn Road, Okemos MI 48864
517-337-4988; Fax: 517-337-4560
Mon. to Sat. 11 to 6, Sun 12 to 6
Southeast corner Hagadorn & Jolly Road.
Large multi-level facility, over 50 dealers, 10,000 square feet.
Pottery, porcelain, furniture, books, jewelry, vintage clothing, 50's, Art Moderne and more.

Okemos:

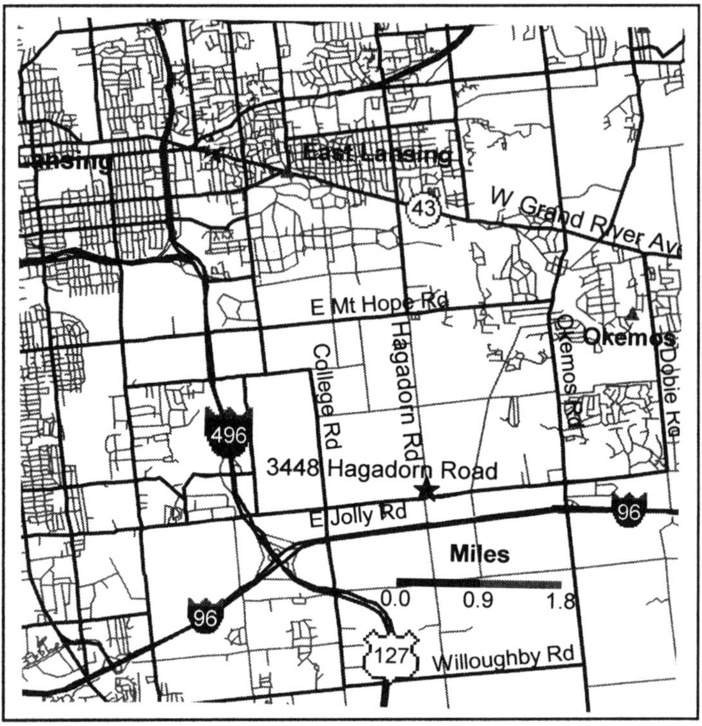

8 Spud's Shop
3448 S, Hagadorn Road, Okemos MI 48864
517-351-2140

9 Wooden Skate Antiques, Estate Jewelry & Gems
1259 West Grand River Road, Okemos MI 48864
517-349-1515; FAX 517-349-8628; E-mail:
Web page: www.woodenskate.com

LANSING

10 Treasure Cove
933 W. Jolly, Lansing MI 48910
517-882-8639

11 Cedar Street Antiques
3709 South Cedar , Lansing MI 48910
517-393-1913

12 St. Luke's Antiques
3016 South Cedar, Lansing MI 48910
517-882-5364

13 Triola's Gallery
1114 East Mt. Hope Road, Lansing MI 489120
517-484-5414 Deco and modernism design.

Lansing:

14 Tom's Furniture & Antiques
319 East Grand River, Lansing MI 48912
517-485-8335 Antiques, new & used furniture, etc.

15 Antique Connection
700 East Kalamazoo Street, Lansing MI 48912
517-484-8360

16 Pennyless in Paradise
1918 E. Michigan, Lansing MI 48912
517-372-4526

17 Slightly Tarnished
2008 E. Michigan, Lansing MI 48912
517-485-3599

18 Little Red School House
5002 W. Saginaw, Lansing MI 48917
517-321-6701

19 Mid Michigan Mega Mall
15487 U.S. Highway 27, Lansing MI 48906
517-487-3275
Daily 11 to 6, Thurs. to 8:30
North side of Lansing, two miles south of I-69.
Antiques, new furniture, unique gifts.
Over 200 dealers.

HASLETT

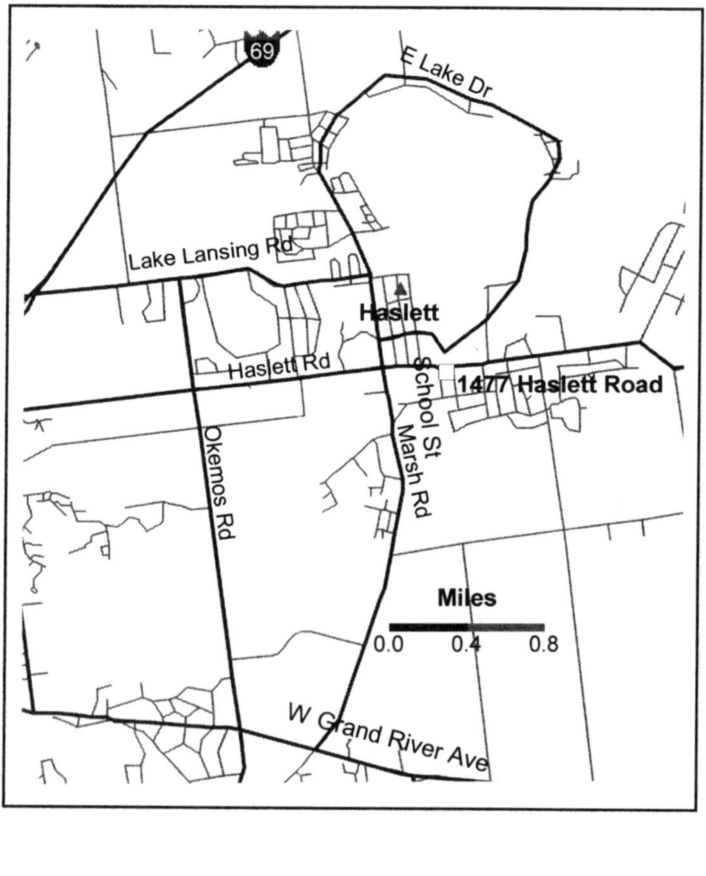

20 Fire House Antiques
1477 1/2 Haslett Road, Haslett MI 48840
517-339-2368
Thurs. to Sat. 10 to 5 - Time might change so call first. From the corner of Marsh and Haslett Roads go east on Haslett, pass the railroad tracks. Turn right on School Street, then left into the alley. The shop is in back of Beal's Refinishing. General line of antiques.

STOCKBRIDGE

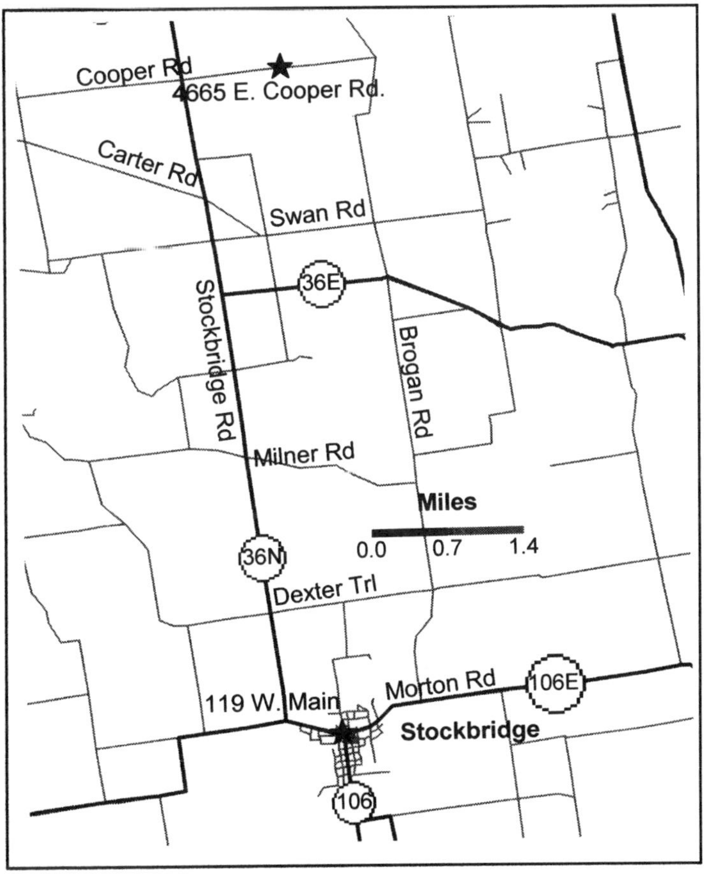

21 Tom Forshee Antiques
119 West Main Street P.O. Box 125, Stockbridge MI 49285
517-851-8114
Fri. & Sat. 10 to 4; Sun. 12 to 4; or by appointment. South side of street. Entrance from the rear parking lot; enter the parking lot from Wood Street southbound. Oriental and English porcelains and American furniture.

22 White Oak Antiques
4665 East Cooper Road, Stockbridge MI 49285
517-851-8151
paunot@vayager.net
7 days, By chance.
7 miles north of Stockbridge on M-52 (or 8 miles south of I-96), and one-half mile east of M-52, on Cooper Road. Antiques, china, glass, books, prints, furniture, plus paper and collectible junk; 3 rooms stuffed full plus a barn.

23 Hafner Antique & Craft Mall
5000 South Clinton, Stockbridge MI 49285
517-851-7677

DANSVILLE

24 Rogers Antiques
1135 Mason Road (M-36), P.O. Box 216, Dansville MI 48819
Phone & Fax: 517-623-6566

25 Red Barn Antiques & Collectibles
1131 Mason Street (M-36), Dansville MI 48819
Phone & Fax: 517-623-6631

WILLIAMSTON

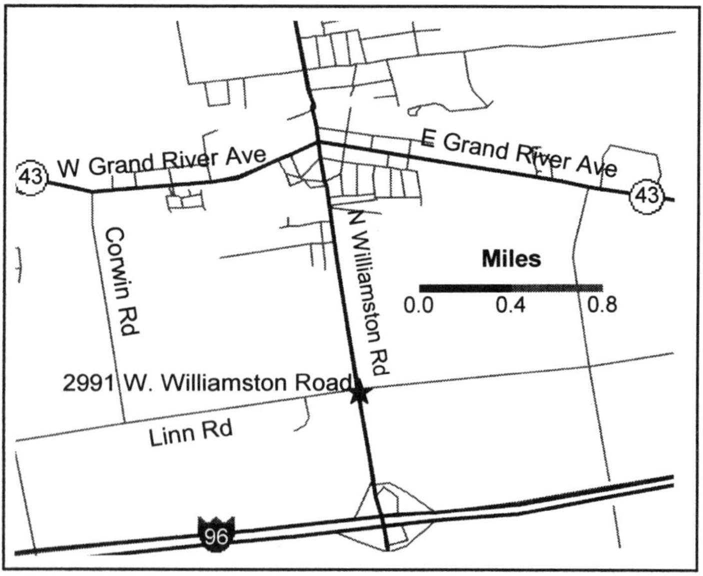

26 Antiques Market of Williamston / Grand River Merchants
2991 Williamston Road
P.O. Box 10, Williamston MI 48895
517-655-1350 gvandusen@voyager.net
www.americanantiquities.com/amwgr.html
Every Day 10 to 6
I-96 Exit 117, then one-third mile north.
70 dealers, 15,000 square feet. "Largest selection of quality antiques in the Lansing Area."

27 Bittersweet Antiques
2200 Howell Road, Williamston MI 48895
517-655-1698

28 Old Plank Road Antiques
126 West Grand River Avenue, Williamston MI 48895
517-655-4273

29 Main Street Shoppe Antiques
108 West Grand River Avenue, Williamston MI 48895
517-655-4005

30 Legends Jewelry
104 West Grand River Avenue, Williamston MI 48895
517-655-4221

31 Corner Cottage
120 High Street, Williamston MI 48895
517-655-3257

32 Putnam Street Antiques
122 South Putnam Street, 2nd floor, Williamston MI 48895
No telephone listed.

33 Lyons Den Antiques
132 South Putnam, Williamston MI 48895
517-655-2622

34 All Good Things
684 West Grand River Avenue, Williamston MI 48895
517-655-6991 Fax: 517-655-8462

35 Things Beer
100 East Grand River Avenue, Williamston MI 48895
517-655-6701

36 Old Village Antiques
125 East Grand River Avenue , Williamston MI 48895
517-655-4827

37 Happicats Antiques
133 East Grand River Avenue, Williamston MI 48895
517-655-1251; 517-223-8039

38 Sign of the Pineapple Antiques
137 East Grand River, Williamston MI 48895
517-655-1905

39 House of Trivia
138 East Grand River Avenue, Williamston MI 48895
517-655-5570

40 The Rectory
326 East Grand River, Williamston MI 48895
517-655-6268

WEBBERVILLE

41 Iron Horses
4412 Grand River Road East, Webberville MI 48892
517-521-4200

42 Re-Use It Antiques, Consignments & Collectibles
120 West Grand River, Webberville MI 48892
517-521-4390

Pinckney:

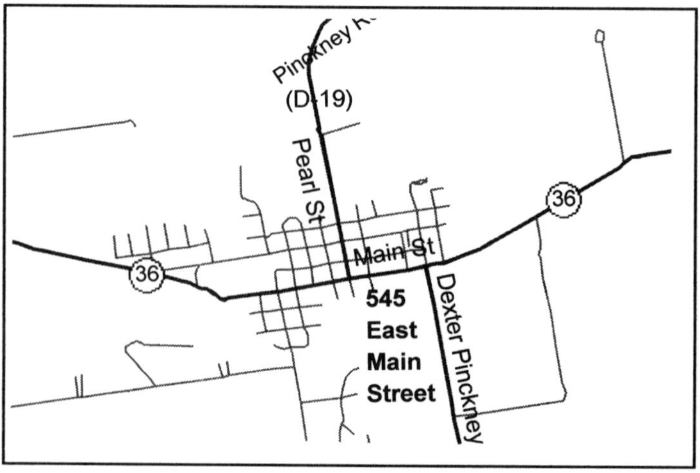

3.5 Livingston County

PINCKNEY

(Map on previous page.)

1 Bloomers Antiques & Collectibles

545 East Main Street (M-36), P.O. Box 105, Pinckney MI 48169
734-878-8957
Bloomers@provide.net
Tues. to Sun. 11 to 5
One block east of D-19 on M-36 (Main Street).
Charming turn-of-the-century Victorian house showcasing an eclectic blend of antiques, collectibles and primitives. Visa and Mastercard accepted.

HOWELL

2 Antiques on the Avenue
315 North Michigan Avenue, Howell MI 48843
517-552-1080

3 Indian Hills Antiques
9480 Wiggins Road, Howell MI 48843
517-546-8792

4 Lake Chemung Oldies
5225 East Grand River Road, Howell MI 48843
517-546-8875

HARTLAND

5 Stillmeadow Shop
3568 Hartland Road, Hartland MI 48029
810-632-5560

BRIGHTON

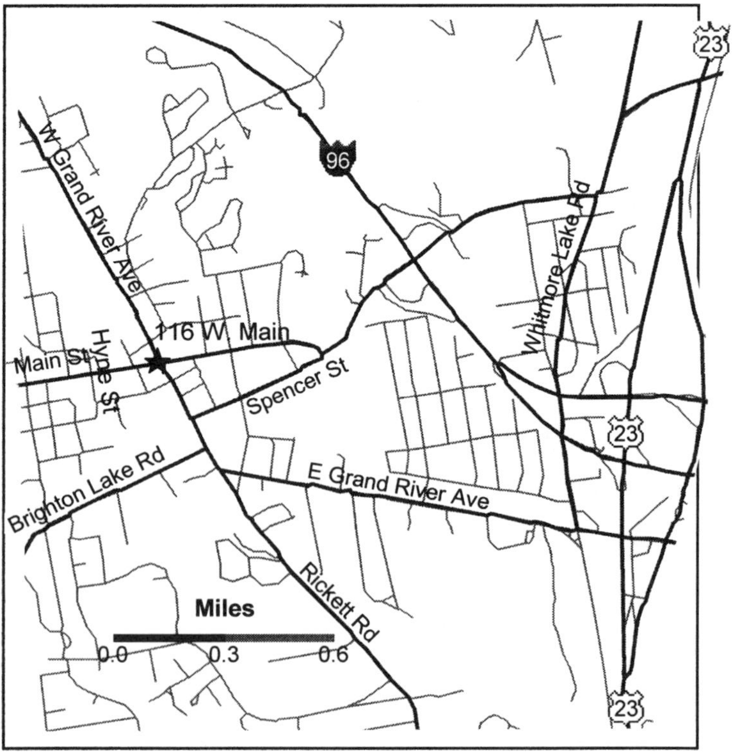

6 Nostalgia
116 West Main Street, Brighton MI 48116
810-229-4710; see2@webtv.net
Mon. to Wed. 10 to 7; Thurs. & Fri. 10 to 8; Sat. 10 to 6; Sun. 12 to 5 by chance or appointment.
Downtown Brighton.
Furniture and a general line of antiques & collectibles. Petite cafe with imported coffees & espresso; live music on Friday; 1800's theme.

7 The Quaker Shoppe Antiques
210 Hyne Street, Brighton MI 48116
810-229-6558

8 Somewhere In Time
316 West Main Street, Brighton MI 48116
810-227-5797

9 History Town Antique Mall
6080 Grand River Avenue, Brighton MI 48114
517-545-9225

HAMBURG

10 The Hamburg Store
10596 Hamburg Road, P.O. Box 96, Hamburg MI 48139
810-231-6940

3.6 Oakland County

WALLED LAKE

(Map on following page.)

1 Town Peddler Craft & Antique Mall
1154 East West Maple Road, Walled Lake MI 48390
248-926-8650 www.townpeddler.com
Mon. to Thurs. 10 to 6, Fri. & Sat. 10 to 8, Sun. 11 to 6
East of Pontiac Trail, West of Decker
One of two locations for Town Peddler Mall.

NOVI

2 Antiques & Pine Design
43443 Grand River Avenue, Novi MI 48375
248-380-7777

Walled Lake:

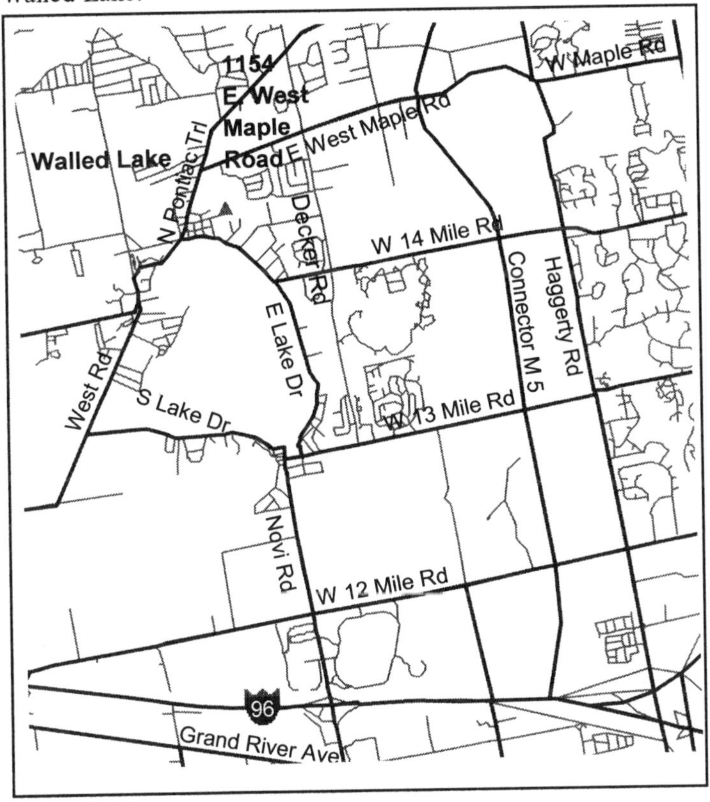

FARMINGTON

3 Craftique Craft & Antique Mall
33300 Slocum, Farmington MI 48336
248-471-7933
www.craftique.com

SOUTHFIELD

4 The McDonnell House
19860 West 12 Mile Road, Southfield MI 48076
248-559-9120

CLINTON TWP.

5 Gloria's Resale Boutique Antique
24394 Crocker, Clinton Township MI 48036
810-463-0857

FRANKLIN

6 D & J Bittker, Ltd.
26111 West 14 Mile Road, Suite 102, Franklin MI 48025
248-932-2660 By Appointment Only

7 Artistry of the Ages
23712 West 13 Mile Road, Franklin MI 48025
248-644-8700

BERKLEY

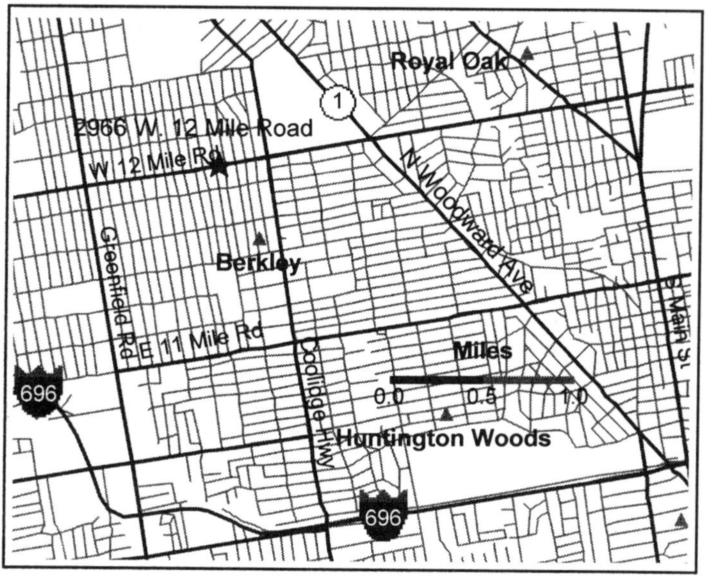

8 Timeless Antiques
2733 Woodward, Berkeley MI 48072
248-582-1510

9 Antiques Unlimited
2656 11 Mile Road, Berkley MI 480
248-545-4488

10 Twice Around Resale Shop
2966 West 12 Mile Road, Berkley MI 48072
248-545-6600
Tues. through Sat. 11 to 4
Downtown Berlkey, north side of the street, next to Rite Aid Pharmacy, same block as Berkley Theatre.
Antiques, collectibles, vintage jewelry.

11 Second Season
3860 12 Mile Road, Berkley MI 48072
248-414-9026

FERNDALE

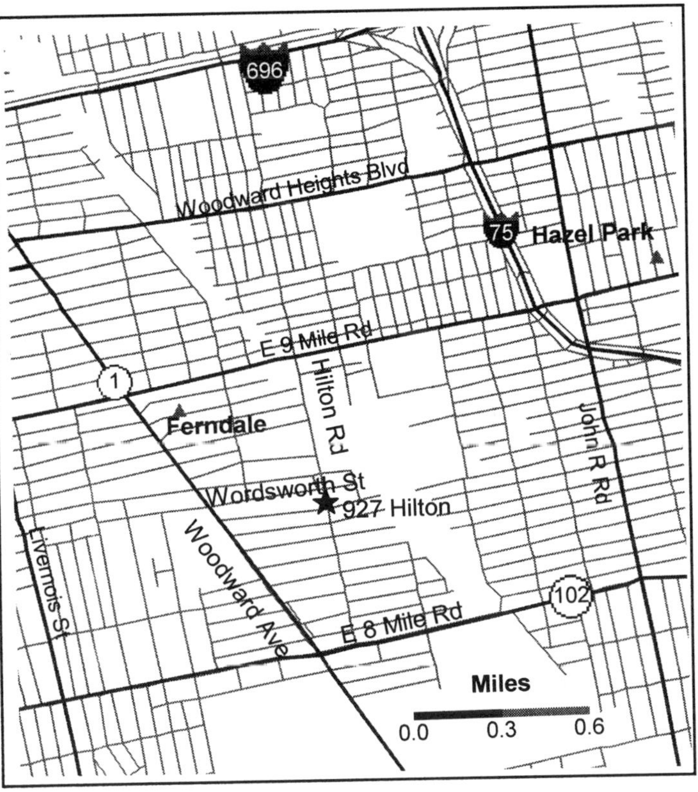

12 Antiques on the Avenue
22446 Woodward, Ferndale MI 48220
248-399-0339

13 EuropeDirect WareHouse Inc.
927 Hilton Road, Ferndale MI 48220
248-691-9155 info@edwh.com
www.edwh.com
Tues. to Sat. 10 to 5
On Hilton Road at 8 1/2 Mile Road.
Largest importer of European antiques and reproductions in Michigan; new shipments from England & France weekly; custom furniture including kitchen & cottage pine, farm tables and chairs.

(See Display Ad on Following Page)

14 Harper Gallery
306 W. Nine Mile Road, Ferndale MI 48220
Moved from Detroit to Ferndale in 2000.

ROYAL OAK

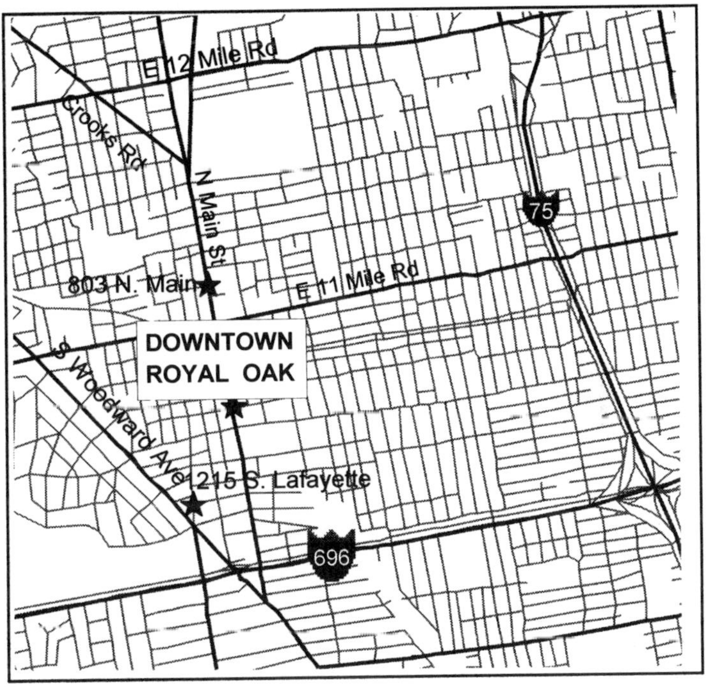

15 Jeff Fontana Designs
1215 Lafayette South, Royal Oak MI 48067
248-543-8370; Fax: 248-543-8372
Mon. to Fri. 11:30 to 5, Sat. 12 to 4
Lafayette & Woodward, across from the Detroit Zoo.
Design studio & European antiques & accessories.

16 Del Giudice Gallery
16 South Lafayette Street, Royal Oak MI 48067
248-399-2608

17 The Dandelion Shop
114 West Fourth Street, Royal Oak MI 48067
248-547-6288

18 Royal Oak Farmers Market
316 East 11 Mile Road, Royal Oak MI 48067
248-548-8822 Sunday; some dealers open during week.

Downtown Royal Oak:

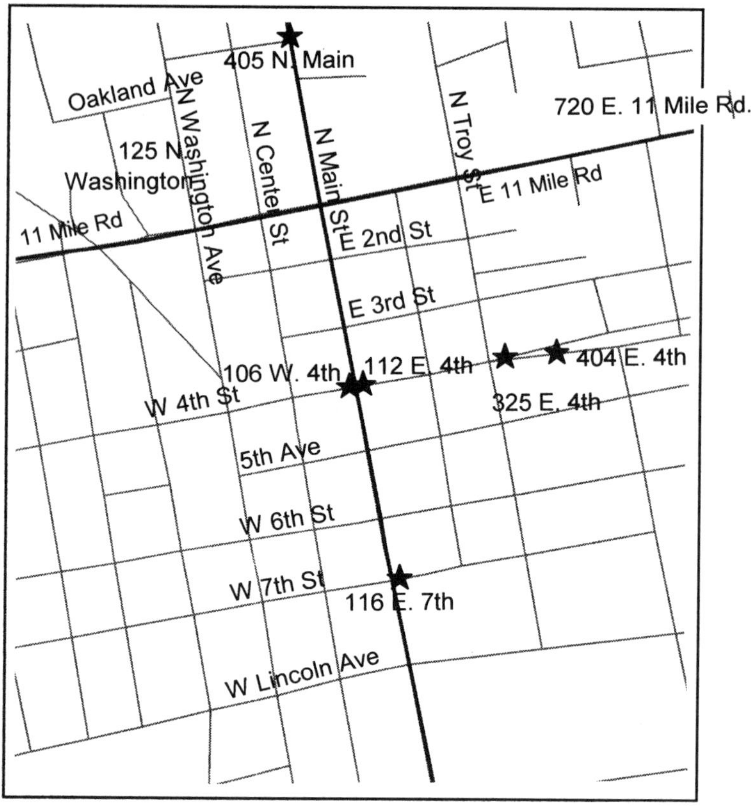

19 Deco Doug
106 West Fourth Street, Royal Oak MI 48067
248-547-3330
Mon. to Sat. 12 to 6
Downtown, North side of street.
Art Deco accessories, barware, vintage watches, clocks, lamps.

20 Heritage Company II Architectural Artifacts &Design
Boutique also at this location: A Rose is a Rose
116 East 7th Street, Royal Oak MI 48067
248-547-0670 heritage@megsinet.net
Tues. to Sat. 11 to 5, Sun. 12 to 4
South of downtown just east of Main Street.
Architectural, garden, antiques, primitives & custom architectural fabrication. A Rose is a Rose has china, linens, garden, gifts.

21 Washington Place
517 South Washington, Royal Oak MI 48067

22 Vertu Deco and Fifties
511 South Washington, Royal Oak MI 48067
248-545-6050

23 Carol Grant Decorative Arts
510 S. Washington, Royal Oak MI 48967
248-398-1411; Fax: 248-586-1104
Arts & crafts furniture and pottery; primitive painted furniture; antique garden accessories.

24 Daves Comics & Collectibles
407 South Washington, Royal Oak MI 48067
248-548-1230

25 Milieu
416 South Washington, Royal Oak MI 48067
248-542-9119

26 Yellow House Antiques
125 North Washington, Royal Oak MI 48067
248-541-2866
Tues. thru Sat. 11 to 5, Sun. 12 to 5, Mon. by chance
West side of street, north of 11 Mile Road.
Primitives, Fifties, decorative accessories, Victorian, and a general line.

27 Vertu II
433 North Washington, Royal Oak MI 48067
248-547-3062

28 Antiques on Main
115 South Main Street, Royal Oak MI 48067
248-545-4663

29 Lulu
405 North Main Street, Royal Oak MI 48067
248-542-6464
Mon. thru Sat. 11 to 5.
Downtown, west side of street, two blocks north of 11 Mile Road.
Buttons, primitives, ceramics, and eclectic, garden items.

30 Histoire De Famille
803 North Main, Royal Oak MI 48067
In the rear of House on Main Antiques.
French antiques.

31 House on Main
803 North Main Street, Royal Oak MI 48067
248-541-3069
Mon. to Sat. 12 to 4, closed Tues.
North of downtown, west side of the street, at Austin Street between 11 and 11 1/2 Mile Roads, across from the Hollywood Market.
Pottery, vintage photographs, silver, glass, textiles etc. A shop in the rear has French Antiques.

32 Paris
112 East Fourth Street, Royal Oak MI 48067
248-542-9594
Mon. to Sat. 10 to 6, Sun. 11 to 5; open to 5:30 in the winter.
South side of the street, one building east of Main Street. A unique blend of French, nouveau, deco, linens, lace, and more. Also: Art deco, furniture, vintage clothing, and textiles. Formerly The Cherub's Chest and In The 20th Century.

33 Simpley Charming Antiques
325 East Fourth Street, Royal Oak MI 48067
248-541-9840
Tues. to Sat. 11 to 4, or by appointment.
Sterling, Flow Blue, Majolica, chandeliers, sconces.

34 Jeffrey's 4th Street Antique Mall
404 East 4th Street, Royal Oak MI 48067
248-584-2220 mail@jeffreyclay.com
www.jeffreyclay.com
Wed. to Sat. 11 to 7, Thurs. to 9; Sun. 12 to 5, Mon. by appointment.
Largest collection of vintage American art pottery in the state. Arts & crafts mission furniture.

35 Grandma's Good-Stuff
405 East Fourth Street, Royal Oak MI 48067
248-543-2335

36 Red Ribbon Antiques
418 East Fourth Street, Royal Oak MI 48067
248-541-8117

37 Lovejoy's Antiques
720 East Eleven Mile Road, Royal Oak MI 48067
248-545-9060 luvjoy720@aol.com
Tues. to Sun. 10 to 5
South side of the road.
General line, specializing in reverse painted lamps.

38 Bogart's Antiques & Collectibles
600 East 11 Mile Road, Royal Oak MI 48067
248-398-0646

39 Antique Connection
710 East Eleven Mile Road, Royal Oak MI 48067
248-542-5042; Fax: 248-542-3660
www.quikpage.com/a/antiqueconn

40 White Elephant Antique Shop
724 West Eleven Mile Road, Royal Oak MI 48067
248-543-5140

41 Royal Antiques
1106 East Eleven Mile Road, Royal Oak MI 48067
248-548-5230
Daily 9 to 6
Between Main Street and I-75, south side of the street. Fifties items, dolls, and a general line of antiques & collectibles. 35 dealers.

42 Craftique Craft & Antique Mall
30947 Woodward Ave., Royal Oak MI 48073
248-288-4400

BIRMINGHAM

43 Classic Country Antiques
2277 Cole, Birmingham MI 48009
248-258-5140
Mon. to Fri. 11 to 5, Sat. 12 to 4
In a warehouse district between 14 Mile & 15 Mile Road, east of Woodward, just east of Eton.
American & English antique furniture and accessories.

44 Savoir Faire
1157 South Adams Road, Birmingham MI 48009
248-644-0560 tjlotarski@aol.com
Tues. to Fri. 10 to 5:30, Sat. 10 to 4:30, or by appointment. One Block northeast of intersection of Woodward & Adams at the corner of Lincoln (14 1/2 Mile Road.)
Direct importer of French antiques.

45 James Sanders, Antiquarian
725 South Adams Road, Birmingham MI 48009
248-540-0044

Birmingham:

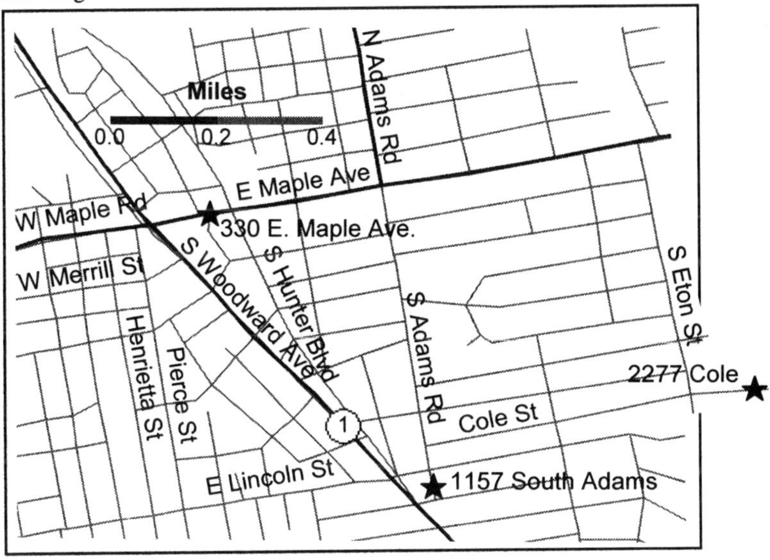

46 L'Esprit
243 West Maple , Birmingham MI 48009
248-646-8822

47 Masterpiece Gallery of Fine Art & Antiques
137 West Maple Road, Birmingham MI 48009
248-594-9470

48 Chase Antiques
251 East Merrill, Birmingham Mi 48009
248-433-1810; 810-543-4511

49 Crimson Rose Antiques
251 Merrill Street, Birmingham MI
248-203-2950

50 Leonard Berry Antiques
251 East Merrill, Birmingham MI 48009
248-646-1996

51 Taylor Antiques
251 Merrill St., Birmingham MI 48009
248-594-8330

52 Merwins Antique Gallery
588 North Old Woodward, Birmingham MI 48009
248-258-3211

53 Watch Hill Antiques & Interiors
330 East Maple, Birmingham MI 48009
248-644-7445; Fax: 248-644-1152
www.watchhillantiques.com
Mon. to Sat. 10 to 6, Thurs. & Fri. to 8; Sun. 12 to 4
South side of street between Woodward and Old Woodward.
Country antiques and accessories from Europe, specializing in original painted furniture, pine TV centers, pine tables, chairs and mirrors.

54 Madeline's Antique Shoppe
790 North Old Woodward, Birmingham MI 48011
248-644-2493

CLAWSON

55 Aquilon Antiques
26 N. Main, Clawson MI 48017
248-577-5255
melliot@mail.customnet.net
Tues. to Sat. 11 to 6
Downtown, just north of 14 Mile Road, east side of the street.
Glassware, jewelry, furniture, gold & silver, etc.

MADISON HEIGHTS

56 Ben Wulff Antiques
918 West 11 Mile Road, Madison Heights MI 48071
248-545-4488

COMMERCE

57 Byers Country Store
213 Commerce Road, Commerce MI 48382
248-363-3638

BLOOMFIELD HILLS

58 Garland Brown Antiquities
1500 Sandringham Way, Bloomfield Hills MI 48301
248-647-9410
Open by appointment only.

PONTIAC

Pontiac:

59 Scott Emporium
196 & 198 West Walton Blvd., Pontiac MI 49770
248-338-4148

60 Modernage Gallery
25 North Saginaw Street, Pontiac MI 49770
248-745-0999; 888 861-8479; Fax: 248-745-9598
E-Mail: kzuc@aol.com

61 First 1/2
43 North Saginaw Street, Pontiac MI 49770
248-334-9660; Fax: 248-253-1883
jcaussin@aol.com
www.machineage.com

62 The Antique Gallery
102 North Saginaw Street, Pontiac MI 49770
248-334-5566 HenkStudio@msn.com
www.HenkStudioAntiques.com
Mon. to Fri. 10 to 5
North of downtown, east side of the street.
Furniture.

63 Dixieland Flea Market
2045 Dixie Highway, Pontiac MI 49770
248-338-3220

TROY

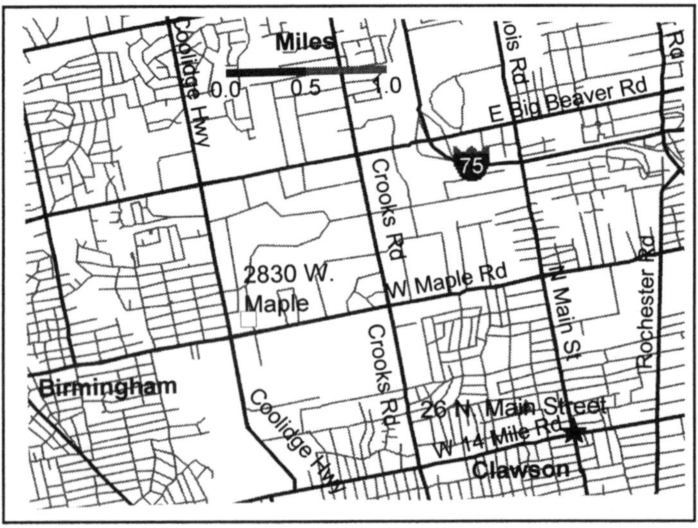

64 Antiques Centre of Troy
2830 West Maple Road, Troy MI 48084
248-649-4399
judy@judyfrankelantiques.com
Tues. thru Fri. 10:30 to 4:30, Sat. 11 to 4
Northeast corner of Maple & Coolege.
Antique decorative furniture, smalls, textiles, fine art, etc.

ROCHESTER

65 Chapman House on Main
311 Walnut Street, Rochester MI 48307
248-651-2157

66 Antiques by Pamela
319 Main Street, Rochester MI 48063
248-652-0866; Fax: 248-652-0866
E-Mail: pjk@speedlink.net
Mon. to Fri. 10 to 6, Sat. 10 to 5, Thurs. to 8
Use Main Street or back parking lot entrances.
Graduate gemologist on staff. Contemporary, vintage and antique jewelry. Victorian through Retro period in furniture, crystal, lighting, sterling; many accessories.

67 Haig Galleries
311 Main Street, Floor Two, Rochester MI 48063
248-656-8333
sales@hsiggalleries.com www.haiggalleries.com
Mon. to Sat. 12 to 6
Downtown, west side of street, two blocks south of Walton.
Ancient, Asian, Tribal antique art.

68 Tally Ho! Antiques
404 Main Street, Rochester MI 48063
248-652-6860
Mon. to Fri. 12 to 6, Sat. 10 to 5, Thurs. to 8
Use Main Street or back parking lot entrances.
Period antiquities in furniture, jewelry, crystal, clocks, books, primitives, sterling and more.

69 Haig Jewelers
436 South Main, Rochester MI 48063
248-652-3660 Antique jewelry.

70 Rochester Design Center and Antique Mall
210 West University Drive, Rochester MI 48307
248-651-5711

WATERFORD

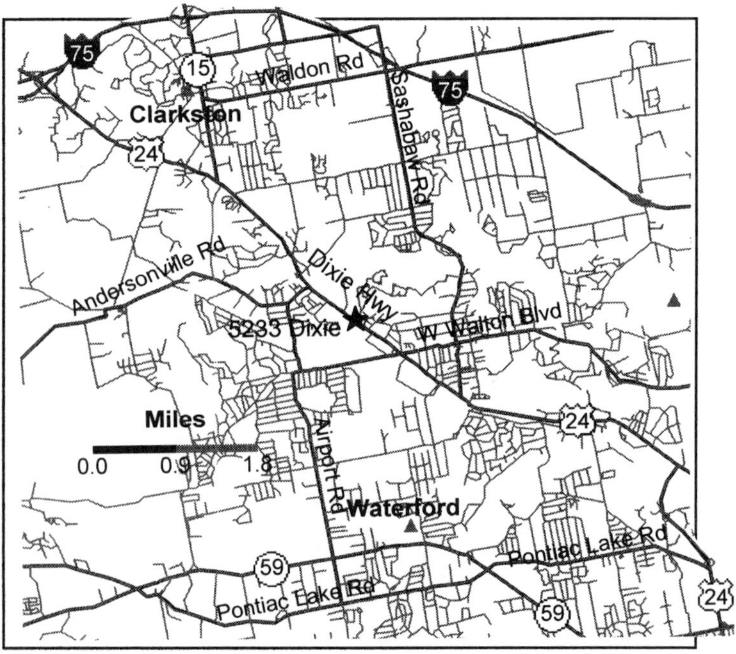

71 The Great Midwestern Antique Emporium
5233 Dixie Highway (U.S. 24), Waterford MI 48329
248-623-7460
Tues. to Sun. 10 to 5
West side of highway, 6 blocks south of Andersonville Road.
50 dealers, 5,500 square feet

72 Shoppe Of Antiquity
7766 Highland (M-59), Waterford MI 48329
248-666-2333

CLARKSTON

73 The Parsonage
6 East Church Street, Clarkston MI 48346
248-625-4340

74 Clarkston Country Store / Main Street Antiques
21 North Main, Clarkston MI 48346
248-625-3122

75 Spinning Jennys
5878 Dixie Highway, Clarkston MI 48346
248-623-3250

HOLLY

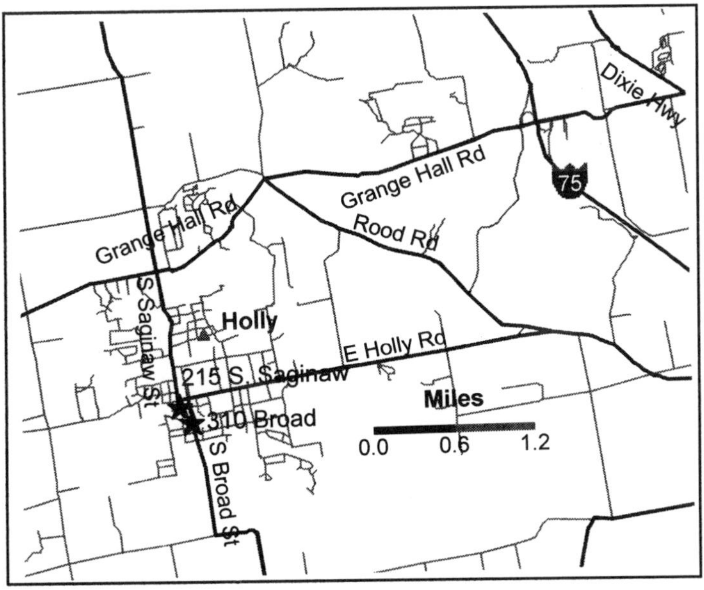

76 Battle Alley Arcade
108 Battle Alley, Holly MI 48442
248-634-8800

77 Sandy's Someplace in Time Antiques
101 South Saginaw Street, Holly MI 48442
248-634-3925

78 Holly Antiques on Main
118 South Saginaw Street, Holly MI 48442
248-634-7696 Fax: 248-634-2583

79 Cottage Antiques
203 South Saginaw Street, Holly MI 48422
248-328-0018

80 Allserv Antique Shop
215 South Saginaw Street, Holly MI 48442
248-634-5500 Fax: 248-634-7957

81 Balcony Row Antiques
216 South Broad Street, Holly MI 48442
248-634-1400

82 Holly Crossing Antiques
219 South Broad Street, Holly MI 48442
248-634-3333

83 Water Tower Antiques Mall
310 South Broad Street, Holly MI 48442
248-634-3500
Tues. to Sat. 10 to 5; Sun. 12 to 5
Downtown, across from the Water Tower.
High quality 18th to 20th Century antiques. Furniture, collectibles, Indian & cowboy artifacts, World War II artifacts.

ORTONVILLE

84 The Stone House
850 Ortonville Road (M-15), Ortonville MI 48462
248-627-5380

OXFORD

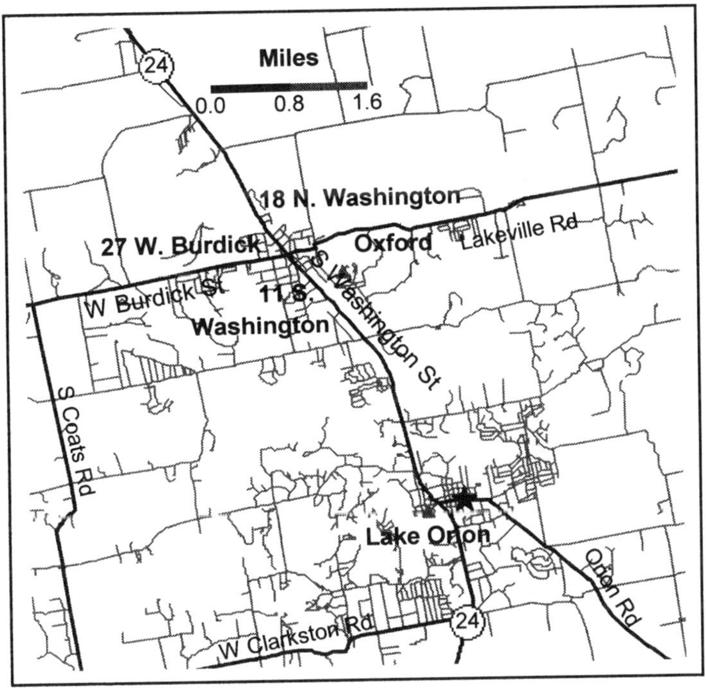

85 Romeo Antique Mall
11 South Washington Street, Oxford MI 48371
248-969-3688
Tues. to Sat. 11 to 5, Sun. 12 to 5
On M-24 between Pontiac and Lapeer.
Two floor of antiques and collectibles with 15 dealers.
Formerly located in the City of Romeo.

86 Sunset Antiques Inc.
22 North Washington Street, Oxford MI 48371
248-628-1111

87 Past Times Antiques
27 West Burdick, Oxford MI 48371
Phone or Fax: 248-628-9939
Thurs. to Sat. 10 to 6
Downtown, just west M-24.
General line of antiques and collectibles.

88 Oxford Antique Mall
18 North Washington Street (M-24), Oxford MI 48371
248-969-1951
sales@oxfordantiquemall.com
www.oxfordantiquemall.com
Every day 11 to 6, Thurs. to Sat. Until 9
Downtown, northeast quadrant.
6,500 square feet of quality antiques.
Dolls, primitives, china, pottery. Large selection of fine furniture, weather vanes, automotive items, advertising, etc., etc.

3.7 Macomb County

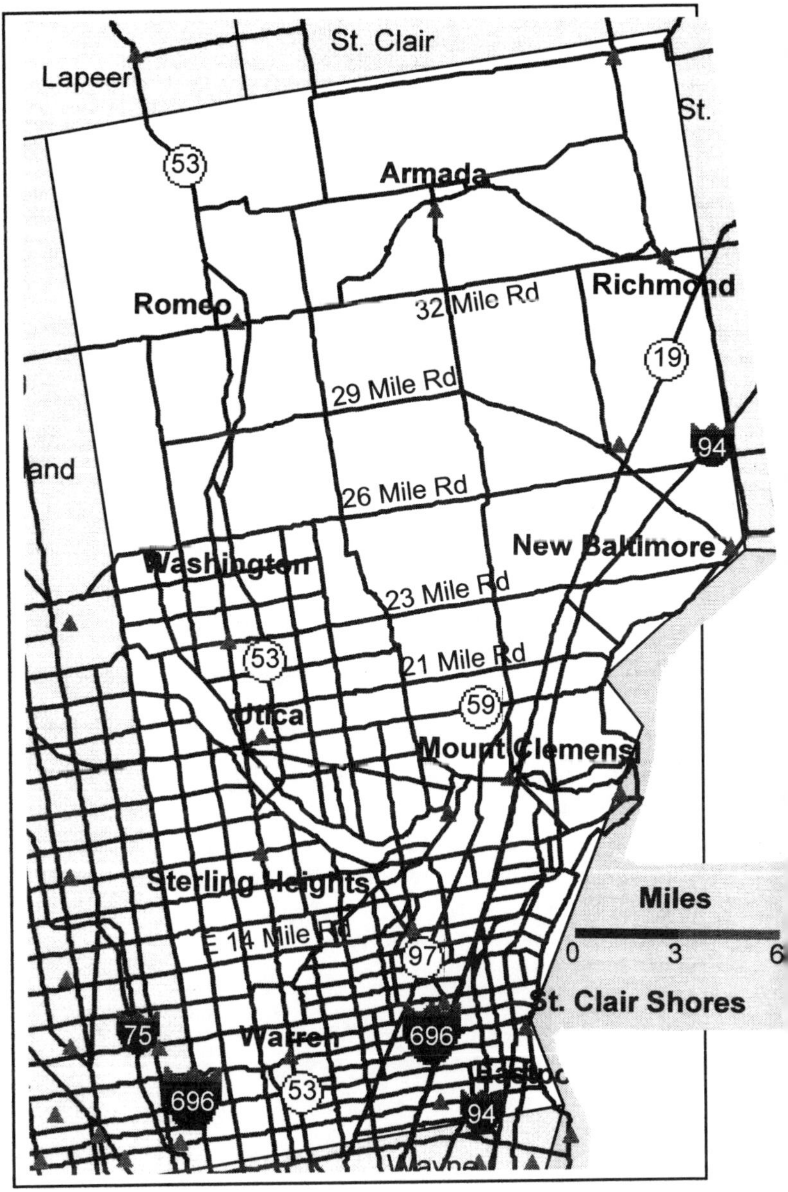

WARREN

1 Fred's Antique Furniture & Antiques
14091 8 Mile Road, Warren MI 48089
810-776-7100

Warren:

2 Silver Quill Antiques
22813 Van Dyke, Warren MI 48089
810-756-8180
Mon. Tues. Fri. & Sat. 12 to 6, Sun. 1 to 6
Two blocks south of Nine Mile Road, northwest corner Maxwell Street.
Glass, china, pottery, jewelry, etc.

3 The Antique Gallery
11564 13 Mile Road, Warren MI 48089
810-751-0063

4 Eclectic Micks
20900 Dequindre Road, Warren MI 48091
810-758-7875

EASTPOINTE

5 Ariel's Enchanted Garden
23712 Gratiot Avenue, Eastpointe MI 48021
810-775-2820

ST. CLAIR SHORES

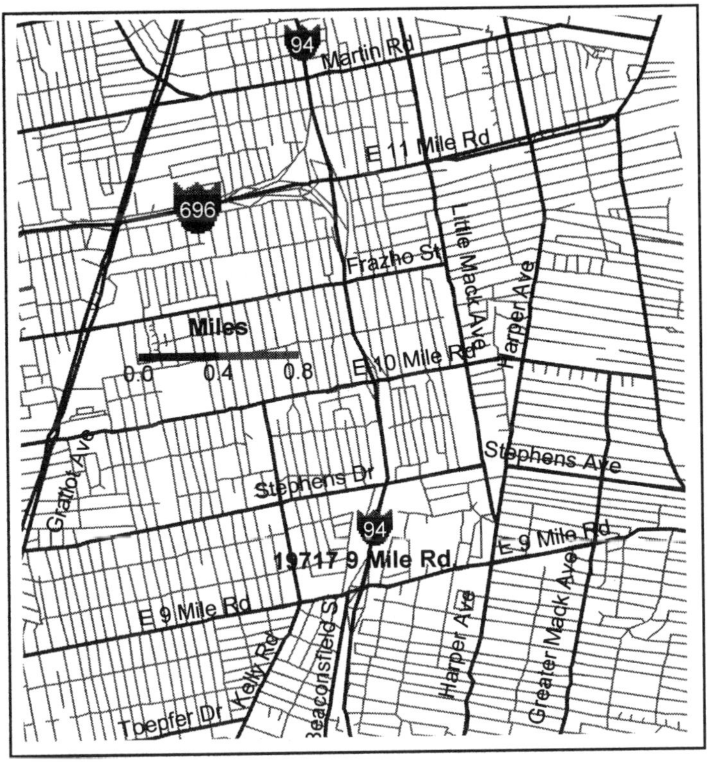

6 Adams English Antiques
19717 Nine Mile Road, St. Clair Shores MI 48080
810-777-1652
Mon. to Fri. 9 to 5, Sat. 10 to 5
6 blocks west of Harper, just east of I-94, north side of road.
Custom harvest tables, wardrobes, and scrub pine specialty.
Very large shop; lots of English furniture.

7 McHugh's Antiques
23215 Nine Mack Loop, St. Clair Shores MI 48080
810-774-9966

MT. CLEMENS

8 Estate Antiques & Resale
1142 Southbound Gratiot Ave., Mount Clemens MI 48043
810-468-9888

STERLING HEIGHTS

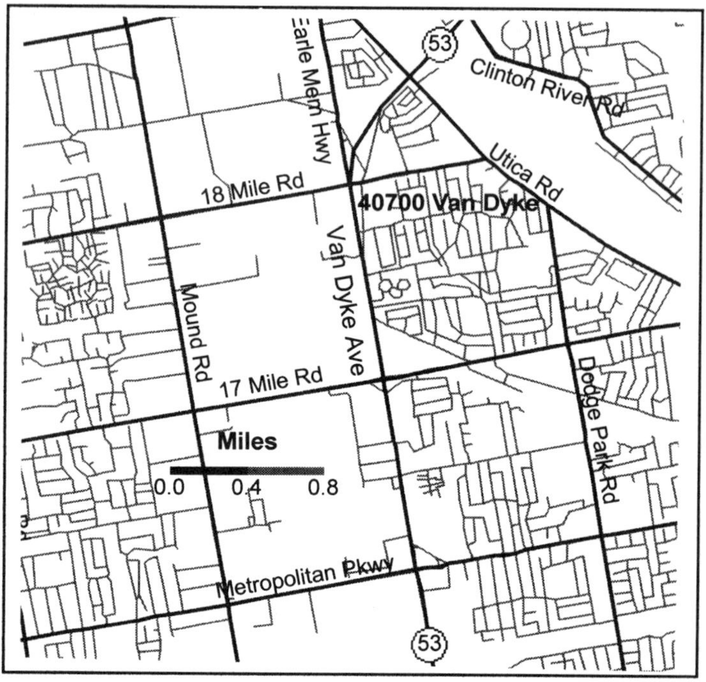

9 Moravian Trail Shop
34355 Moravian Trail, Sterling Heights MI 48313
810-979-4101

10 Countryside Craft Mall & Antiques
40700 Van Dyke Ave., Sterling Heights MI 48313
810-977-1633
Mon. to Wed. & Fri. 10 to 6; Thurs. & Sat. 10 to 8; Sun. 11 to 5
Southeast corner northbound Van Dyke at 18 Mile Road. One of four locations of Countryside Mall.

UTICA

11 Artisans Antiques & Collectibles
13477 Hall Road, Utica MI 48317
810-731-5510

12 Bear Lair
2100 Auburn Rd., Utica MI 48317
810-731-2894
Next to the Hollywood Market.

NEW BALTIMORE

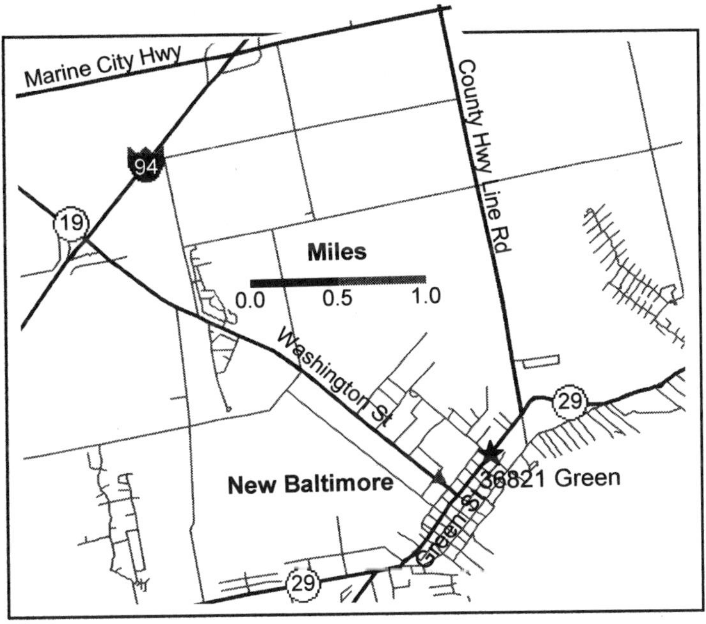

13 Heritage Square Antique Mall
36821 Green Street (M-29), New Baltimore MI 48047
810-725-2453
Tues. to Sat. 10 to 5; Sun 11 to 5
Northeast of downtown on M-29 past the light, north side of street in a large white 1861 mansion.
20 dealers; wide variety of quality antiques.

14 Washington Street Station
51059 Washington Street, New Baltimore MI 48047
810-716-8810

WASHINGTON

15 Bank of Antiques
58415 Van Dyke (M-53), P.O. Box 263, Washington MI 48094 810-781-5647; 810-798-3283

ROMEO

16 A Matter of Taste
105 South Main, Romeo MI 48065
810-752-5652

Romeo:

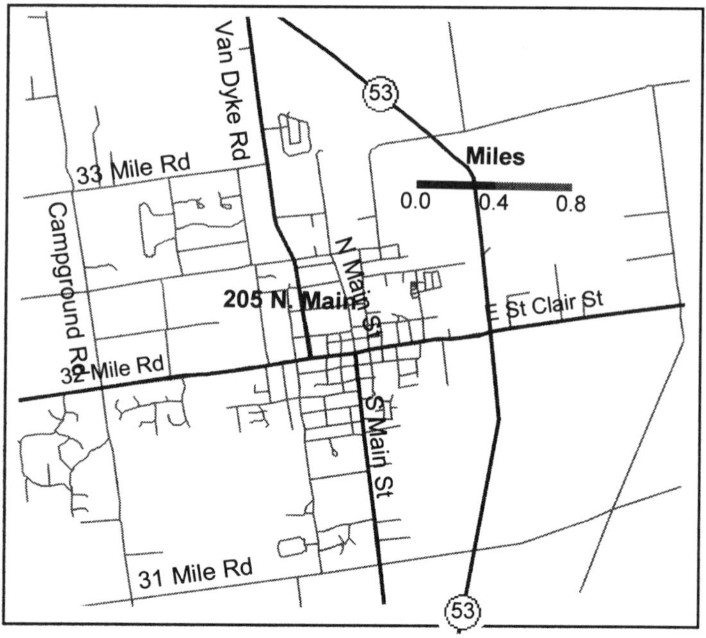

17 Town Hall Antiques
205 North Main, Romeo MI 48065
810-752-5422 townhall@ees.eesc.com
Daily 10 to 6
Downtown, west side of street just north of the light at 32 Mile Road.
50 dealers; quality antiques.

18 Romeo Bargain Barn
230 East St. Clair, Romeo MI 48065
810-752-5060

RICHMOND

19 High Bank Antiques
28689 Armada Ridge Road, Richmond MI 48062
810-784-5302
Fri. to Sun. 12 to 5, Tues. by chance or appointment.
From Richmond on M-19: At the north end of downtown go west on Park Street; this becomes Armada Ridge Road. Continue out of town several miles. The shop is on the north side of the road, midway between Richmond and Armada.
250 antique lighting fixtures; furniture, and miscellaneous.

Richmond:

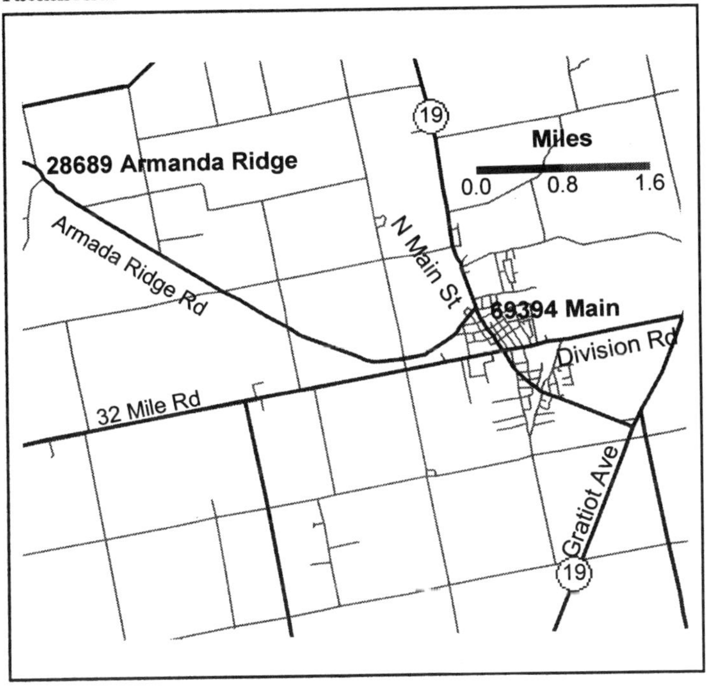

20 Barb's Antique Mall
69394 Main Street (M-19), Richmond MI 48062
810-727-2826 810-727-9724 anytime
Tues. to Sun. 12 to 5
North end of downtown, 3 blocks north of Division Street, east side of street.
Antiques, Depression Glass, OAK & Victorian furniture.

21 Wagon Wheel Antiques
69273 Main Street, Richmond MI 48062
810-727-7474

ARMADA

22 Parkway Antiques
23046 Main Street, Armada MI 48002
810-784-5682

23 Grandfathers Yesteryears
23089 Main, Armada MI 48002
No telephone listed.

TIER 4: GRAND RAPIDS-FLINT-PORT HURON

4.1 Ottawa County

HOLLAND

One shop with a Holland address is located in Allegan County.

1 The Brick House
112 Waukazoo Drive, Holland MI 49423
616-399-9690

2 Twigs
185 South River Avenue, Holland MI 49423
616-392-2775

3 Tulip City Antique Mall
3500 U.S. 31, Holland MI 49424
616-786-4424; Fax: 616-786-4426; E-mail: tcamall@sirus.com
Web Site: www.tulipcityantiquemall.com
Mon. to Sat. 10 to 6; Sun. 12 to 6
Corner of Greenly, east side of the highway, 2 miles north of M-21 interchange.
30,000 square feet, 200 dealers. Dolls, glass, fine china, pottery, radios, Indian artifacts, advertising, quality furniture, jewelry.

4 Harvest Antiques & Collectibles
Holland Outlet Center, 12330 James St., Holland MI 49424
616-395-0823
Mon. to Sat. 10 to 8, Sun. 10 to 6
The Harvest Outlet Center is at U.S. 31 & James Street. Harvest Antiques & Collectibles is located between Eddie Bauer & Bugle Boy at the east end of the mall.
Coca Cola collectibles, Herman Miller furniture, NASCAR, advertising, World Fair goods, glassware, miniatures, etc.

Holland:

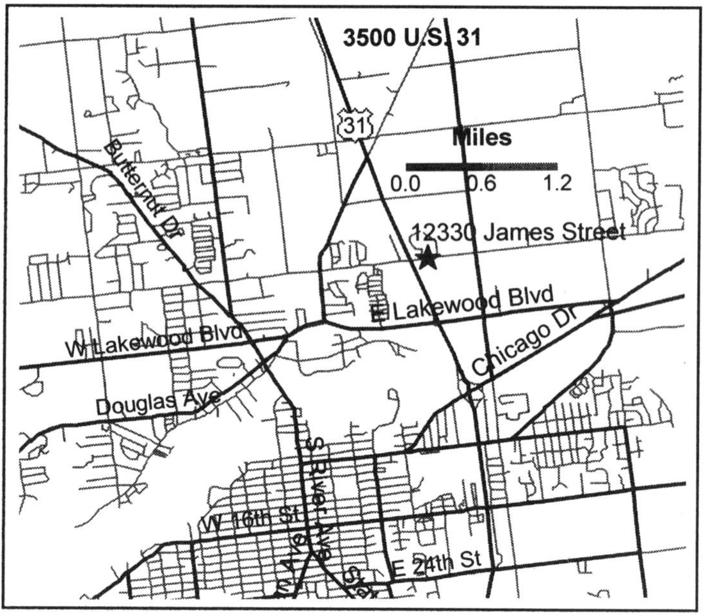

ZEELAND

(Map on following page,)

5 Main Place Antique Mall and Le Cafe

114 East Main Avenue, Zeeland MI 49464

616-748-0510

Mon. to Fri. 7:30 to 5.30, Sat. 9 to 5

Take Zeeland Exit to downtown Zeeland

8,000 square feet of antiques, gifts, collectibles.

Cafe with deli located in front of store.

Main Place Antique Mall

Antiques • Collectables and Gifts

Le Cafe

Coffee & Espresso Bar

Soups • Deli Sandwiches

114 East Main
Zeeland, MI 49464
(616) 748-0510

Zeeland:

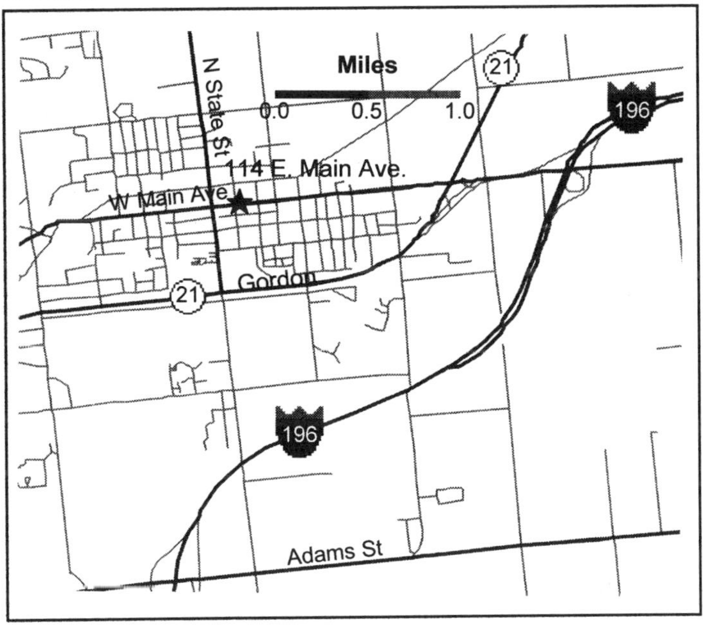

HUDSONVILLE

6 Somewhere In Thyme
2410 Chicago Drive, Hudsonville MI 49426
616-662-1571

WEST OLIVE

(Map on following page,)

7 Whispering Pines Antiques
6427 Butternut Drive, West Olive MI 49460
616-399-6216

8 Lake Shore Antique Shop
10300 U.S. 31, West Olive MI 49460
616-847-2429 Fax: 616-847-7101
Mon. to Sat. 10 to 6; Sun. 12 to 5
Jan. & Feb.: Mon. to Sat. 10 to 5; Sun. 12 to 5
11 North of Holland east side of US 31, or 7 miles south of Grand Haven on US 31.
Quality antiques & collectibles, glqss, pottery, quilts & furniture.

West Olive, Grand Haven & Spring Lake:

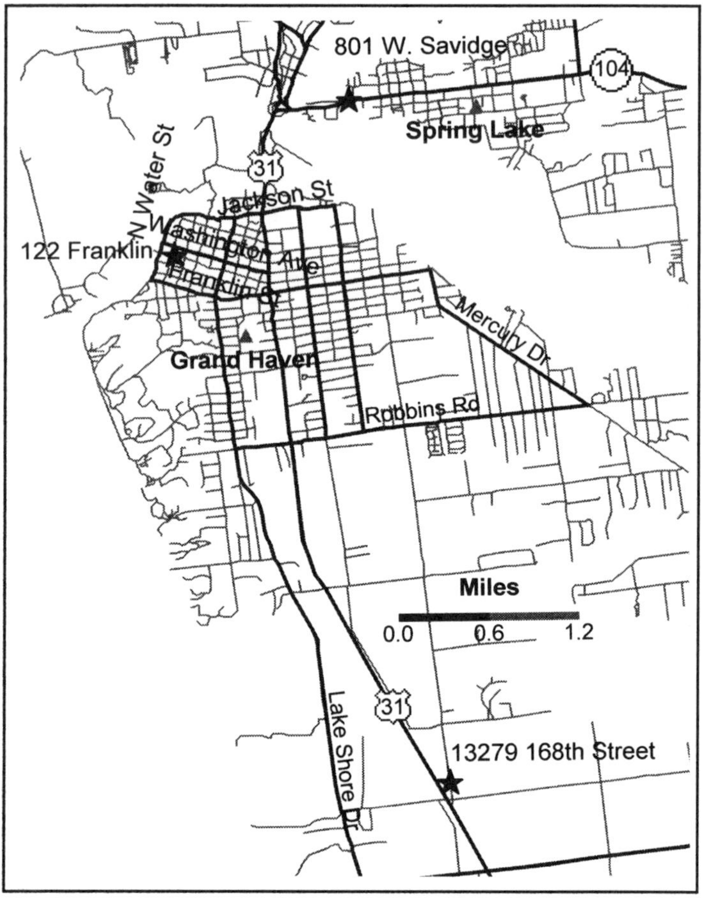

GRAND HAVEN

9 West Michigan Antique Mall
13279 168th Street at U.S. 31 South, Grand Haven MI 49417
616-842-0370
E-mail: Leavittsq@novagate.com
Mon. to Sat. 10 to 6; Sun. 12:30 to 6
On U.S. 31 at Ferris, 2 miles south of Grand Haven.
12,000 square feet.

10 Whims and Wishes
216 Washington, Grand Haven MI 49417
616-842-9533

11 Carriage House Antiques
122 Franklin Avenue, Grand Haven MI 49417
616-844-0580
Tues. through Sat. 11 to 5; Sun. 1 to 5
Downtown location, one block south of Washington between 1st and 2nd Streets.
Victorian, country and mission furniture 1830 to 1930. Estate jewelry. 3.500 square feet of display. Expert assistance. Individually owned and operated.

SPRING LAKE

12 Spring Lake Antique Mall
801 West Savidge (M-104), Spring Lake MI 49456
616-846-1774
Summer: Mon. to Sat. 10 to 6; Sun. 12 to 5;
Winter: Mon. to Sat. 10 to 5, Sun. 12 to 5
North side of road, just east of the Spring Lake bridge . 50 dealers, 4,400 square feet. Glassware, primitives, all types of furniture, collectibles, North Woods, Chitz China, jewelry, marbles, etc.

13 Green Gables Antiques and Collectibles
630 East Savidge Street, Spring Lake MI 49456
616-846-7383

COOPERSVILLE

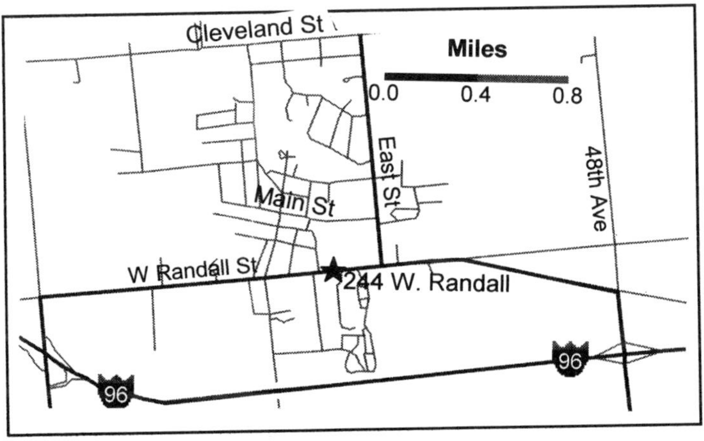

14 Track Side Antiques & Collectibles
248 Main Street, Coopersville MI 49404
616-997-8545

15 Ye Olde Post Office
286 Ottawa Street, Coopersville MI 49404
616-837-9475

16 Main Street Antiques
265 Main Street, Coopersville MI 49404
616-837-1937
Main Street is one-way east-bound.

17 The Re-Find Shop
244 West Randall, Coopersville MI 49404
616-837-5814
Mon. to Fri. 10 to 6, Sat. 10 to 5
South side of Randall between 48th and 68th Streets. Use Exit 16 or 19 from I-96.
Antiques, collectibles, housewares, used furniture.
"An estate Sale in a Showroom."

18 Mostly Antiques
16694 48th Avenue, Coopersville MI 49404
616-837-9695

LAMONT

19 Maple Valley Antiques
13575 42nd Avenue, Lamont, MI 49435
616-677-3422

ALLENDALE

20 Antiques of Allendale
6821 Lake Michigan Drive (Highway M-45), P.O. Box 556, Allendale MI 49401
616-892-6022

21 Ward's Antiques
5187 Lake Michigan Drive (M-45), Allendale MI 49401
616-895-7015 pjward@altelco.net
Open All Year - Thurs. Fri. & Sat. 10 to 5, or by appointment.
Located just west of Grand Valley State University; north side of road.
Two floors of quality furniture, advertising, toys, glassware, etc.

4.2 Kent County

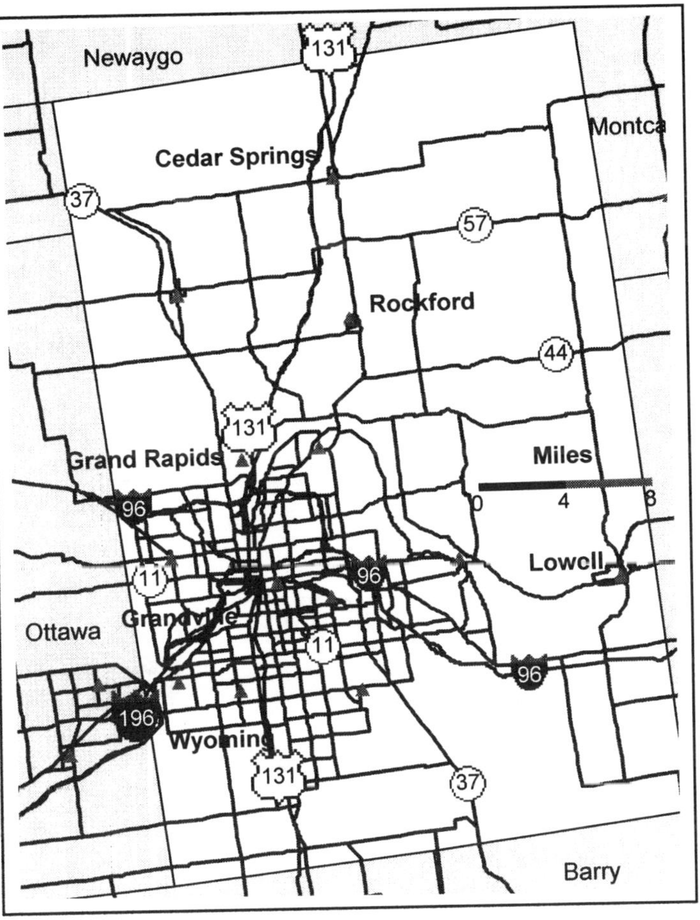

GRAND RAPIDS

1 Plaza Antique Mall
1410 28th Street SE, Grand Rapids MI 49506
616-243-2465
Mon. to Fri. 10 to 7; Sat. 10 to 6; Sun. 1 to 5.
South side of the highway, a block west of Kalamazoo Rd.
68 dealers, 9,000 square feet. Air conditioned; Visa & Master Card Accepted.
Oak furniture, lamps, glassware, china, pottery.

2 Marlene's Antiques & Collectibles
1054 West Fulton, Grand Rapids MI 49504
616-235-1336

Grand Rapids:

3 One Man's Junk
450 Leonard, Grand Rapids MI 49504
616-456-9100

4 Mary's Used Furnishings
730 Leonard NW, Grand Rapids MI 49504
616-774-8792
Mon. to Sat. 10 to 6
1.5 miles west of Highway 131, just past Arnie's Restaurant, at McReynolds Street.
Antiques, accessories, used furniture, art, religious, and collectibles.

5 Tried and True Shop
1200 West Leonard St., Grand Rapids MI 49504
616-774-9052

6 The Green Man Antiques
444 Bridge Street NW, Grand Rapids MI 49504
616-454-5771
Wed. to Sun. 12 to 5;
Oct. to June: closed between 3 & 4 weekdays.
South side of the street, across from Antiques by the Bridge. Fine china, furniture, and a general line of antiques.

7 Antiques by the Bridge
445 Bridge N.W., Grand Rapids MI 49504
616-451-3430
Tue. to Sat. 10 to 5; Sun. 12 to 5
North side of street, just west of Broadway, across the river from downtown.
Note: Bridge Street becomes Michigan Street east of the river.
20 dealers, 9,500 square feet, 3 floors. One of the dealers, Mayfield Antiques, specializes in mission oak.

8 Curiosity Shop
220 Lyon Street NW Suite 215, Grand Rapids MI 49503
616-454-7879

9 A Scavenger Hunt
210 E. Fulton, Grand Rapids MI 49503
616-454-1033
May be moving to new loaction in 2001.

10 Nobody's Sweetheart
953 East Fulton, Grand Rapids MI 49503
616-454-1673

11 East Fulton Antique Mall
959 East Fulton Street, Grand Rapids MI 49503
616-774-3320
Mon. to Sat. 11 to 6
One mile east of downtown in the heart of the East Fulton Business District, near Diamond Street.
Large variety of unusual antiques including primitives, pottery, glass, toys, furniture, etc. Credit cards honored.
NOTE: Show this listing and take 15% off your purchase.

12 Lighthouse Furnishings
1317 East Fulton, Grand Rapids MI 49503
616-458-8212
Tues. to Fri. 11 to 4:30, Sat. 11 to 3

13 Heartwood
956 Cherry Street SE, Grand Rapids MI 49506
616-454-1478
Mission; Art Deco; and other 20th Century decorative arts.

14 Old Stuff Antiques
722 Wealthy Street SE, Grand Rapids MI 49503
616-459-1940; 616-459-2550; Fax: 616-459-8687

15 Acauthus Antiques
1035 Wealthy Street SE, Grand Rapids MI 49503
616-235-3467

16 Curious Antiques
1052 Wealthy Street, Grand Rapids MI 49503

17 Cobblestone Antiques
1500 Wealthy Street SE, Grand Rapids MI 49503
616-774-3483

18 Blue Door
1440 Wealthy Street SE, Grand Rapids MI 49503
616-456-7888

19 Theadora's
2166 Wealthy Street, East Grand Rapids MI 49506
616-458-4755

20 A Cut Above Antiques
507 Glenwood, Grand Rapids MI 49506
616-454-8793

21 Turn of the Century Antiques
7337 South Division, Grand Rapids MI 49508
616-455-2060

22 Koning's Wood Products, 7226 South Division , Grand Rapids MI 49508
616-455-1780

23 The Antique Gallery, Inc.
3545 28th Street SE; Eastbrook Mall, Grand Rapids MI 49512 616-977-0981; Fax: 616-977-0985

24 Home Sweet Home
2717 Kraft SE, Grand Rapids MI 49512
616-949-7788; Fax: 616-949-7076 Antiques & gifts.

WYOMING

25 Antique Mall
4907 S. Division, Wyoming MI 49548
616-249-0588; Fax: 616-249-0780
Former site of Pack Rat Antique Mall.

GRANDVILLE

26 Sheri's Antiques
3948 30th Street Suite A, Grandville MI 49418
616-249-8066

LOWELL

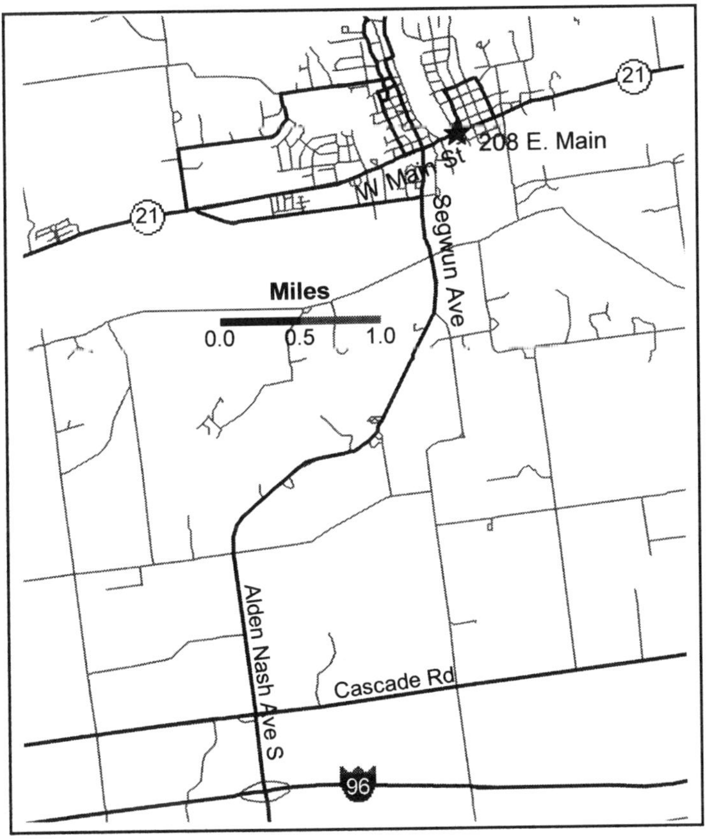

27 Flat River Antique Mall
212 West Main Street, Lowell MI 49331
616-897-5360 Fax: 616-897-0097

28 Cranberry Urn Antiques
208 East Main, Lowell MI 49331
616-897-9890; (616-897-9145 res.)
Tue. Wed. Fri. & Sat. 11 to 5
South side of street, east end of downtown; pull into the parking lot just east of the bridge.
Glass lamp shades, dolls, clocks, furniture, art glass, and a general line of antiques.

29 Main Street Antique Mall
221 West Main Street, Lowell MI 49331
616-897-5521

ROCKFORD

30 Red Pump Antiques
11630 14 Mile Road, Rockford MI 48838
231-754-8991

31 Rockford Antique Mall
54 Courtland, Rockford MI 49341
616-866-8240
www.rockfordantique.com

32 Time Travelers
480 Northland Drive, Rockford MI 49341
616-866-9368

CEDAR SPRINGS

33 Red Flannel Antique Co.,
128 North Main Street, Cedar Springs MI 49322
616-696-9599

34 Mercantile of Yesterday
17 North Main Street, Cedar Springs MI 49319
616-696-9945

4.3 Ionia County

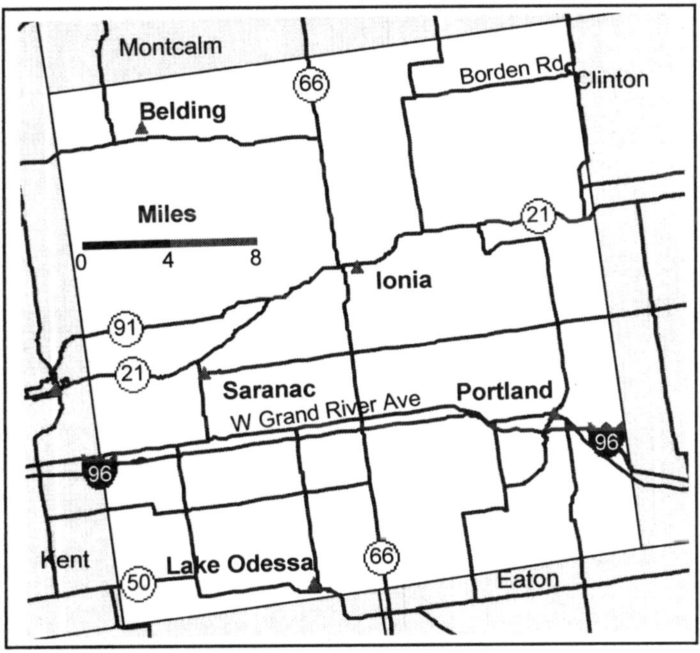

LAKE ODESSA

1 Lake-O Downtown Mall Antiques & Collectibles
1012 4th Avenue, Lake Odessa MI 48849
616-374-3089

2 Robinson's Antiques
763 West Bippley Road, Lake Odessa MI 48849
517-647-6155
www.robinsonsantiques.com
antiquehardware@robinsonsantiques.com
Antique hardware; mirror resilvering; etc.

SARANAC

3 Saranac Antique Exchange
28 Vosper , Box 187, Saranac MI 48881
616-642-6291
www.theantiquexchange.com

Saranac:

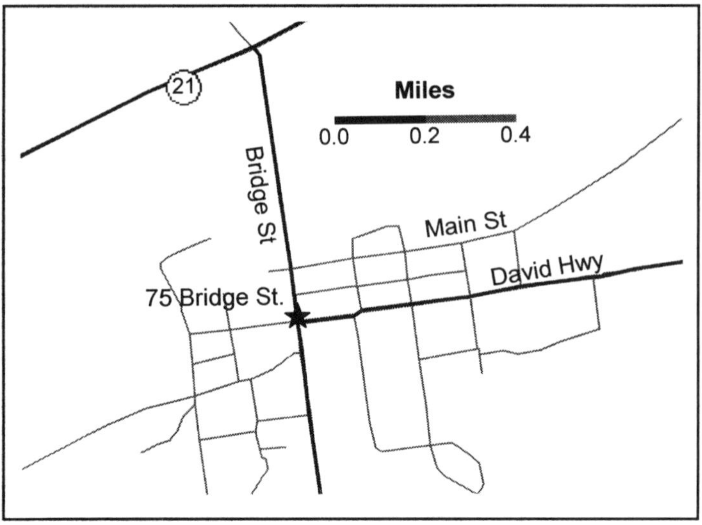

4 Pine Ridge Antiques & Collectibles
75 Bridge Street, P.O. Box 277, Saranac MI 48881
616-642-0362
Wed. to Sat. 11 to 5; closed Dec. 25 through Jan. 1.
Other hours by chance or appointment.
Located downtown, west side of the street, in an 1880's building approximately 1/2 mile south M-21.
General line of antiques including furniture, glassware & pottery, post cards, and linens. Visa/Mastercard accepted. Additional parking a block west.

BELDING

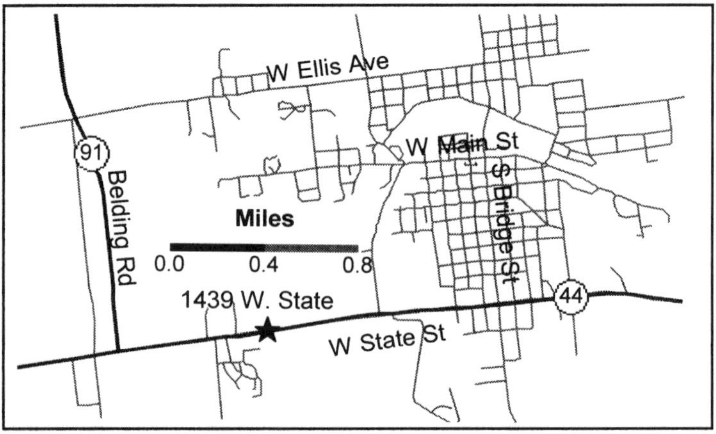

5 Sentimental Journey
304 West Main Street, Belding MI 48809
616-794-9947

6 Countryside Floral Gifts & Antique Shop
224 West State (M-44), Belding MI 48809
616-794-0921 or 1-800 842-3137
Gifts, flowers, primitive furniture and country accessories.

7 Mari-Mar Sales
1439 W State (M-44), Belding MI 48809
616-794-2423
Mon. to Wed. and Fri. & Sat. 10 to 5
Red barn set back from road; south side of M-44 between Bridge St. & M-91.
Furniture; glassware; dolls; jewelry and collectibles.

IONIA

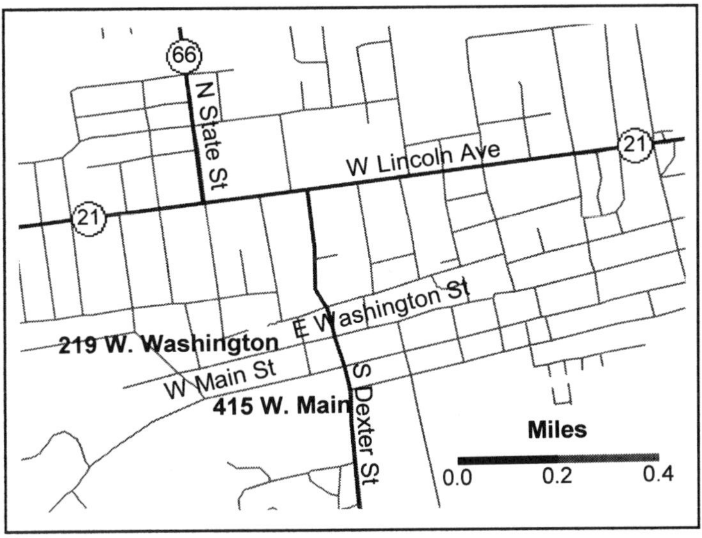

8 Keynote
316 West Main Street, Ionia MI 48846
616-527-2262

9 Checkerboard Antiques
524 West Lincoln Ave., Ionia MI 48846
616-527-1785
E-mail: checkers@iserv.net

10 Ionia Corners
7190 South State St., Ionia MI 48846
616-522-0634

11 Ionia Antique Mall
415 West Main, Ionia MI 48846
616-527-6720
Mon. to Sat.: 10 to 5, Fri. to 6:30, Sun. 11 to 5
Downtown, south side of the street a half block from M-66. One dealer specializes in fishing lures and all forms of hunting & fishing collectibles, tools, and men's stuff. A quality mall without modern collectibles.

12 Fire Barn Antiques
219 West Washington Street, Ionia MI 48446
616-527-2240
Wed. to Sat. 10 to 5, Fri. to 6; Sun. 12 to 5
South side of street, next to Post Office, 1 block off Main Street -- in an old fire station.
General line of antiques.

PORTLAND

13 McMillen & Wife Antiques
9073 South State Road, Portland MI 48875
616-374-8088

14 Two Peas in a Pod
170 Kent Street, Portland MI 48910
517-647-6577

15 McMillen & Husband
11464 McCrumb Road, Portland MI 48875
517-627-2794

4.4 Clinton County

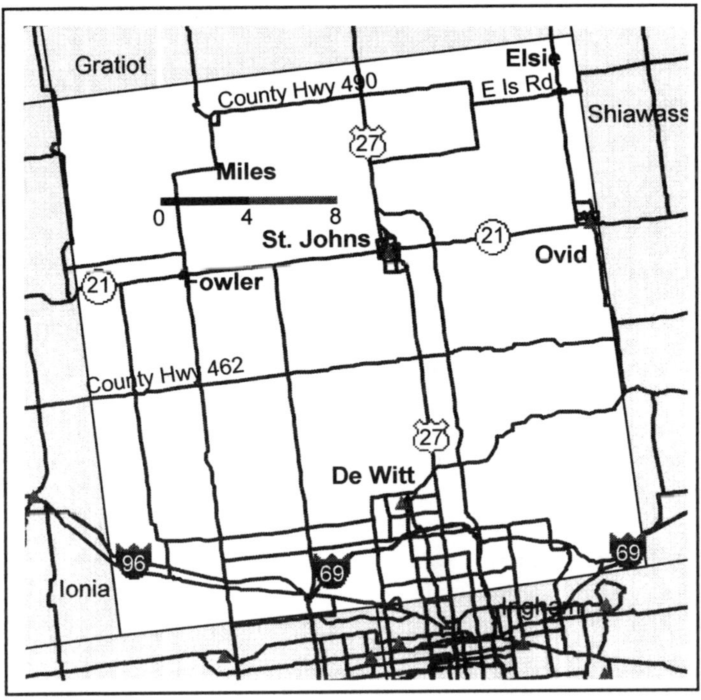

DeWITT

1 Liberty Antique Mall
1161 East Clark Road (#310), DeWitt MI 48820
517-669-4050; Fax: 517-699-3499
Lansing Factory Outlet Stores

FOWLER

2 Savannah's Secret Garden
108 Main St., P.O. Box 253, Fowler MI 48835
517-593-3012
Gifts, crafts, antiques.

ST. JOHNS

3 Banner Grange
3257 Banner Grove Road, St. Johns MI 48879
517-224-4473

4 Antiques & Friends
115 Clinton Avenue North, Saint Johns MI 48879

5 Irrer Antiques
201 West McConnell, St. Johns MI 48879
517-224-4085

6 Antiques & Collectibles
601 West Cass Street, St. Johns MI 48879
517-224-3864

7 Jerry Nickel Antiques
1300 N. Lansing Street, St. Johns MI 48879
517-224-6248
Bibles, books, gifts, music, antiques.

8 County Line Antiques
2021 South County Line Rd, St. Johns MI 48879
517-224-6285, res: 517-838-2526

9 Barnside Antiques
1991 County Line Road, St. Johns MI 48879
517-224-8212
June to Sept., Fri. to Sun.
Northwest corner U.S. 27 and County Line Road, 8 miles north of St. Johns.
Furniture, cabinets, etc.

St. Johns:

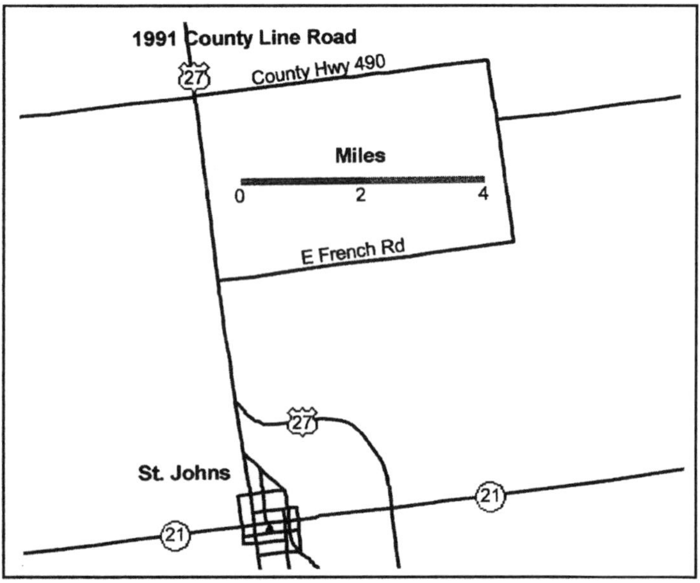

OVID

10 Parkers Furniture
108 North Main Street, Ovid MI 48866
517-834-2287
Some antiques.

ELSIE

11 Melvin Antiques & Clock Shop
8401 Island Road, P.O. Box 459, Elsie MI 48831
517-862-4322

DRIVING DISTANCES IN THE LOWER PENINSULA:

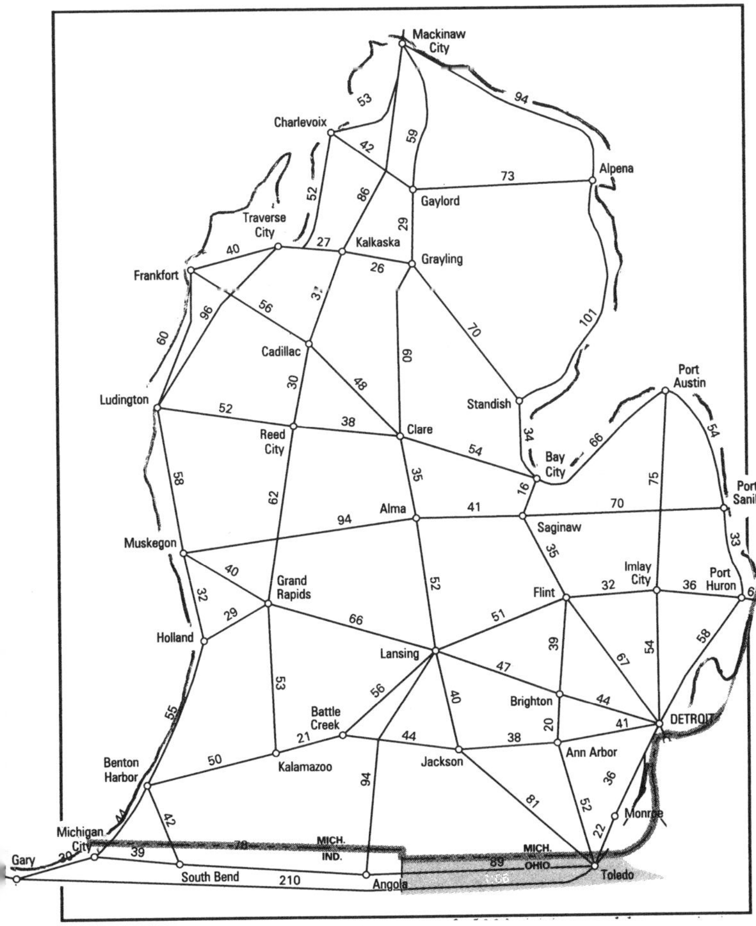

4.5 Shiawassee County

PERRY

1 Bobbie's Gifts & Collectibles
10980 South M-52, Perry MI 48872
517-625-7817

2 Victorian Gallery
807 W. Braden, Perry MI 48872
517-487-0913

LAINGSBURG

3 Found Object
11600 Woodbury Road, Laingsburg MI 48848
517-675-5188
Open by appointment only.

OWOSSO

4 My Little Shop
West Main Street, Owosso MI 48867

5 Curiosity Shop
113 North Washington, Owosso MI 48867
517-725-1589

6 Midtown Antiques Mall
1426 North M-52, Owosso MI 48867
517-723-8604

CORUNNA

7 Ken's Consignment Resale Shop
231 North Shiawassee (M-71), Corunna MI 48817
517-743-5744

DURAND

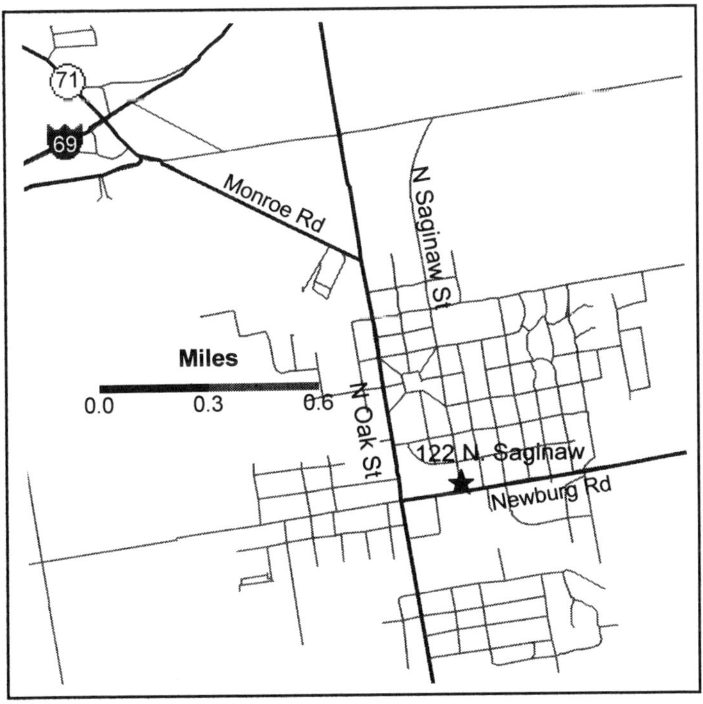

8 Our Place
122 North Saginaw, Durand MI 48429
517-288-5856
Mon. to Sat. 10 to 6, Sun. 11 to 5
Downtown.
Antiques & crafts.

9 Collectors Knot
218 West Main Street, Durand MI 48449
810-621-4014
By appointment only.

10 The Country Cupboard
10260 East Bennington Road, Durand MI 48429
517-288-3659

Linden:

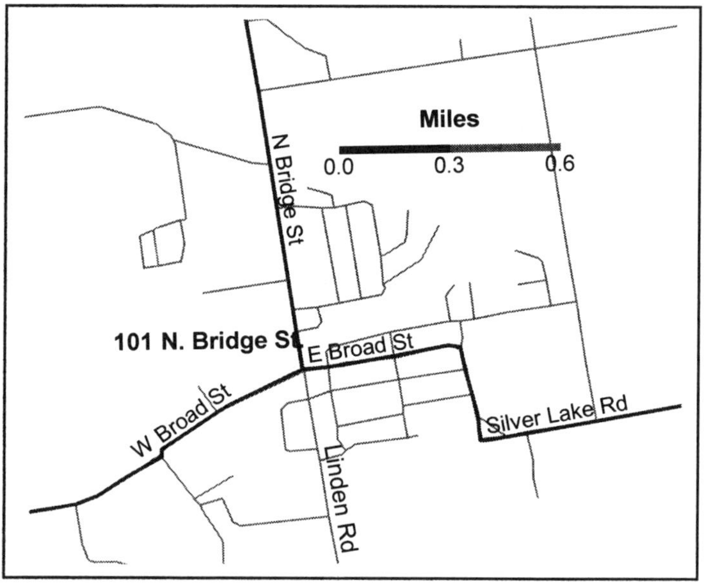

4.6 Genesee County

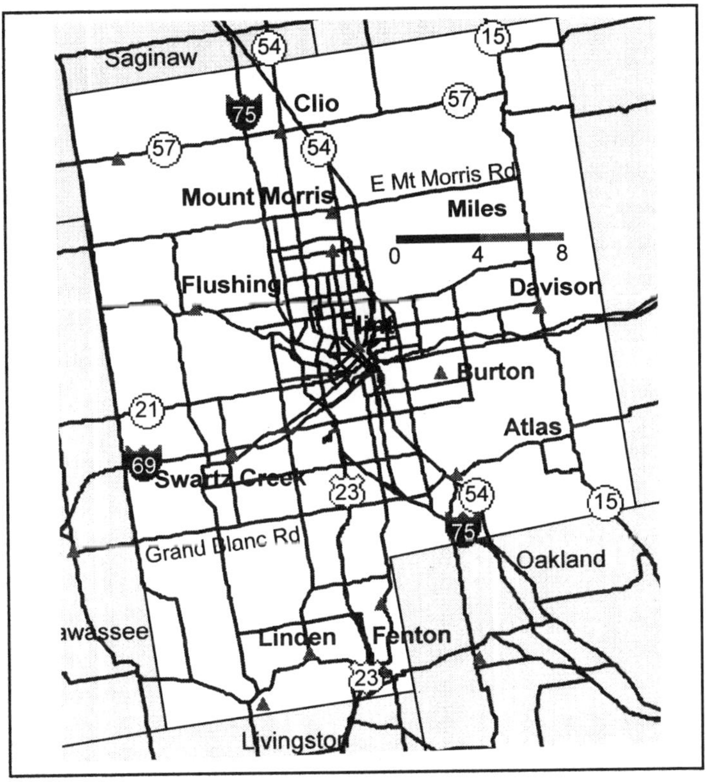

LINDEN

1 Thimbleberry Antiques
101 North Bridge Street, P.O. Box 183 , Linden MI 48451
810-735-7324
Tues. to Sat. 11 to 5; Sun. 12 to 5; Fri. & Sat. evenings on occasion.
Downtown at the light, three miles west of U.S. 23, Silver Lake Road exit.
Antiques, art glass, gifts, furniture, lamps, and Old World Christmas. Now an authorized Fenton Glass dealer.

2 The Tangled Vine Antiques & Gifts
109 North Bridge Street, P.O. Box 734, Linden MI 48451
810-735-4611

3 Susan's Woven Seats
116 West Broad Street, Linden MI 48451
810-735-5854, 810-735-5832

4 This & That Shop Antiques & Things
416 West Broad Street, Linden MI 48451
810-735-4234

FENTON

5 Stuff 'N Such
11440 Torrey Road, Fenton MI 48430
810-629-4613

6 The Iron Grate
103 West Shiawassee Avenue, Fenton MI 48430
810-629-3434

7 The Gathering
115 Mill, Fenton MI 48430
810-750-0877

8 Fenton Bean Company
234 North Leroy, Fenton MI 48430
810-750-4595

9 Yesterday's Treasures
300 South Leroy, Fenton MI 48430
810-714-2600

SWARTZ CREEK

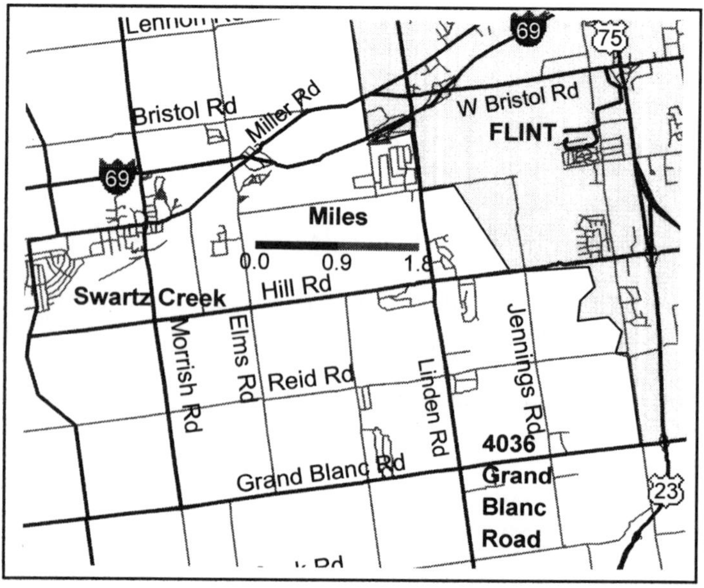

10 Memories Antique Mall
4036 West Grand Blanc Road, Swartz Creek (Rankin) MI 48473
810-655-8306
Tues. to Sat. 11 to 6, Sun. 12 to 5
North side of the road, a mile west of U.S. 23.
Outdoor flea markets in summer months. General line of antiques, and select accessories for the home.

ATLAS

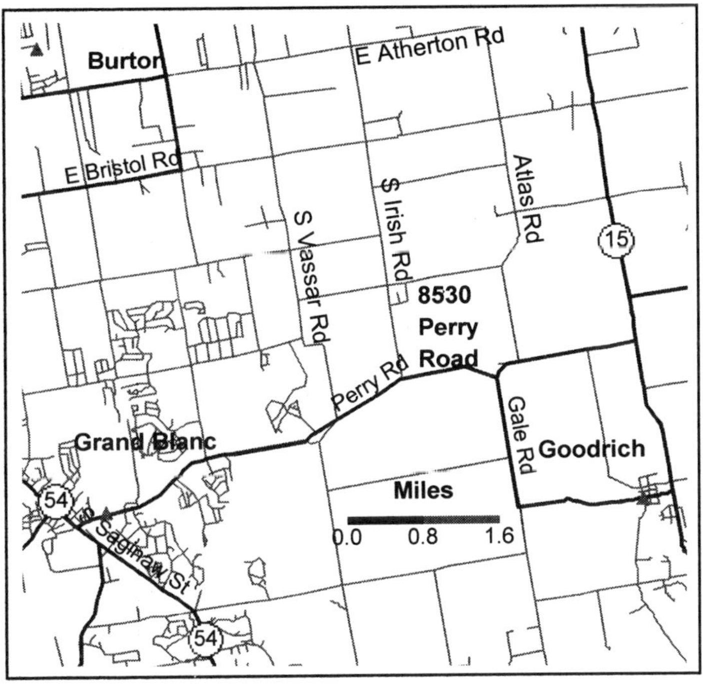

11 Maurice Reid Antiques
8470 Perry Road, P.O. Box 132, Atlas MI 48411
810-636-2414

12 Under the Dust
8530 Perry Road, Atlas MI 48411
810-636-2665 underthedust@aol.com
Fri. & Sat. 11 to 4:30, Sun. 1 to 4:30 and by appointment
Three miles east of Grand Blanc on Perry Road; two miles northwest of Goodrich.
The shop is in a restored 19th Century community hall. General line of antiques.

FLINT

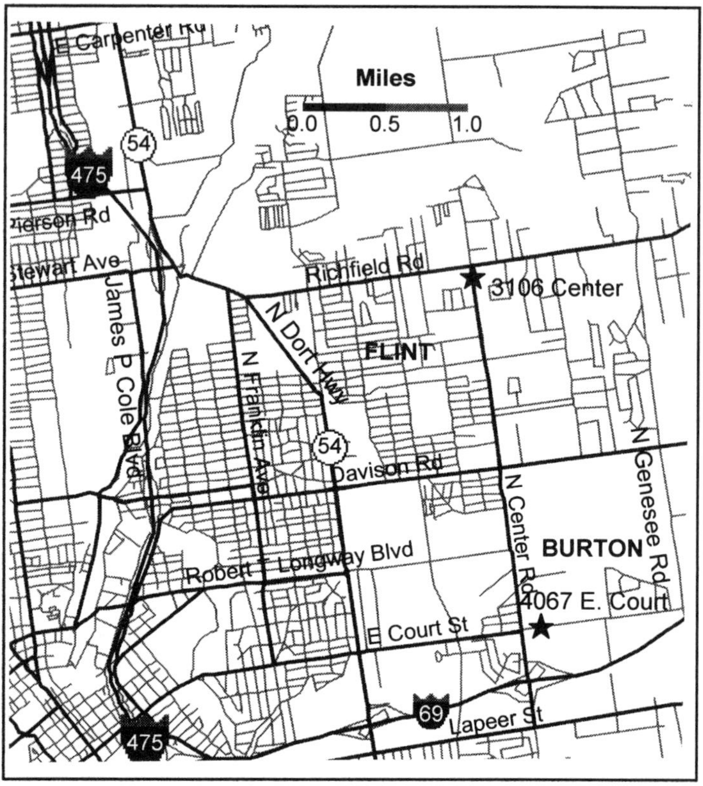

13 Countryside Crafts Mall & Antiques
4333 Miller Road, Flint MI 48507
810-230-0885

14 Rebel's Junque
4442 Torrey Road, Flint MI 48507
810-238-0882

15 Neva's Antiques and Collectables
2818 North Franklin Avenue, Flint MI 48506
810-233-7183

16 Antiques By Cecilia
G-3106 North Center Road, Flint MI 48506
810-736-0800
Mon. to Fri. 11 to 7, Sat. 11 to 5
In strip mall east side of Center Road, 1/2 block south of Richfield.
Glass, porcelain, lamps, dolls, furniture and general line.

17 Westwood Antiques & Gifts
4135 West Coldwater Road, Flint MI 48504
810-785-1300 Fax: 810-787-9569

FLUSHING

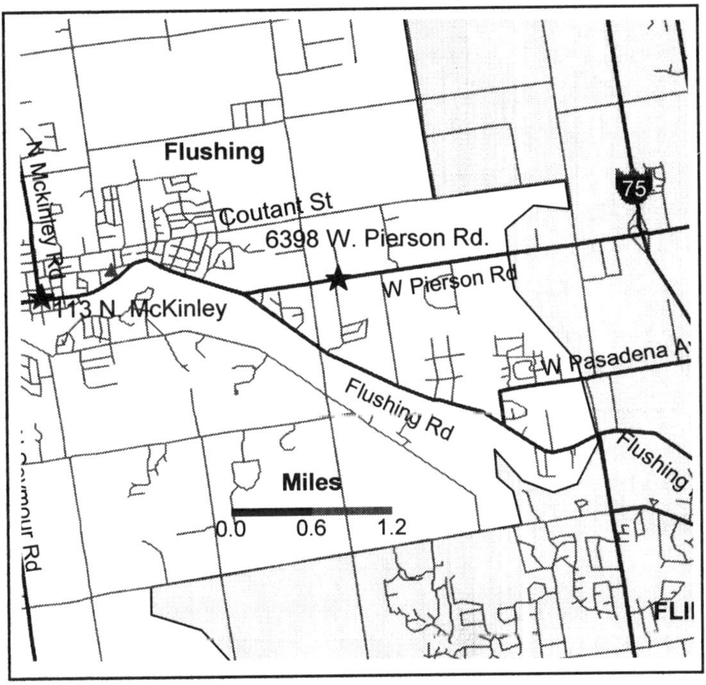

18 Up In the Attic at Village Wallcovering
114 East Main Street, Flushing MI 48433
810-659-6313

19 Trudy's Antiques & N. Dean Mosey Jr. Woodworks
113 North McKinley Road, Flushing MI 48433
810-659-9801

20 R & J Needful Things Antique Center, Inc.
6398 West Pierson Road, Flushing MI 48433
810-659-2663
www.antiqueit.com
Seven Days 10 to 5
North side of street, 2 1/2 miles west of I-75, Exit 122.
170 dealers.

BURTON

21 Esquire
3140 East Atherton Road, Burton MI 48509
810-742-4968

22 My Country Home
4067 East Court Street, Burton MI 48509
810-742-6570 \ 810-742-0433

DAVISON

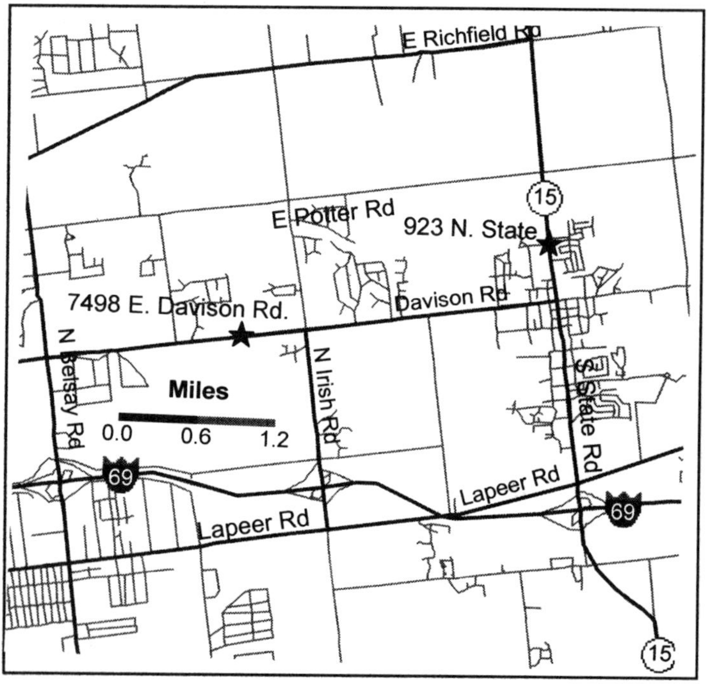

23 Village Square Antiques
305 North State (M-15), Davison MI 48423
810-653-2447

24 Small Town Coins & Collectibles
7498 East Davison Road, Davison MI 48423
810-658-1992
http://small-town.cnchost.com
Mon. to Fri. 10 to 4, Sat. 10 to 3
In small mall, one mile north of I-69, southwest corner Irish & Dacison Roads.
Coins, antique toys, pedal cars & Pez.

CLIO

25 Brothers and Sisters
14100 North Saginaw (M-54), Clio MI 48420
810-687-1294

26 Matthew's Antiques
G 12180 North Saginaw, Clio MI 48420
810-686-5148

27 Ye Ole Country Store
12140 N. Saginaw, Clio MI 48420
810-564-2449

Mt. MORRIS

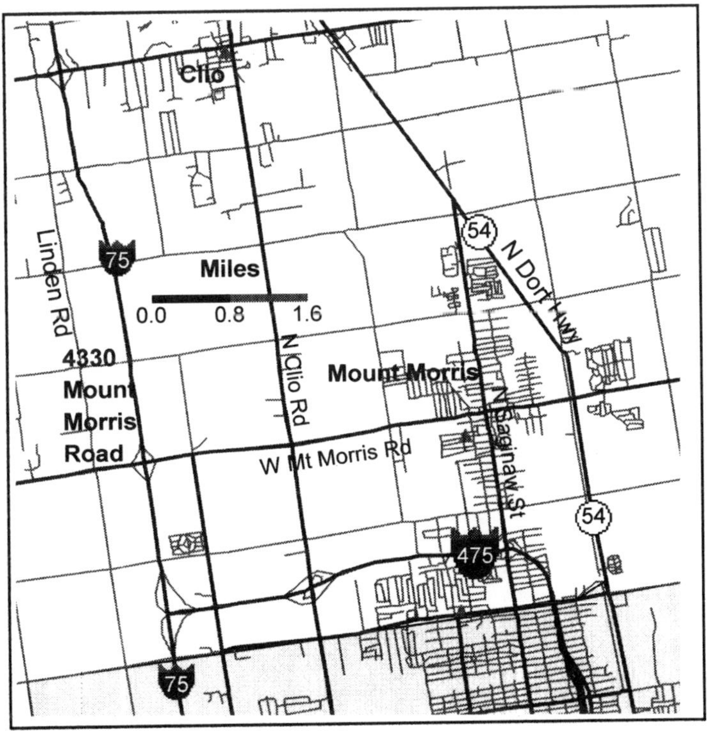

28 Attic Memories
G 9394 North Saginaw, Mt. Morris MI 48458
810-687-4804

29 Antique Mall America
4330 W. Mount Morris Road, Mt. Morris MI 48458
810-564-1056
Sun. thru Thurs. 10 to 6; Fri. & Sat. 10 to 8
Northwest corner, I-75 (Exit 126) & Mt. Morris Road, two exits south of Birch Run.
"Something for everyone."

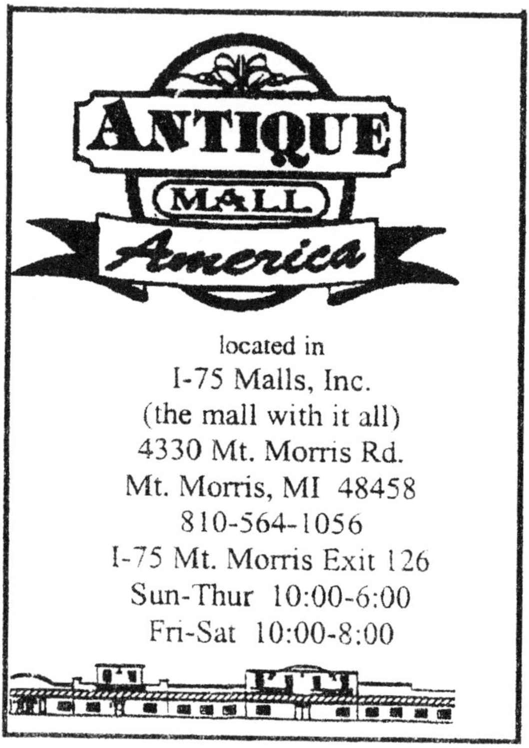

4.7 Lapeer County

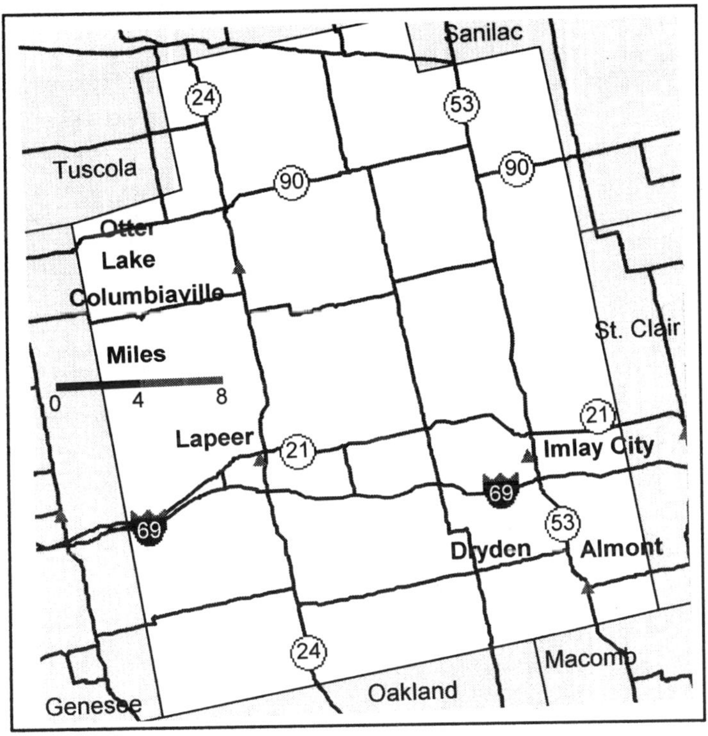

OTTER LAKE

1 Collectibles of Yore
6405 Detroit Street, Otter Lake MI 48464
810-793-1321

COLUMBIAVILLE

2 Christina's Antiques & Things
5155 Stanley Road, Columbiaville MI 48421
810-793-2762

LAPEER

(Map on page 173.)

3 Kingsmill Antiques
340 West Nepessing, Lapeer MI 48446
810-245-0971

4 Remember When Antiques
2080 North Lapeer Road, Lapeer MI 48446
810-664-7650

5 Past Tense
1965 Farnsworth Road, Lapeer MI 48446
810-664-5559

DRYDEN

6 A Basket of Violets
3960 North Mill Road, Dryden MI 48428
810-796-3244

ALMONT

7 Stoney River Mercantile Antiques at the Shops of King's Mill
622 South Main Street, P.O. Box 601, Almont MI 48003
810-798-8214

8 Enchanted Alley
114 South Main Street, Almont MI 48003
810-798-2944

9 Christy's Country Store
3070 Van Dyke, Almont MI 48003
810-798-3748

IMLAY CITY

(Map on following page,)

10 Memory Junction
244 East Third Street, Imlay City MI 48444
810-724-4811; Fax: 810-724-6590
E-mail: antiques@cardina.net
Mon. to Sat. 10 to 5, Sun. by chance.
Exit 168 from I-69, north on M-53 1.5 miles, then one block west on Third Street.
General line, Staffordshire, furniture, pattern glassware, Depression Glass, etc.

11 Re-Sale Shop
7567 Imlay City Road (Old M-21), Imlay City MI 48444
810-724-1082

Imlay City:

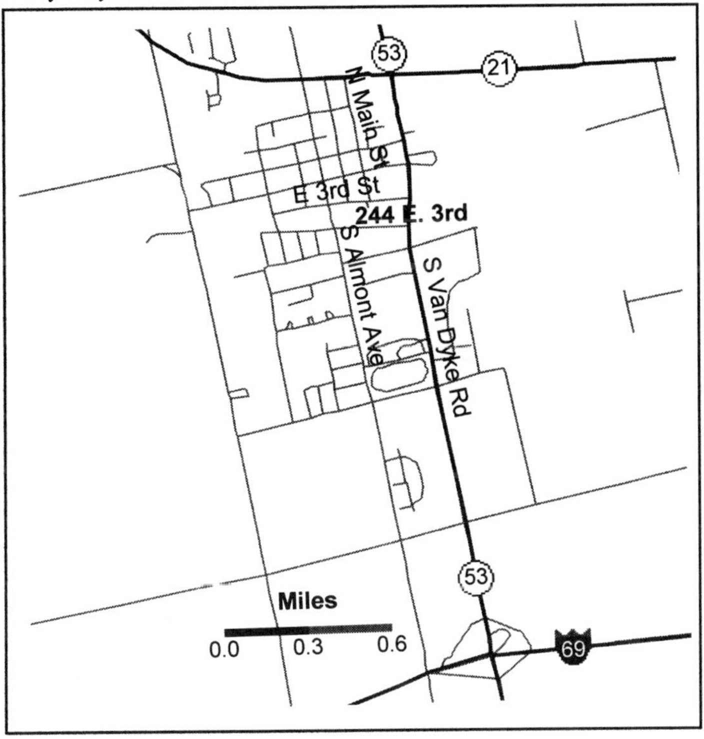

Lapeer:

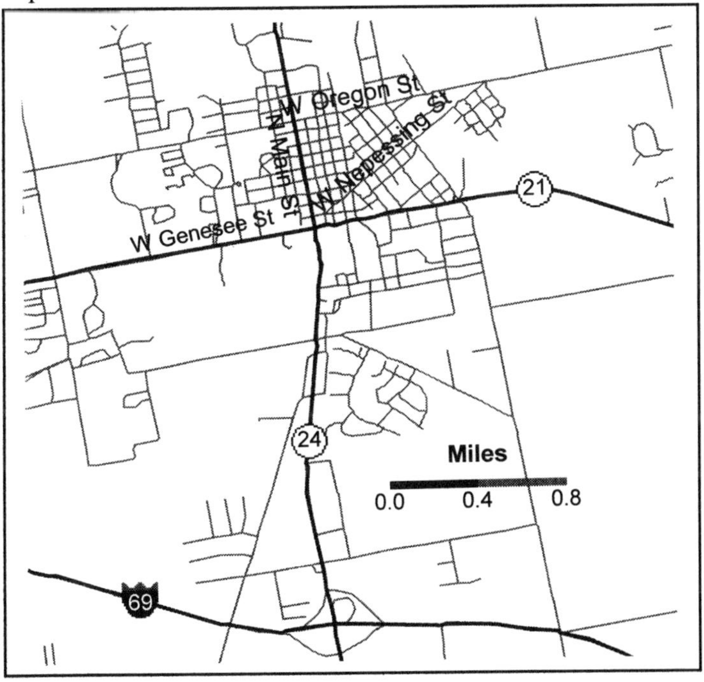

4.8 St. Clair County

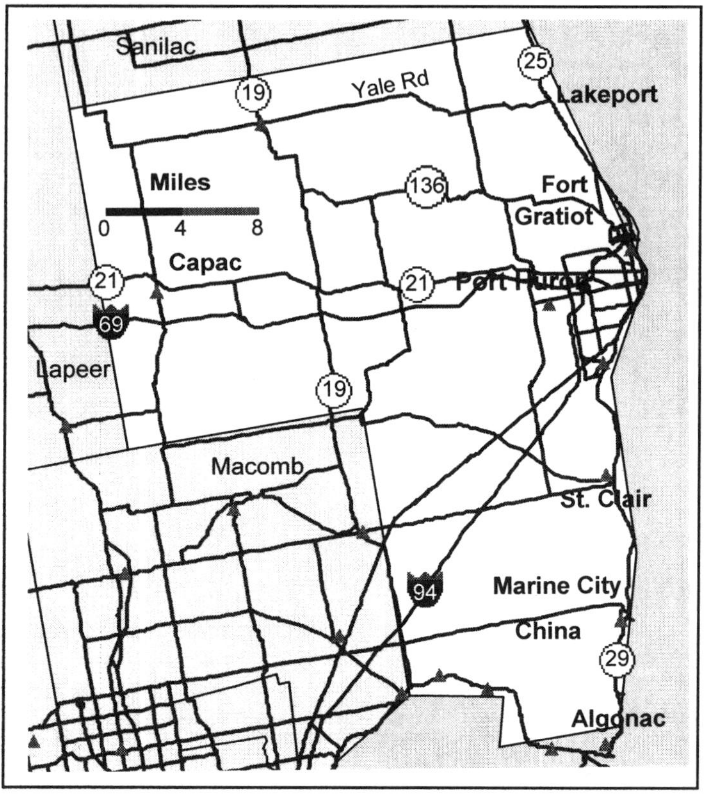

CAPAC

1 Yesterday's Shadows
107 North Main Street, P.O. Box 514 , Capac MI 48014
810-395-4100
Tue. & Thurs. 12 - 5; Wed. Fri. & Sat. 10 - 5; Sun. 1 - 5
Downtown, west side of street.
Antiques, crafts, and collectibles.
Space for rent, consignments accepted.

2 Treasures in the Rough
126 North Main Street, Capac MI 48014
No telephone listed.

Capac:

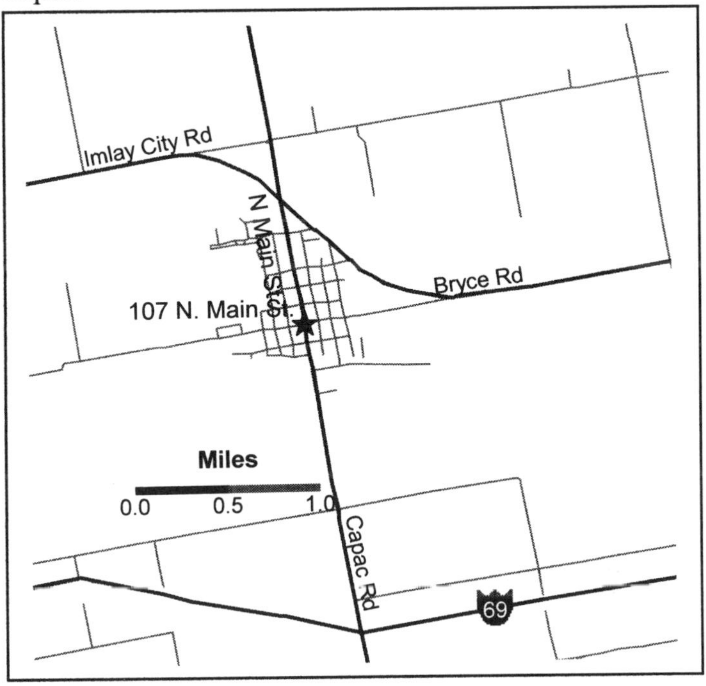

LAKEPORT

3 Antique Workshop
7077 Lakeshore (M-25), Lakeport MI 48059
810-385-4344

FORT GRATIOT

4 Robins Egg Blue
7102 3rd Street, Fort Gratiot MI 48059
810-385-1799

PORT HURON

5 Colonial Used Furniture Outlet
1219 Military Street, Port Huron MI 48060
810-987-4001
Mon. to Fri. 10 to 5:30, Sat. 10 to 5, Sun. 11 to 4
South of downtown; west side of street between Court and Union.
Used furniture, antiques and collectibles. "A litle bit of everything."

Port Huron:

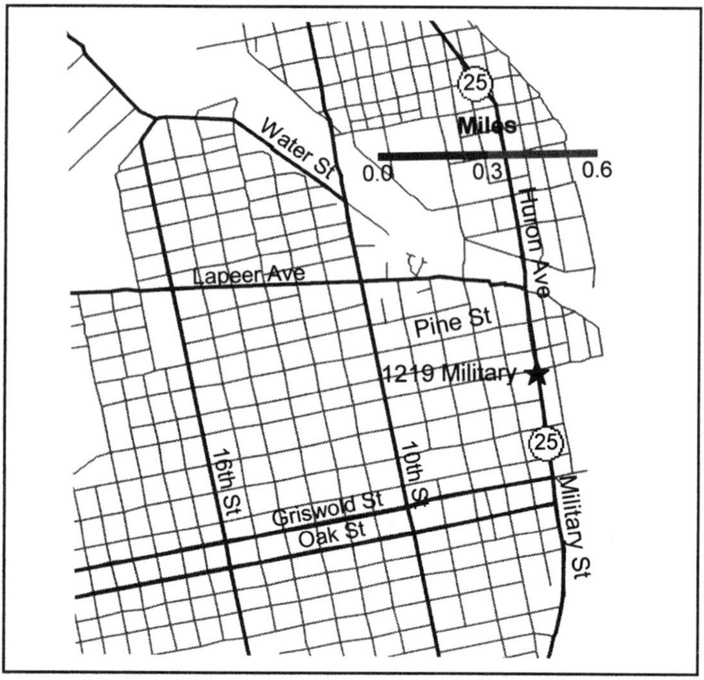

6 The Wooden Spool
2513 10th Avenue, Port Huron MI 48060
810-982-3390

7 Antique Collectors Corner
1603 Griswold Street, Port Huron MI 48060
810-982-2780; Home: 810-984-2932

8 K & T's Antiques
716 Lapeer Road, Port Huron MI 48060
810-966-3951

9 Yesterday's Treasures
4490 Lapeer Road West, Port Huron MI 48060
810-982-2100

ST. CLAIR

10 Jennifer's Trunk
Riverview Plaza Shopping Center
201 North Riverside, St. Clair MI 48079
810-329-2032
In Riverview Plaza Shopping Center.

11 John Moffett Antiques
1102 South 7th Street, St. Clair MI 48079
810-329-3300

MARINE CITY

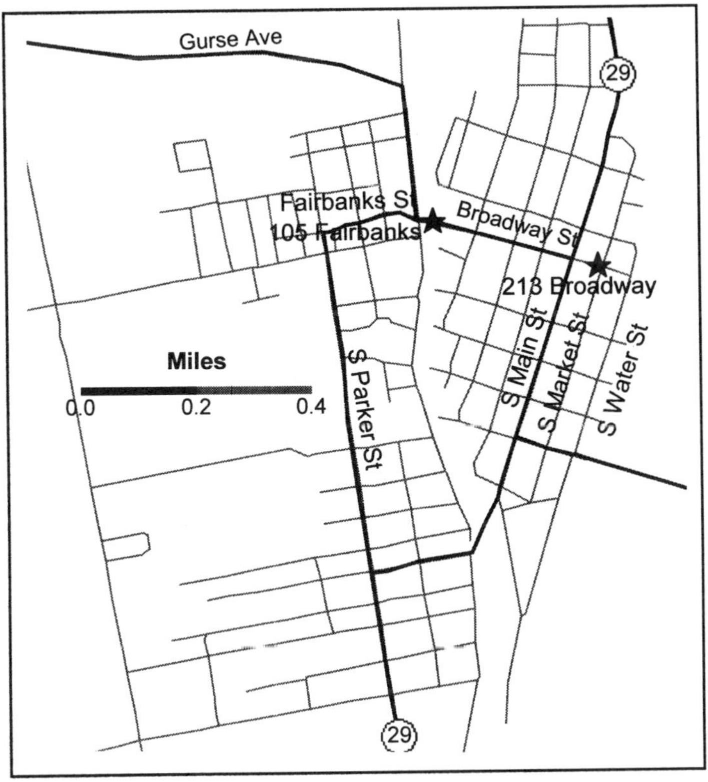

12 The Centennial Co.
105 Fairbanks Suite 2, Marine City MI 48039
810-765-6454
Jewelry & silver.

13 Marine City Antique Warehouse
105 Fairbanks (M-29), Marine City MI 48039
810-765-1119
Mon. to Sat. 10 to 5, Sun. 1 to 5
In the Bell River Plaza, just west of the bridge, south side of the highway.
Two floors of the largest selection of fine antiques and collectibles in the Tri-County area.

14 Old Times N Such
213 Broadway Street, Marine City MI 48039
810-765-9577
Thurs. to Sat. 12 to 5, Sun. by chance.
Off M-29 east.
Depression Glass, Fiesta, pottery.

15 The Snuggery
8540 North River Road (MI Route 29), Marine City MI 48039
810-765-4737

CHINA

16 Red Barn Antiques, Crafts & Collectibles
4950 King Road, China MI 48054
810-765-9453 redbarm@firststep.net
Fri. to Mon. 10 to 4
King Road is a mile west of downtown Marine City; north on King Road to just past Meisner Road; west side of road.
2.500 square feet of quality merchandise

TIER 5:
THE M-46 ROUTE

5.1 Muskegon County

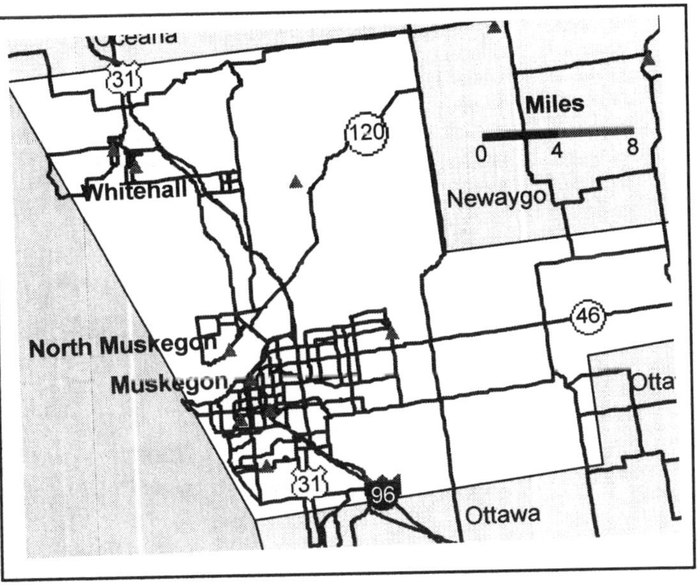

MUSKEGON

1 Airport Antique Mall
4206 Grand Haven Road, Muskegon MI 49441
231-798-3318
Mon. to Sat. 11 to 6; Sun. 12 to 6
South from Muskegon on Business U.S. 31, exit on Grand Haven Road; the mall is several blocks south at the southeast corner of Airport Road.
Antiques & collectibles; mostly glassware & smalls.
25 dealers, 5,000 square feet.

2 Hole In the Wall Antiques
1321 Division Street, Muskegon MI 49441
231-722-7218

3 Mandy's Antiques
1950 East Laketon Avenue, Muskegon MI 49441
231-777-1428

Muskegon:

4 Downtown Muskegon Antique Mall
1321 Division, Suite 10, Muskegon MI 49441
231-728-0305
Mon. to Sat. 11 to 6; Sunday 1 to 6
Lakeview Center, west of downtown, across from Muskegon Lake.
From U.S. 31 go west on Laketon to Division, then north.
Old Shaw Walker Building at Western & Division.
20,000 square feet.
In the winter of 2000 the mall may be moving to Grand Haven Road between the Pontaluns and Sternberg exits, south of Muskegon.

5 Station Antiques
2204 McCracken, Muskegon MI 49441
231-759-6708

6 Old Grange Mall
2783 Apple Avenue, Muskegon MI 49442
231-773-5683

7 Western Ave. Coffee House & Antiques
477 Western Avenue, Muskegon MI 49440
231-727-9953

8 Strippers of Muskegon
3535 Getty, Muskegon MI 49441
231-733-2201 or 231-733-2824 May be closing late 2000.

NORTH MUSKEGON

9 Memory Lane Antique Mall
2073 Holton Road, North Muskegon MI 49445
231-744-8510
Seven days 10 to 6
Northwest corner M-120 & U.S. 31 Expressway. Enter from Roberts Road a block west of U.S. 31.
37 dealers, 6,000 square feet.

WHITEHALL

10 Pages & Friends Antique Shop
121 W. Colby , Whitehall MI 49461
231-894-5980

11 From Time to Time Gallery
214 East Colby, P.O. Box 457, Whitehall MI 49461
231-894-9569
Antiques and art.

12 Martha's Vineyard Antiques
4075 Lakewood Road, Whitehall MI 49461
231-894-6602

Greenville:

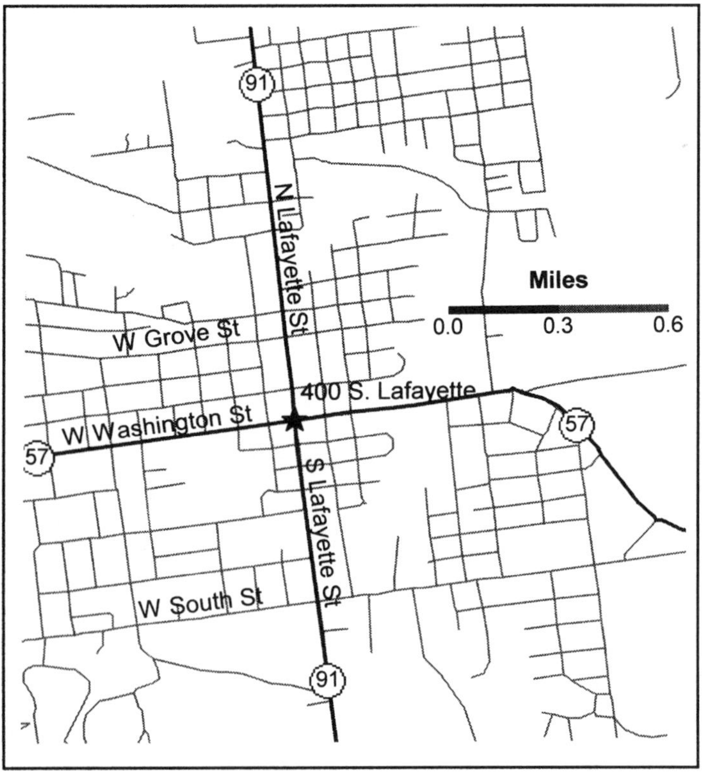

5.2 Montcalm County

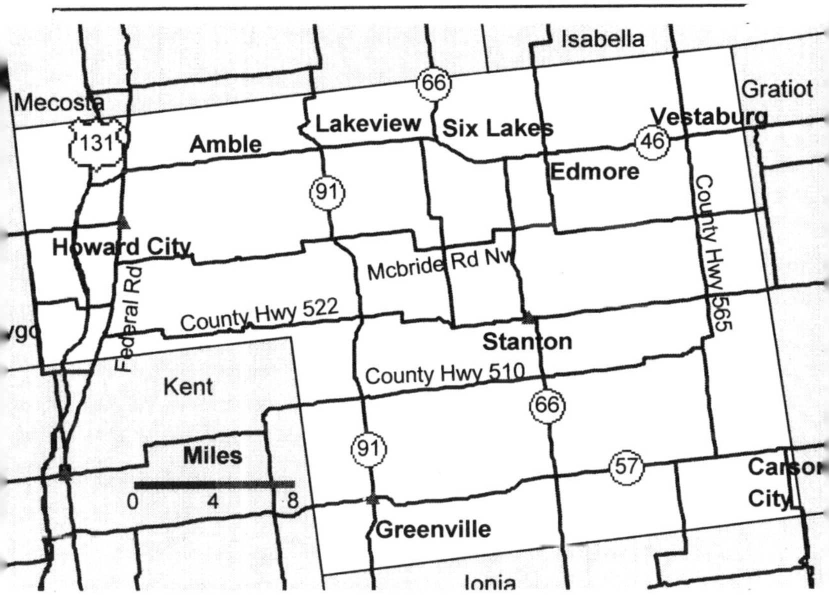

GREENVILLE

(Map on preceding page.)

1 Greenville Antique Center
400 South Lafayette Street, Greenville MI 48838
616-754-5540 gac@pathwaynet.com
Sat. 10 to 8, Sun. 12 to 6, Mon. thru Thurs. 11 to 6, Fri. 11:30 to 8
Corner of M-57 & M-91, just south of downtown; loft building on east side of street.
5 floors, 35,000 square feet, 85 dealers.

CARSON CITY

2 Cook's Crossing
105 west Main Street, Carson City MI 48811
517-584-3677

STANTON

3 Antique Stuff
2990 1/2 Sheridan Road, Stanton MI 48888
517-831-8063; 800 572-6703

Stanton:

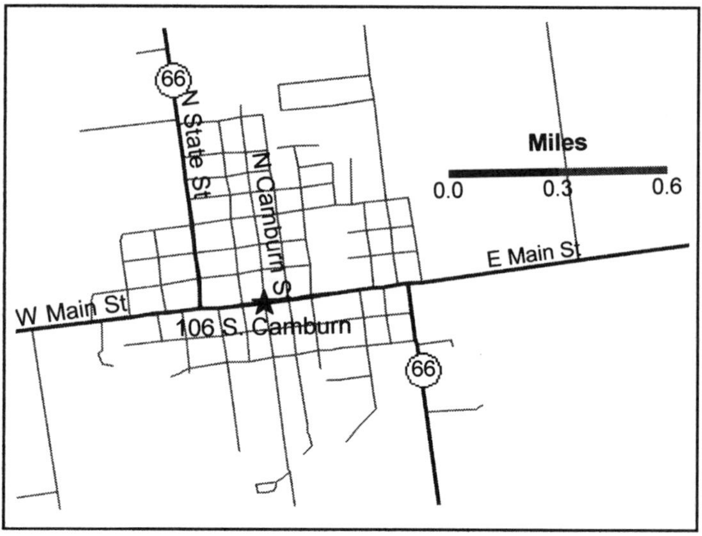

4 Hotel Montcalm
106 S. Camburn, Stanton MI 48888
517-831-5055
Every day 12 to 6
Downtown, Main Street (M-66) & Camburn Street.
Unique Setting in historic hotel; reasonable prices. Newly opened ice cream parlor and restaurant.

VESTABURG

5 Ora Deila Antiques
9881 Cannonsville, Vestaburg MI 48891
517-268-5143
By chance or appointment.

HOWARD CITY

6 Pine Lodge Antiques & Collectibles
19358 West Howard City-Edmore Road (M-46), Howard City MI 49329 231-937-9400

7 Haack's Antiques
413 Muenscher, Howard City MI 49329
231-937-4494

AMBLE

8 Amble Antiques and Collectibles
14766 M-46, Amble MI 49322
231-762-4548

LAKEVIEW

9 Tara II Antiques and Stuff
531 Lincoln, P.O. Box 173, Lakeview MI 48850
231-937-5148
Open by chance.

10 Granny's Antiques
9535 Fitzner Rd, Lakeview MI 48850
517-352-6030
By chance or appointment.

11 Welcome Inn
7477 M-46, Lakeview MI 48886
517-352-6393 By chance or appointment.

SIX LAKES

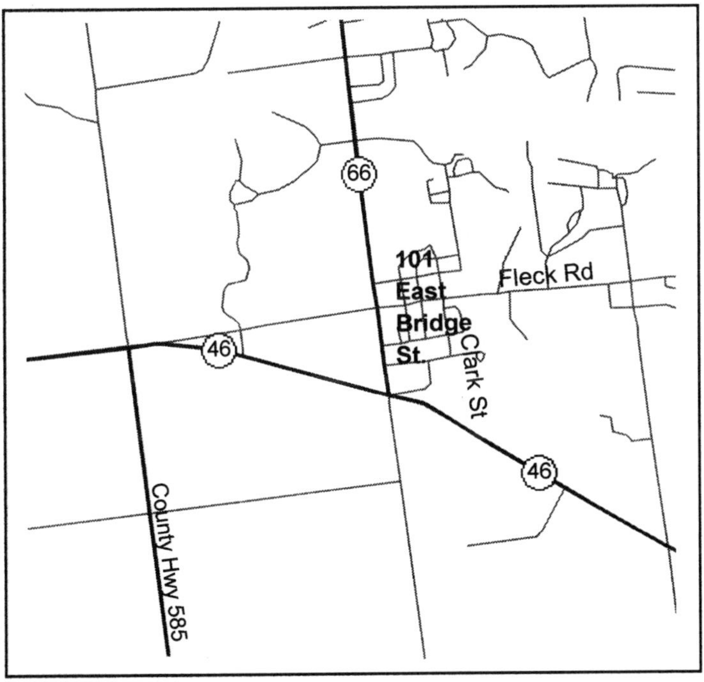

12 The Intersection
101 East Bridge Street, P.O. Box 152, Six Lakes MI 48886
517-365-3773
Mon. to Sat. 10 to 5:30
Three blocks north of M-46, three blocks east of M-66, at Clark Street.
Antiques & collectibles. Stained glass art studio - residential and commercial commissions and restoration.

13 The Potato Been
3572 West Fleck Road, Six Lakes MI 48886
517-365-3477

EDMORE

14 Moore's Antiques
406 East Main Street, Edmore MI 48829
517-427-3378

15 Country Charm
5167 East Howard City Road, Edmore MI 48829

5.3 Gratiot County

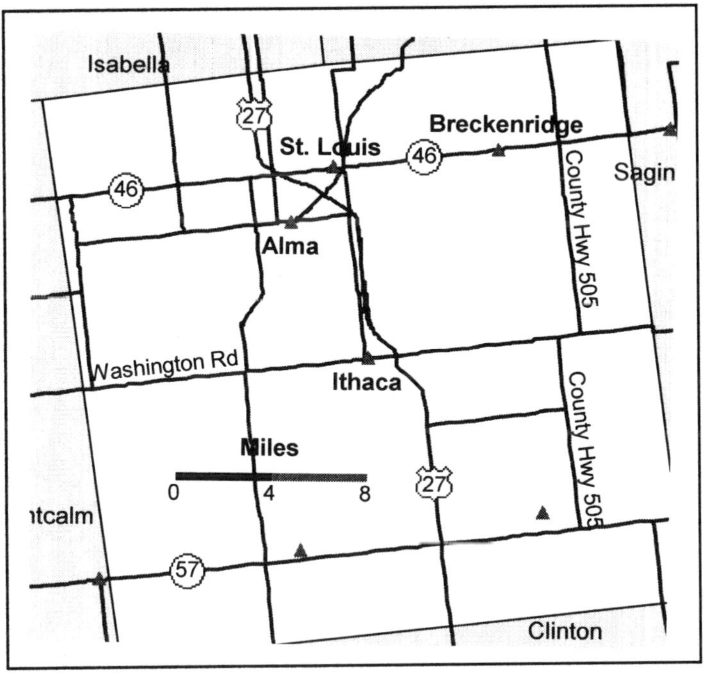

ELWELL

1 Mac Lachlan House Antiques
6482 North Pingree Road, Elwell MI 48832
517-463-1512

ITHACA

2 North Star Trader
3036 South Bagley Road, U.S. 27, Ithaca MI 48847
517-875-4341 or 517-838-4409
Oak reproductions, & antiques; 25 % of the items are antiques.

3 My Sister's Closet
127 E. Center Street, Ithaca MI 48847
517-875-4096

4 Countryside Antiques
2024 South Bagley (U.S. 27), Ithaca MI 48847
517-875-2349

WHEELER

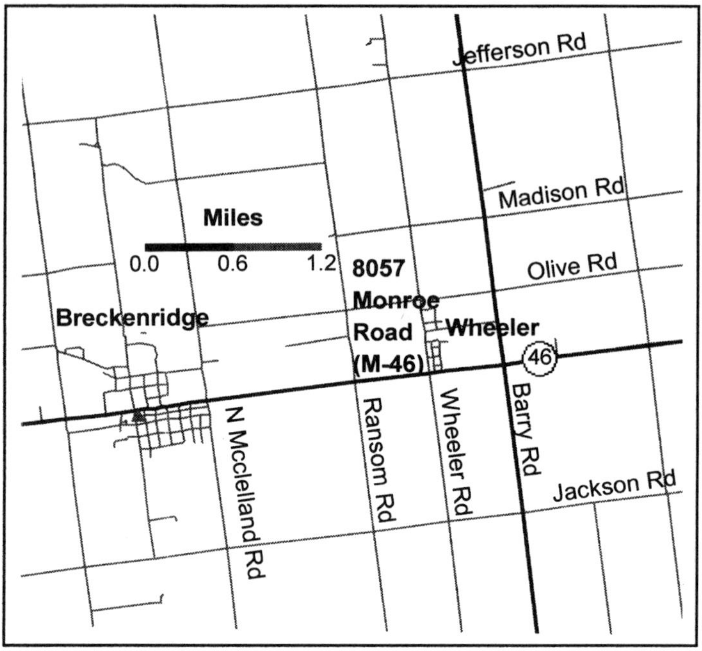

5 Auntie Q's
8150 North Mason, P.O. Box 56, Wheeler MI 48662
517-842-5862

6 Rohde's Antiques and Collectibles
8057 Monroe Road (M-46), Wheeler MI 48662
517-842-5456 old-stuffnj@webtv.net
Fri. Sat. Sun. 10 to 5
One mile east of Breckenridge, corner of Ransom Road. 37 dealers with a good selection of antiques and collectibles, including "guy" things like motorcycles, old guns, fishing lures, marbles, kinves, etc. New "old" stuff added weekly.

ST. LOUIS

7 Tried and True Antique Mall
1694 West Monroe Road (M-46), St. Louis MI 48880
517-681-2487
Mon. to Sat. 10 to 5, Sun. 12 to 5
One mile east of U.S. 27, north side of the highway. Large variety of antiques and collectibles.

St. Louis:

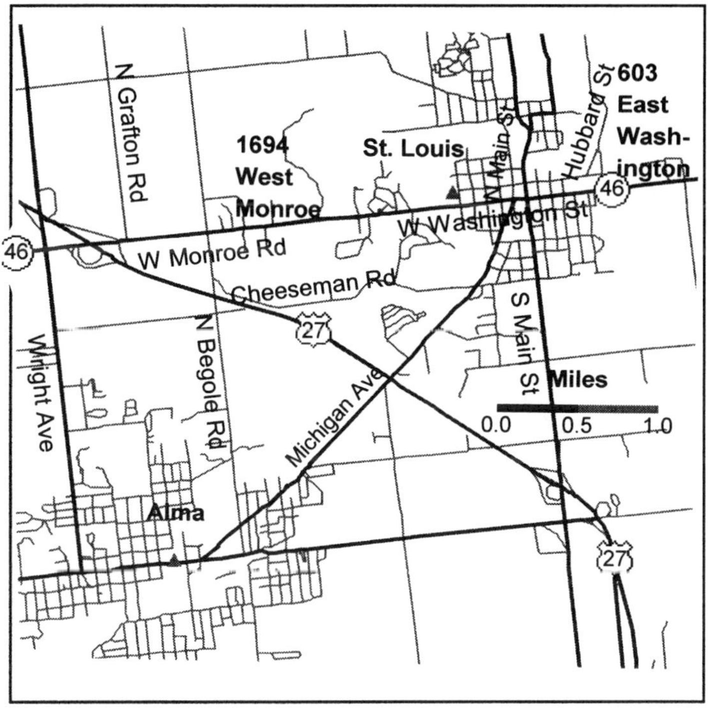

8 Middle of the Mitten Antiques

603 East Washington (M-46), St. Louis MI 48880
517-681-3536
Mon. to Sat. 10 to 5, Sun. 12 to 5
East city limits, 6 blocks East of stoplight.
Furniture and a general line of antiques.

Downtown Saginaw:

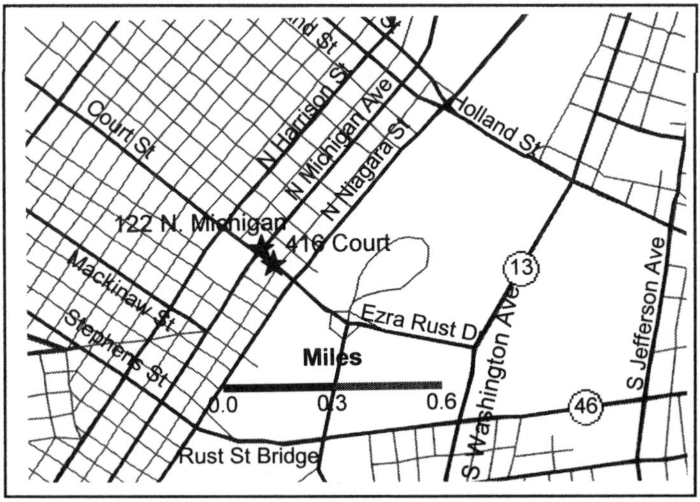

5.4 Saginaw County

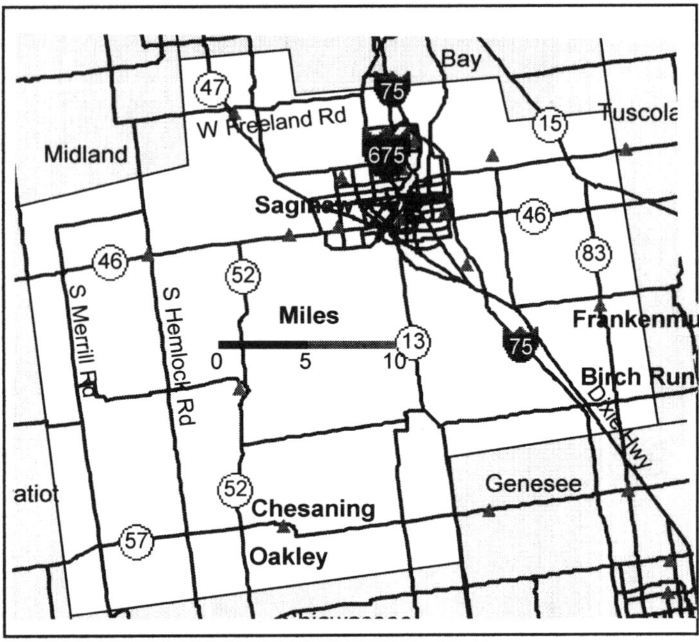

SAGINAW

(Downtown Saginaw map on preceding page.)

1 Adomaitis Antiques
412 Court Street, Saginaw MI 48600
517-790-7469

2 Court House Square Antiques
122 N. Michigan Street, Saginaw MI 48600
517-249-0827
Mon. to Sat. 10 to 5, Sun. 12 to 5
Old Town Saginaw.
Group mall with a general line & glass, china, and early American pattern glass.

3 Little House Antiques
416 Court Street, Saginaw MI 48602
517-792-9622
Wed. to Sat. 11 to 4
In Historic Old Saginaw City.
Depression Glass, kitchenware, elegant glass, collectibles, etc.

North Side Saginaw:

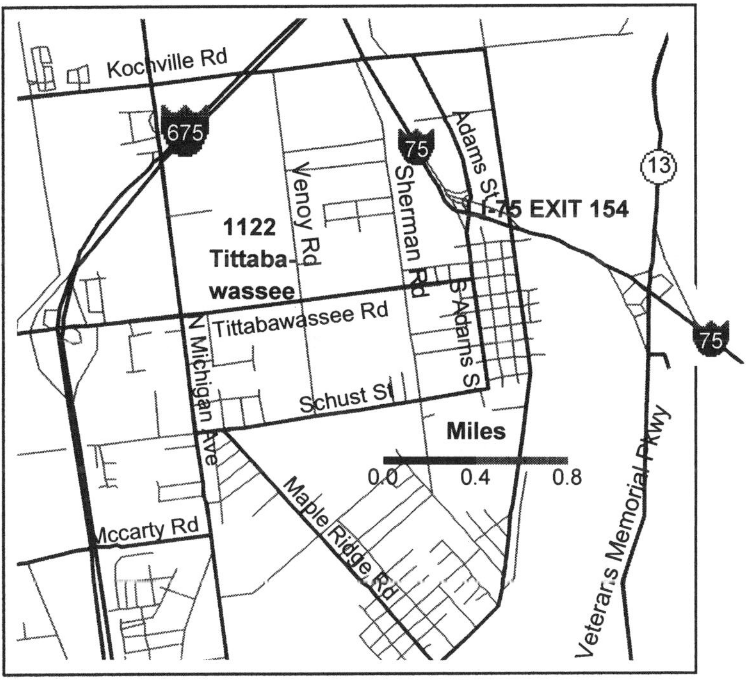

4 Antique Warehouse
1122 Tittabawssee Road, Saginaw MI 48602
517-755-4343
Mon. to Sat. 10 to 6, Sun. & Holidays 12 to 6
From I-75: Exit 154 exit right one half mile to Tittabawssee, then right one mile; north side of the road, midway between I-75 and I-675. (1.5 miles east of Fashion Square Mall.)
Seventy quality dealers; lunch and 12 specialty shops; 20,000 square feet.

5 Ron's Antiques
12025 Gratiet Road, Saginaw MI 48609
517-642-8479

FRANKENMUTH

6 B-C Antiques
8470 West Tuscola Road, Frankenmuth MI 48734
517-652-2116
By chance.

BIRCH RUN

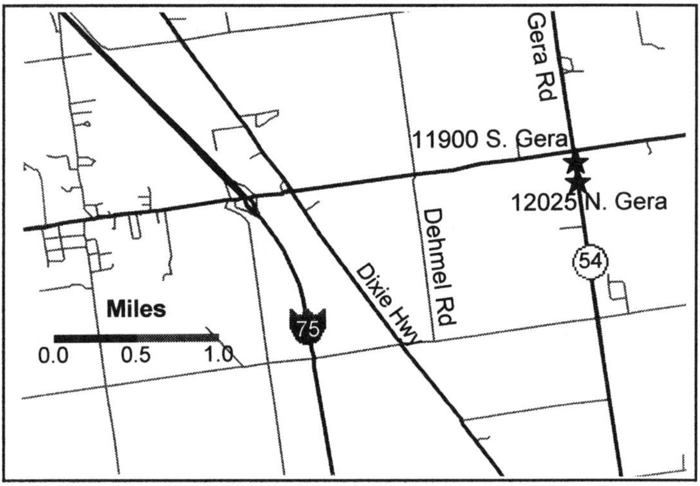

7 The Collector's Corner
11900 South Gera Road (MI Route 83), Birch Run MI 48415
517-624-4388
Daily 10 to 5
One block north of Birch Run Road, west side of highway.
Cookie jars, and a general line of antiques & collectibles.

8 Red Beard's Antiques & Collectibles
12025 North Gera Road, Birch Run MI 48415
517-624-5211 888-202-3877
Daily 10 to 6
Southeast corner Gera & Birch Run Roads, south of Frankenmuth.
"We buy old stuff."

OAKLEY

9 "I REMEMBER THAT!"
304 South Main Street (Highway M-52), Oakley MI 48649
517-845-4940
Mon. to Sat. 10 to 5, closed Wed. & Sun.
Ten miles north of Owosso, three miles south of M-57.
Watch for bright pink sign.
The shop has relocated from Owosso to Oakley. Still a small mall with a large variety; something sure to make you say: "I Remember That!"

5.5 Tuscola County

MILLINGTON

1. Millington Antique Depot
8484 State Street, P.O. Box 511, Millington MI 48746
517 871-3300; Fax: 517 871-7228
Every day 10 to 5, except holidays.
Downtown, west side of the street.
50 dealers.

2 Enduring Reflections
8516 State Street, Millington MI 48746
517-871-5080
Antiques, gifts, collectibles, furniture.

3 Millington Antique Co-Op Mall
8549 State Street (M-15), Millington MI 48746
517-871-4597
Every day 10 to 5, except holidays.
East side of street, a block south of the Millington Antique Depot.

Millington:

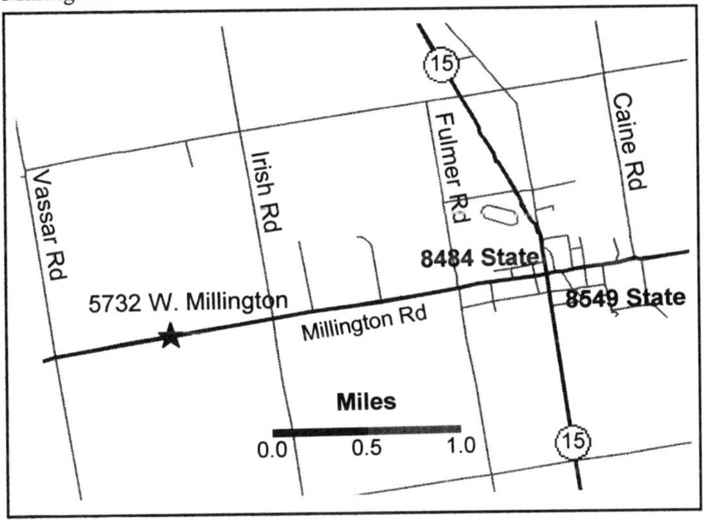

4 Jim's Antiques
8590 State Street , Millington MI 48746
517-871-3523 Barn in back of Country Shops Gift Store.

5 Mike's Antiques and Old Goodies
5732 West Millington Road, Millington MI 48746
517-871-4479 cody+@qtds.net
Evenings & weekends; days by chance.
West from the light Two miles.
Furniture refinished and in the rough; tall oak beds & farm wagons always on hand.

VASSAR

6 Village Antiques & Collectibles
231 Goodrich Street (M-15 South), Vassar MI 48768
517-823-3003

CARO

7 Quilt Talk Antiques
209 North State St., Caro MI 48723
517-673-7994

8 This That and Then Some
1146 Caro, Caro MI 48723
No telephone listed.

9 Gallery Unique
1333 East Caro Road, Caro MI 48723
517-673-5118

KINGSTON

10 Barron's Antiques
5969 State Street (M-46), Kingston MI 48741
517-683-2750

Croswell:

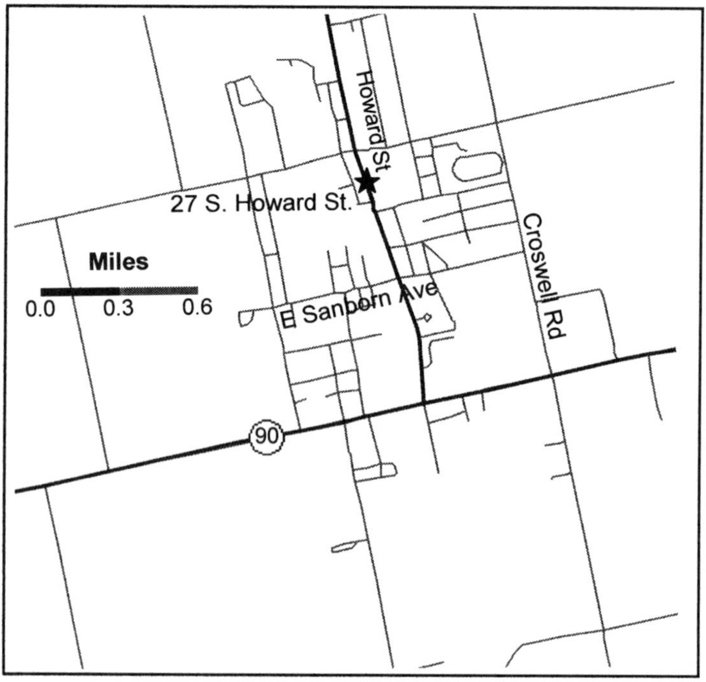

5.6 Sanilac County

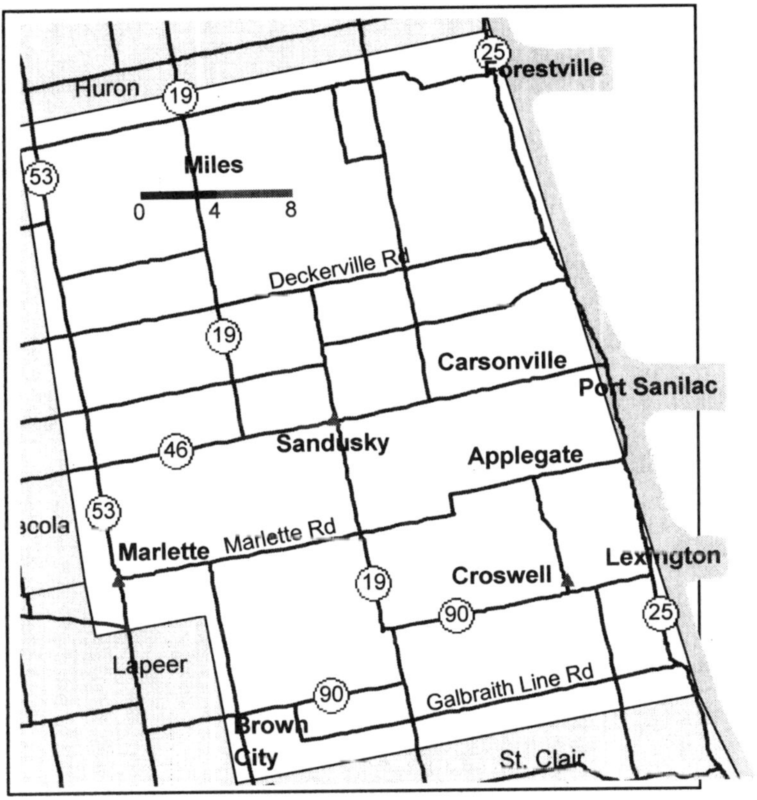

BROWN CITY

1 Timeless Creations
4223 Main (M-90), Brown City MI 48416
810-346-3747

2 Antiques Barn - Outback
Main & St. Mary's Streets, Brown City MI 48416
810 346-2331
By chance or appointment.

3 Evergreen Farm Antiques
15055 Dudley Road, Brown City MI 48416
810-346-3598
By chance or appointment; closed winter.

CROSWELL

(Map on page 196.)

4 Neal's Floral Shop & Antiques
14 N. Howard Ave., Croswell MI 48422
810 679-3554 Flowers; a few antiques.

5 Granny's Attic
27 South Howard Street, Croswell MI 48422
810-359-4462; 810 359-7563
Sun. 11 to 5 or by appointment.
East side of street, three blocks north of M-90. Croswell is four miles west of Lexington.
General line, furniture, pottery, glassware, etc.
Interested in buying an antique business? Call Joan Smith of Granny's Attic. The shop, inventory, and 2 bedroom apartment are available for purchase.

6 Black River Hobbies
80 North Howard Avenue, P. O. Box 215, Croswell MI 48422
810-679-4750

7 Allen & Louise Dodd
4691 Croswell Road, Croswell MI 48422
810 679-2936

APPLEGATE

8 Carol's Antiques
Main Street, Applegate MI 48422
810 679-3399
Open Sun.

9 Beverly Martin Antiques
4769 Main Road, Applegate MI 48079
810-329-9193

10 Keay's Antiques
4769 Main Road, Applegate MI 48422
810-679-3660 By appointment only.

11 Julia Ostrowski Antiques
4762 Main Street, Applegate MI 48401
810 633-9479 Open Sun.

LEXINGTON

12 Village House Antiques
5666 Main Street, Lexington MI 48450
810 359-7733
Weekends by chance.

13 Hunter House
5654 Main Street (M-25), P.O. Box 246, Lexington MI 48450
810 359-8016

14 B & L Antiqurie Inc.
6217 Lakeshore, Lexington MI 48450
810-359-8623
Curved glass, beveled mirrors, antique glass.

15 Time Will Tell
7245 Huron Avenue, Lexington MI 48450
810 359-2046
Weekends

16 Bob Hobbs Gifts & Antiques
7262 Huron Street, Lexington MI 48450
810 359-8386

CARSONVILLE

17 Jan's Antiques
560 Goetze Road , Carsonville MI 48419
810-657-9786 E-mail: jantique@greatlakes.net

PORT SANILAC

18 Sarah's Colony & Crown Antiques
173 South Ridge (M-25), Port Sanilac MI 48469
810 622-9020
Memorial Day to end of Oct.

19 Old Red Barn Antiques
P.O. Box 79, 235 Ridge Road (M-25), Port Sanilac MI 48469
810 622-8297 oldred@greatlakes.com
Sat., Sun. Holidays 9 to 5
Eleven miles north of Lexington across from Sanilac Museum. Specializing in country oak.

Port Sanilac:

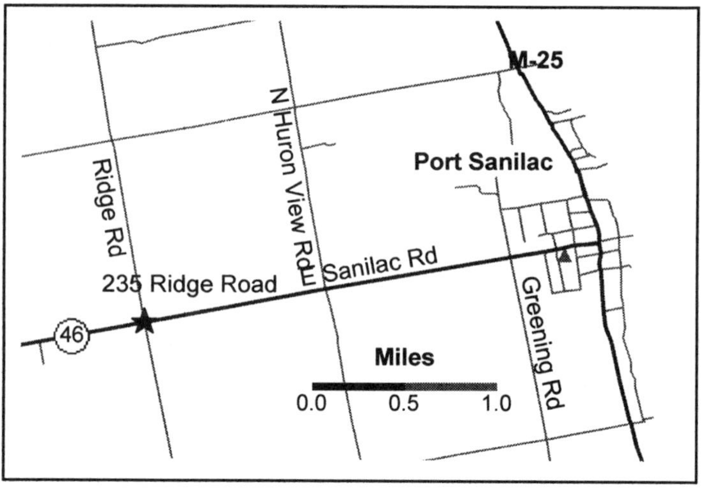

20 Liberty Rose Antiques & Refinishing Supplies
56 South Lakeshore Road, Port Sanilac MI 48469
810-622-9500

21 Gull Cottage Antiques
2096 S. Lakeshore (M-25), Port Sanilac MI 48401
810 622-9883

22 Lalla Rookh Antiques
185 North Ridge Road (M-25), Port Sanilac MI 48469
810 622-7966 Weekends

SANDUSKY

(Map on following page.)

23 Denise Kelley Antiques
26 Austin Street, Sandusky MI 48471
810-648-4183
Tues. to Fri. 1 to 5, Sat. 10 to 5, or by appointment.
Just off M-46 on Austin Street, behind Apria Healthcare (just south of the State Police Post) in the green house. Little bit of everything from the 30's to 50's: wall pockets, pottery, costume Jewelry, furniture, and household items. Also pillows and Christmas items made from vintage fabric and trims.

24 Back Alley Antiques Etc.
17 Lincoln Street, Sandusky MI 48471
810 648-5084

Sandusky:

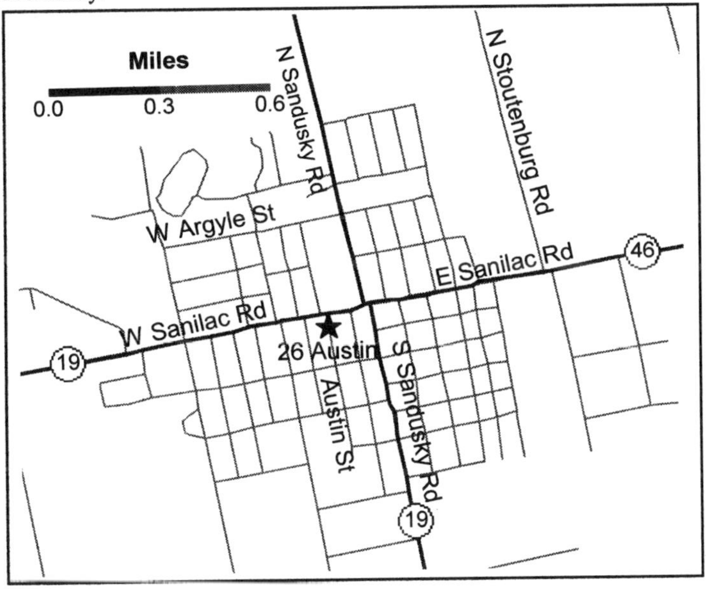

FORESTVILLE

25 Farmhouse Antiques
7914 Lake Road
Forestville, MI 48234 Dennis & Joan Kickhofel
May 30 to Oct. 30: Sat/ & Sun. 11 to 5
Off M-25, behind St. John's Catholic Church (on Lake Huron).
Depression glass, Fiestaware, pottery, 30's & 40's kitchen collectibles, oak furniture

TIER 6: THE M-20 ROUTE

6.1 Oceana County

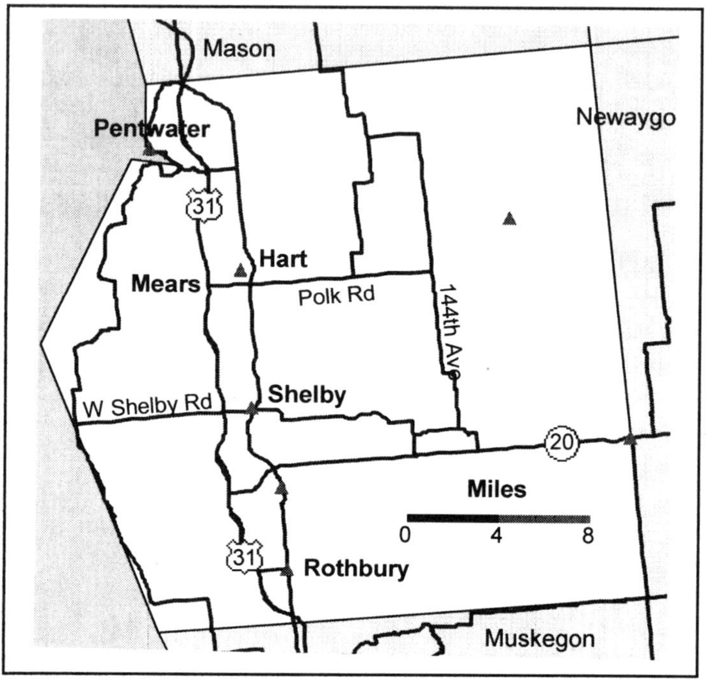

SHELBY

1 Nielsen's Nest
1021 South Oceana Dr. (Old U.S. 31), Shelby MI 49455
231-861-4920 May through Oct.

2 The Barn Antiques
141 South 24th Avenue, Shelby MI 49455
231-861-5038 kap@westmichigan.net Seasonal hours.

MEARS

3 Silver Hills Antique Mall
6780 West Fox Road, Mears MI 49436
231-873-3905 Memorial Day to Labor Day

HART

4 Courtland House
16 Courtland Street, Hart MI 49420
231-873-4746

5 The Flower Bin
27 South State Street, Hart MI 49420
231-873-0222 Flowers and antiques.

PENTWATER

6 The Carriage House Antique Mall
50 Second Street, Pentwater MI 49449
231-869-0222 Closed Dec. 31 to April 1

6.2 Newaygo County

GRANT

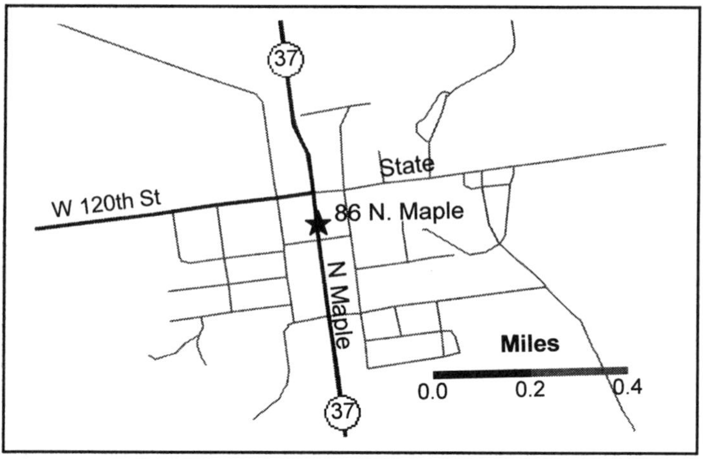

1 Homefront Antiques & Collectibles
73 South Front Street, P.O. Box 168, Grant MI 49327
231-834-9440

2 Big Apple Antique Mall
86 North Maple, P.O. Box 341, Grant MI 49327
231-834-8088; Fax: 616-887-9151
Mon. to Sat. 11 to 5; Sun. 1 to 5
East side of M-37, north of downtown.
Many dealers with full line of unique antiques and collectibles.

NEWAYGO

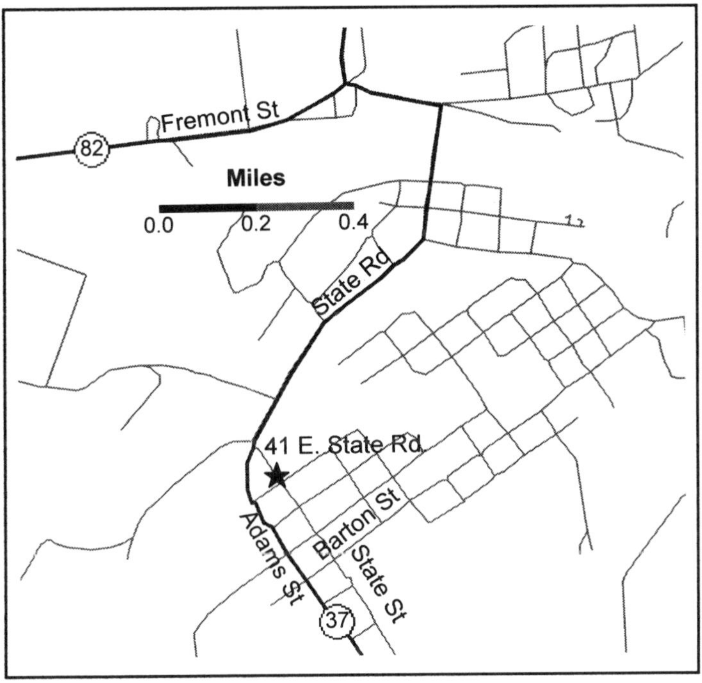

3 River Valley Antique Mall
41 East State Road (M-37), P. O. Box 192, Newaygo MI 49337
231-652-4519
April to Dec: Mon. to Sat. 10:30 to 5:30, Sun. 1 to 4;
Jan. to March: Fri. Sat. & Sun. only.
Heart of Downtown Newaygo.
4,000 square feet floor space. Quality antiques, collectibles, books, furniture, post cards paper memorabilia, dolls and primitives.

FREMONT

4 Rolling Ladders Antiques
10 East Main Street, Fremont MI 49412
231-924-0420
Mon. to Fri. 10 to 5:30. Sat. 10 to 5.
Downtown at Division & Main.
General line.

Fremont:

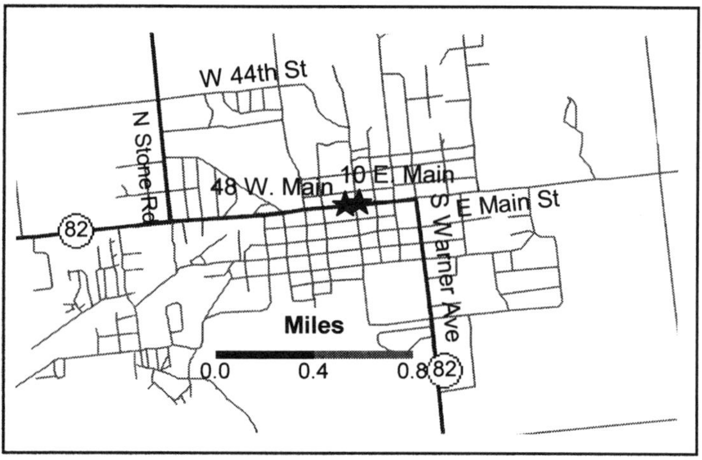

5 The Treasure Chest
11 East Main, Fremont MI 49412
231-924-6143

6 Brass Bell Antique Mall
48 West Main, Fremont MI 49412
231-924-1255
Mon. to Sat. 10 to 5:30, Sun. 12 to 5
Downtown
Four showrooms of quality antiques, plus Espresso Bar & country gifts.

WHITE CLOUD

7 The Heritage Shop
2357 West One Mile Road (M-20), White Cloud MI 49349
231-689-1876

8 Rosy Green's Antiques
901 North Evergreen (M-37), White Cloud MI 49349
231-689-5849

6.3 Mecosta County

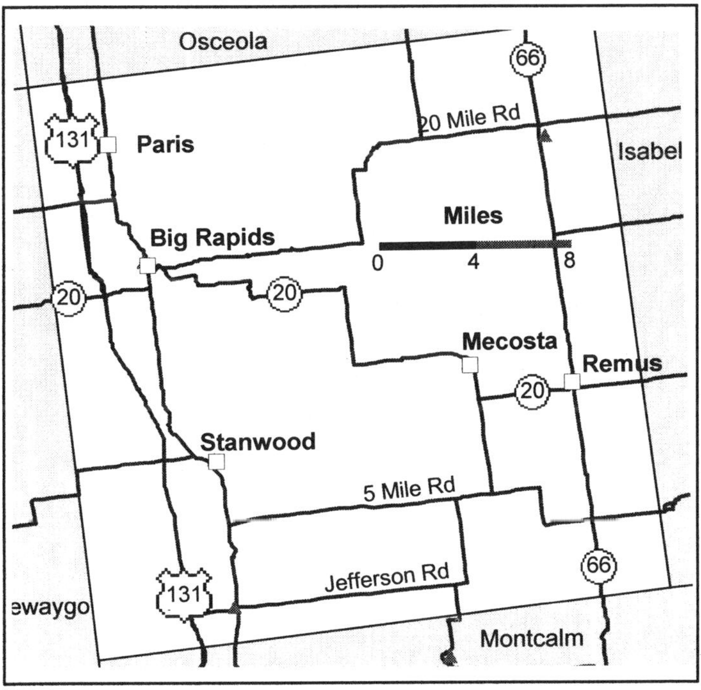

BIG RAPIDS

1 Big Rapids Antique Mall
107 S. Michigan, Big Rapids MI 49307
231-796-4100 ctiger3@yahoo.com
Mon. to Sat. 10 to 5, most Sun. 12 to 4.
Downtown, one block east of Business Loop U.S. 131 in historic Nisbett Building.
Specialties: oak furniture, knives, coins, vintage clothing, pottery & glassware, books, toys, jewelry.

PARIS

2 R. & M. Log Cabin
22920 Northland Drive (Old 131), Paris MI 49338
231-832-2941
New furniture & reproductions; few antiques.

3 Paris Country Shop
22203 Northland Drive (Old U.S. 131), Paris MI 49338
231-832-4533

MECOSTA

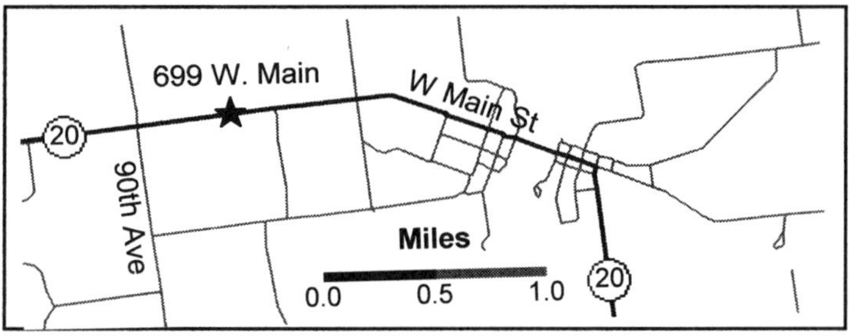

4 The Tamarack Shoppe Crafts & Collectiques
699 West Main Street (M-20), Mecosta MI 49332
231-972-4222
Fri., Sat. & Mon 10 to 5; Sun. 12 to 5 (except one month at year end).
West of downtown, southeast corner Franklin and Main Streets.
Dolls, Furniture, quilts, depression, pattern & Fenton glass, Griswold iron, lots of antiques and crafts.
Layaways: 10% down, 10% a month.

REMUS

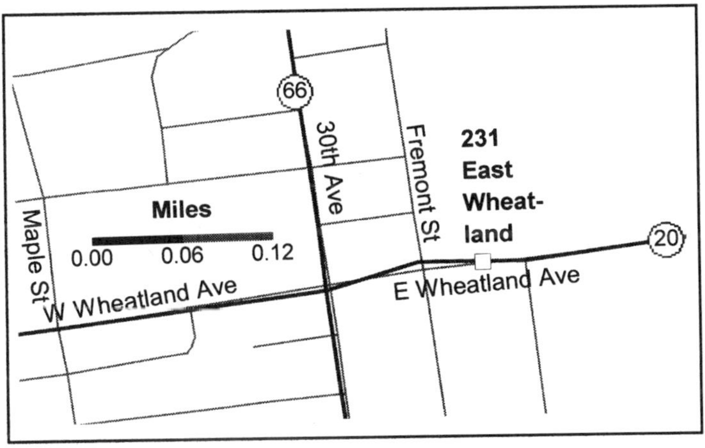

5 The Barn - Hilltop Heirlooms
231 East Wheatland (M-20 East), Remus MI 49340
517- 967-3402
May 15 to Nov. 15: Daily 8 to 5;
East on M-20, big barn on north side of the road.
Furniture; primitives; glassware; smalls.

6 Wheatland Trading Post Craft & Antique Mall
298 W. Wheatland, P.O. Box 352, Remus MI 49340
517-967-3400

Mt. Pleasant:

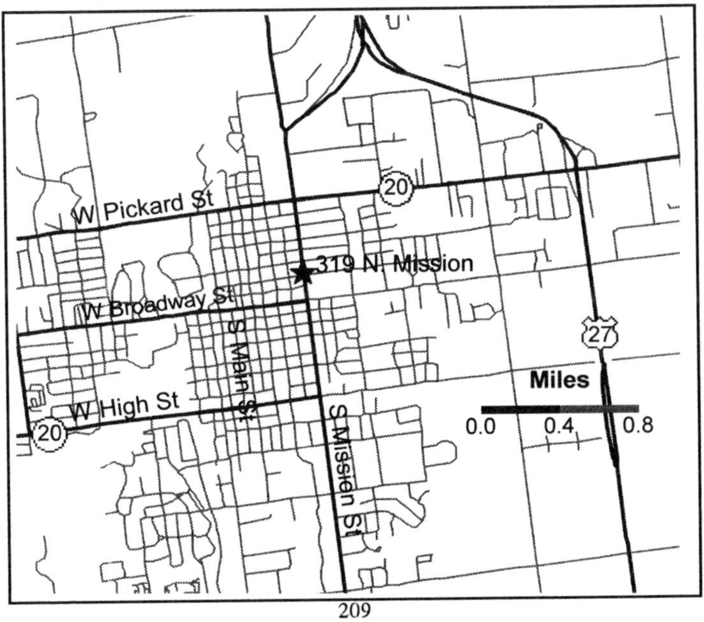

6.4 Isabella County

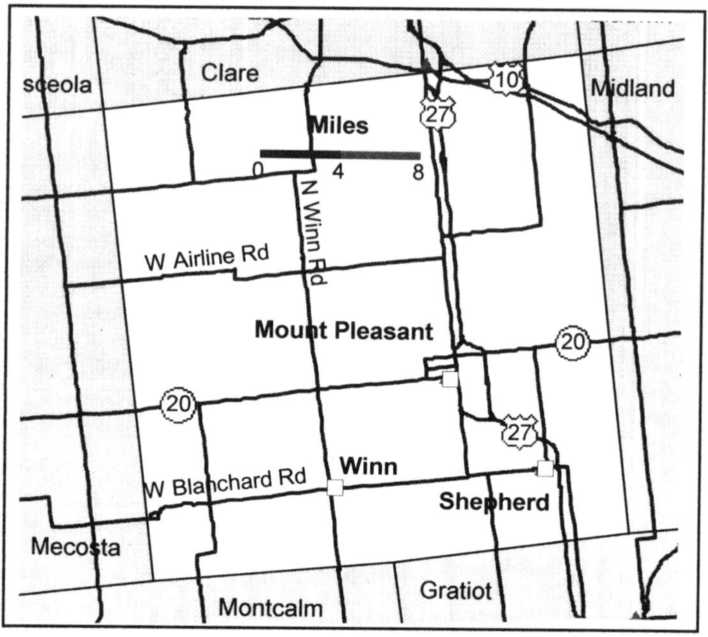

MT. PLEASANT

1 Antiques on the Side
1833 West Millbrook Road, Mt. Pleasant MI 48858-8521
517-866-2527; Fax: 517-866-2749

2 Antiques Center of Mt. Pleasant
1718 South Mission, Mt. Pleasant MI 48858
517-772-2672

3 Mt. Pleasant Antiques Market
319 North Mission, Mt. Pleasant MI 48858
517-779-0000 www.antiquemkt.com

4 Antiques & Collectibles
1005 North Mission, Mt. Pleasant MI 48858
517-772-0073

SHEPHERD

5 Cedar Valley Antiques & Collectibles
2835 W. Blanchard Road, Winn MI 4896
517-866-6155

6.5 Midland County

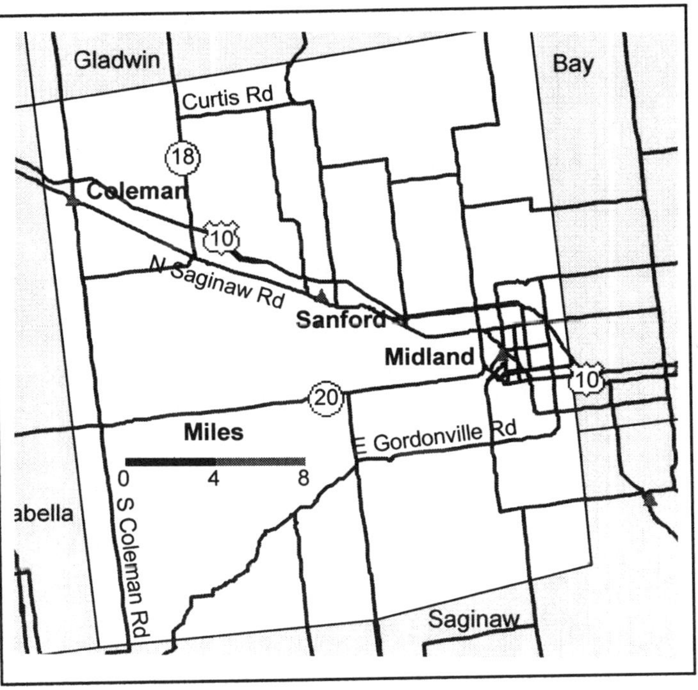

MIDLAND

1 D.A.D.'s Antiques
3004 Poseyville Road, Midland MI 48640
517-835-7483

2 Linda's Cobble Shop
2900 Isabella Street, Midland MI 48640
517-832-9788

3 Corner Cupboard
2112 East Wheeler Road, Midland MI 48642
517-835-6691

4 King Solomon's
201 East Main Street, Midland MI 48640
517-837-5464
Mon. to Fri. 10 to 6, Sat. 10 to 5
Downtown, just east of M-20.
Gifts, Antiques, Christian books & Jewish items.

Midland:

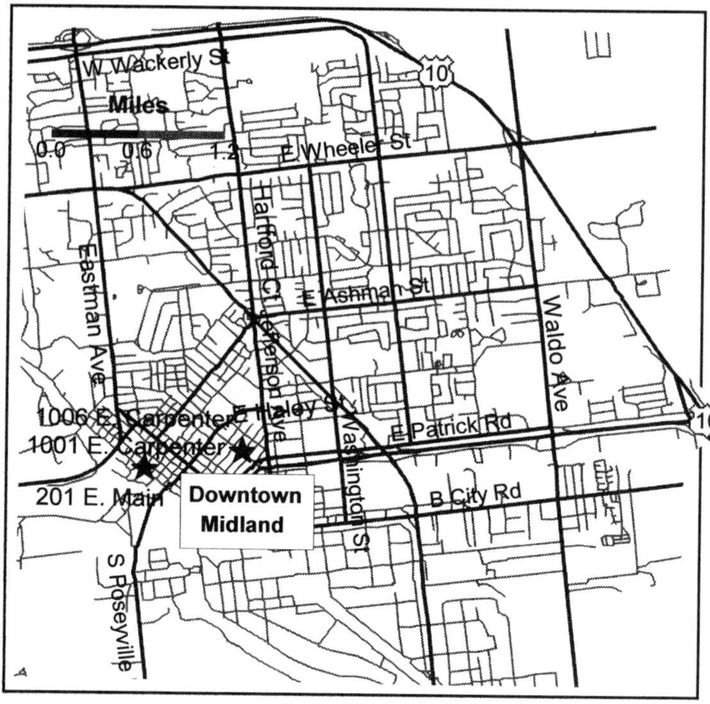

5 Second to None

1001 East Carpenter, Midland MI 48642
517-832-6067
Mon. to Fri. 10 to 5, Sat. 11 to 4
Haley & Carpenter Streets, just east of downtown.
General line of antiques; also consignments & second hand furniture.

Downtown Midland:

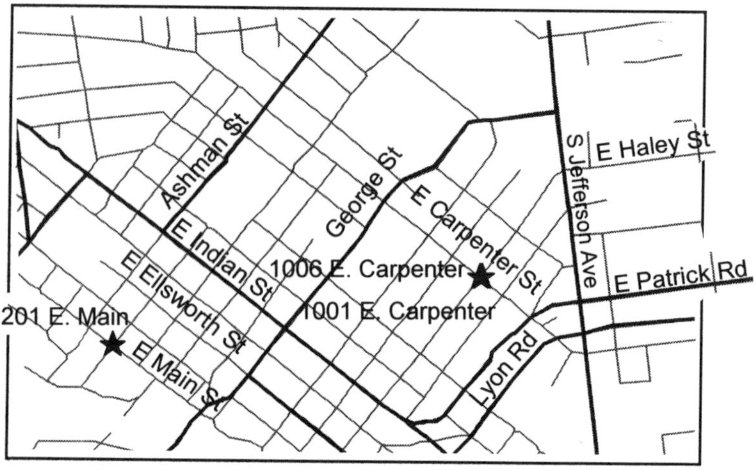

6 Antiques, Uniques, Collectibles
1006 E. Carpenter, Midland MI 48642
517-839-9153
Tues. and Thurs. to Sat. 10 to 5
Haley & Carpenter Streets, just east of downtown.
Antique glassware, Fireking dishes, Fairy Lamps, etc.

7 Yorkshire Emporium
1621 East Wheeler, Midland MI 48642
517-923-0364

Bay City:

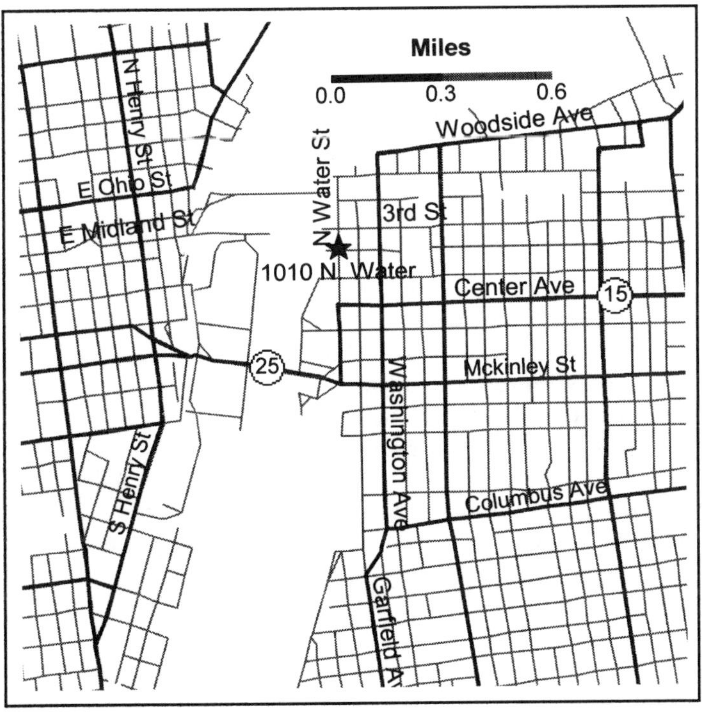

6.6 Bay County

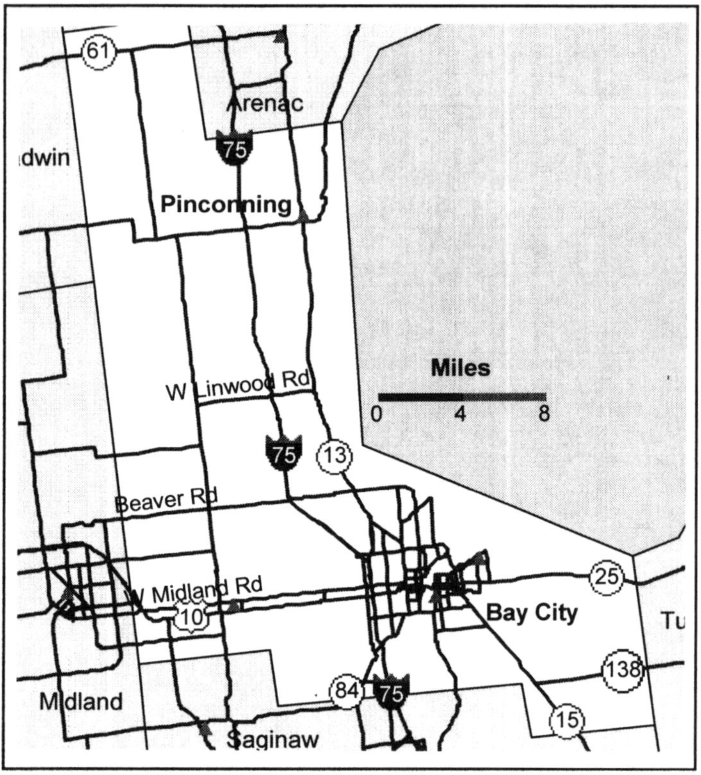

BAY CITY

1 Bay City Antiques Center
1010 North Water Street, Bay City MI 48708
517-893-0251 Fax: 517-893-1424
www.antiquecenteronline.com
Mon. to Sat. 10 to 5, Fri. till 8; Sun. 12 to 5
Downtown, southeast corner Third & Water Streets. From 1-75 exit at 162-A toward downtown, take the first left after the river - Saginaw Street; go six blocks north to Third Street, then left one block to Water Street, then left. Entrance is under the blue awning.
53,000 square feet. Block long building with three floors. Always free coffee.

2 Phoenix Antiques
113 3rd Street, Bay City MI 48708
517-892-3246

3 Gathered Traditions
115 3rd Street, Bay City MI 48708
517-891-0255 Primitives; gifts.

4 Ames Bargain Center
800 Garfield, Bay City MI 48706
517-893-0527 Re-opening Winter of 2000.

5 Mid Michigan Retail Sales
614 Garfield , Bay City MI 48706
517-893-6537
Antique used furniture & collectibles.

6 Little House
924 North Water, Bay City MI 48706
517-893-6771
Gifts, only a few antiques.

7 My Secret Garden
923 1/2 North Water Street, Bay City MI 48706
517-891-2000

8 Americana Company
912 North Water Street, Bay City MI 48706
517-891-8721

9 A Weathered Gate Antiques & Gifts
920 North Water, Bay City MI 48708
517-895-7902
Gifts, crafts, antiques.

10 Hen in the Holly
110 Third Street, Bay City MI 48708
517-895-7215
Antiques and folk art.

11 Trinkets & Treasures
113 Third Street, Bay City MI 48708
517-893-7143

12 Cottage Thyme
207 3rd Street, Bay City MI 48708
517-892-0005

13 Owl Antiques
703 East Midland Street, Bay City MI 48706
517-892-1105

PINCONNING

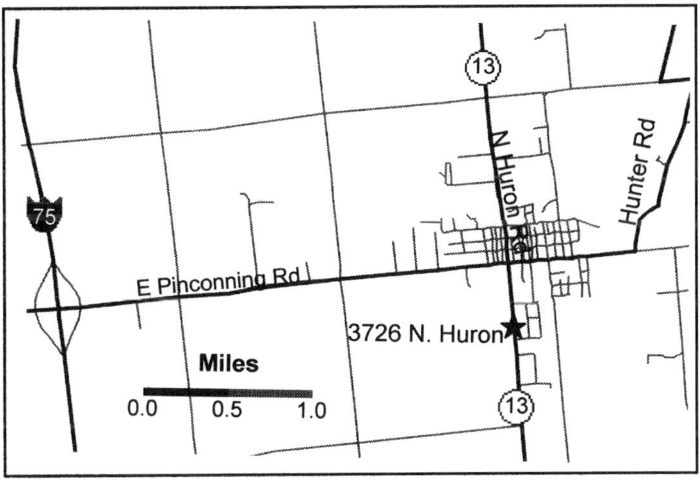

14 E & J Antique Mall
3726 North Huron Road (M-13) , Pinconning MI 48650
517-879-3300
E-mail: cjs@journys.com
Mon. to Sat. 10 to 5:30, Sun. 12 to 5
East side of the highway, 1/4 mile south of light.
Over 300 pieces of furniture; 7,000 square feet of antiques.
Complete restoration and repair services.

Sebewaing:

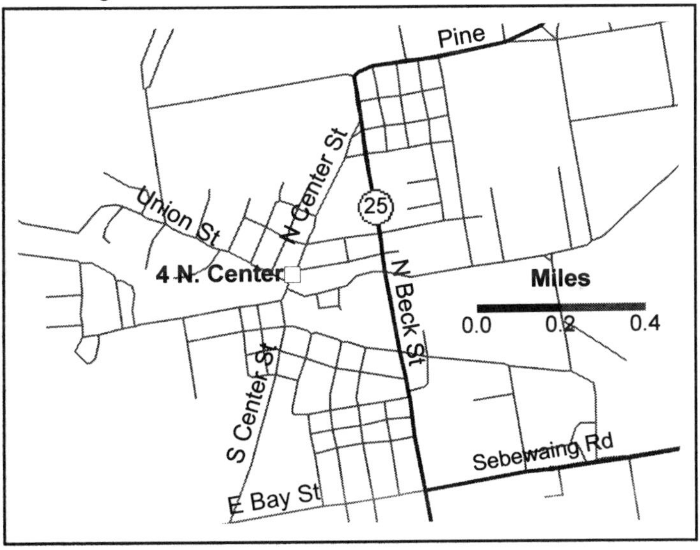

6.7 Huron County

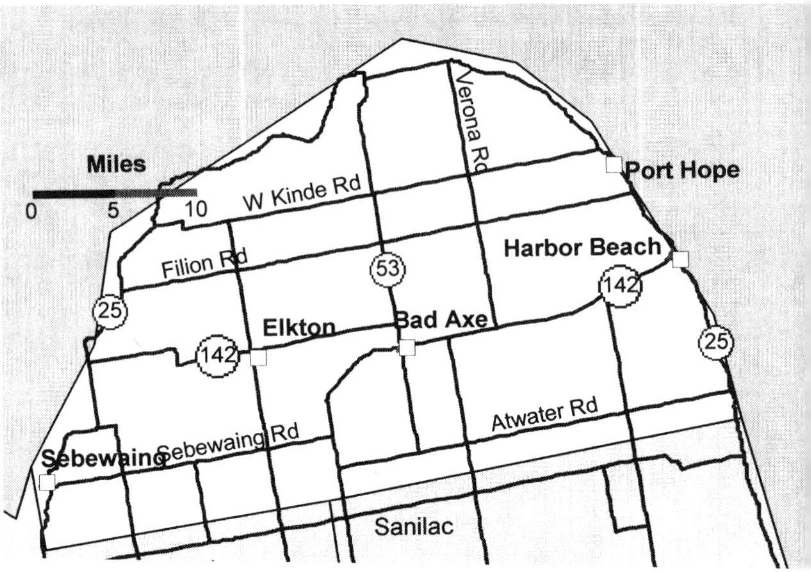

SEBEWAING

(Map on preceding page.)

1 Antiques By-The-Bridge
4 North Center Street, Sebewaing MI 48759
517-883-9424
Summer: Daily 10 to 5;
Rest of Year: Thurs. to Sat. 10 to 5, Sun. by chance.
Five large rooms full of antiques in renovated historic 1895 building. The Antique Inn Bed & Breakfast is located on the second floor. Also: Kay's Cafe, an old fashioned soda fountain.

2 Armiger's
11 N. Center Street, Sebewaing MI 48759
517-883-9055

ELKTON

3 Antiques & More
36 North Main Street, Elkton MI 48731
517-375-2426 rginter@avci.net
Fri. & Sat. 9:30 to 5
Downtown
10 dealers

Elkton:

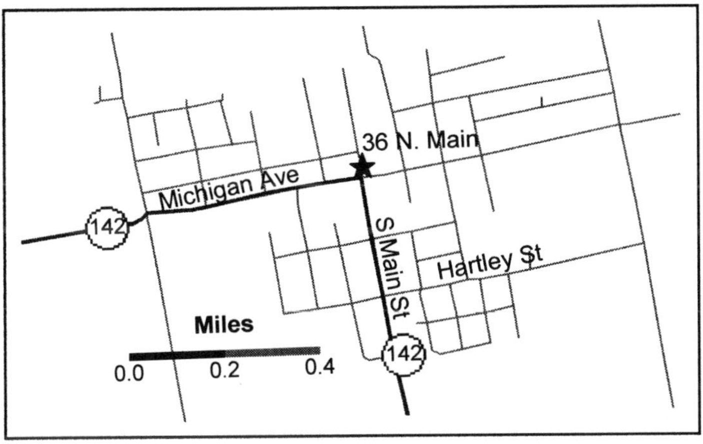

4 Mckenzie's Gifts & Antiques

30 North Main Street, P.O. Box 365, Elkton MI 48731
517-375-2750
April to Jan.: Mon. to Sat. 9 to 5
Feb. to March: Fri. & Sat. 9 to 5
Downtown, east side of street.
Furniture, glassware, jewelry, and collectibles.

BAD AXE

5 The Old Mill Antiques

M-53, P.O. Box 323 , Bad Axe MI 48413
517-269-9254
Seasonal, Summer 7 days, Fall 4 days, Winter Sat. & Sun.
Just south of Filion, 5 miles north of Bad Axe, southeast corner Van Dyke (M-53) & Crown Road.
Antiques, collectables, gifts, and an old-fashioned ice cream parlor in season.

6 Main Street Mercantile
163 East Huron, Bad Axe MI 48413

PORT HOPE

7 Main Street Antiques
4432 Main Street, Port Hope MI 48468
517-428-4925

TIER 7: LUDINGTON-GLADWIN-STANDISH

7.1 Mason County

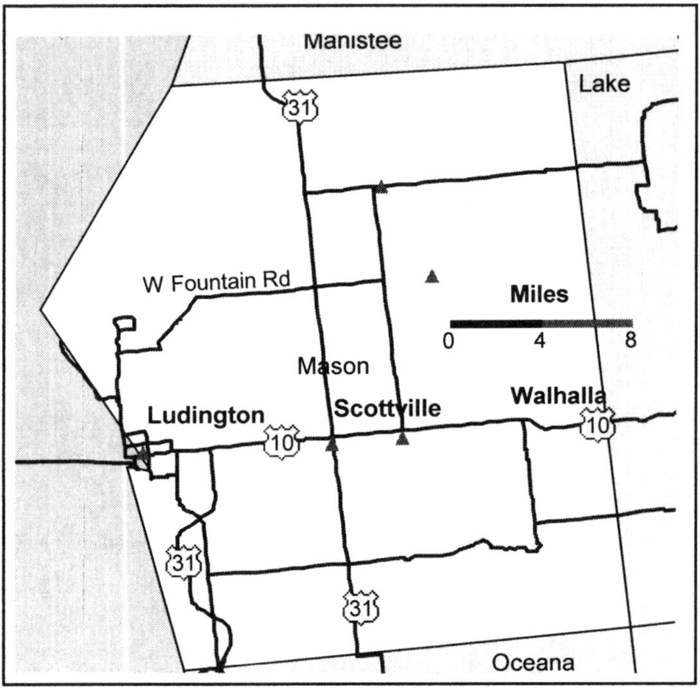

LUDINGTON

1 Cole's Antiques Villa
322 West Ludington Avenue, Ludington MI 49431
231-845-7414 Fax: 231-845-8667
Feb. March April Nov. & Dec.: Wed. to Sat. 10 to 5, Sun. 1 to 5
May to August: Mon. to Sat. 10 to 5, Sun. 12 to 5;
Sept. & Oct.: Tues. to Sat. 10 to 5, Sun. 1 to 5; closed Jan.
West end of downtown, just east of the House of Flavors Restaurant.
2,400 square feet. Quality furniture, pottery, glass, fine jewelry, advertising, lighting, price guides, decoys, fishing, clocks, graniteware, ephemera.

Ludington:

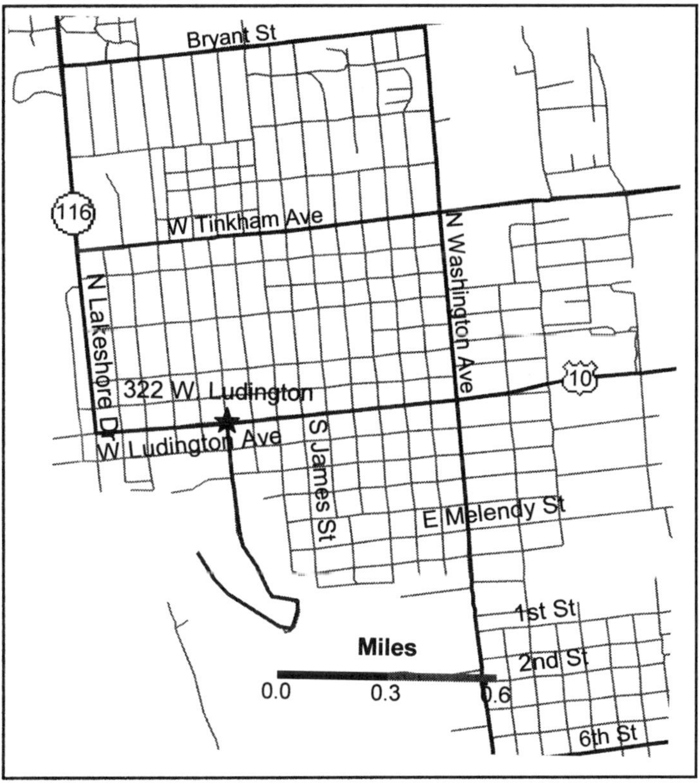

2 Sandpiper Emporium
809 West Ludington Avenue, Ludington MI 49431
231-843-3008

3 Country Charm
119 West Ludington Avenue, Ludington MI 49431
231-843-4722
Gift shop, with a few antiques.

4 The Antique Store
127 South James, Ludington MI 49431
231-845-5888; (708 852-8170 off season)

5 Sunset Bay Antiques
404 South James Street, Ludington MI 49431
231-843-1559

6 Elliott's Antiques
900 South Washington, Ludington MI 49431
231-845-5944

7 Washington Antiques
1001 South Washington Avenue, Ludington MI 49431
231-843-8030

8 Christa's Antiques & Collectibles
1002 South Madison, Ludington MI 49431
231-845-0075

9 Always Antique Mall
2144 Johnson Road, Ludington MI 49431
231-843-8781

SCOTTVILLE

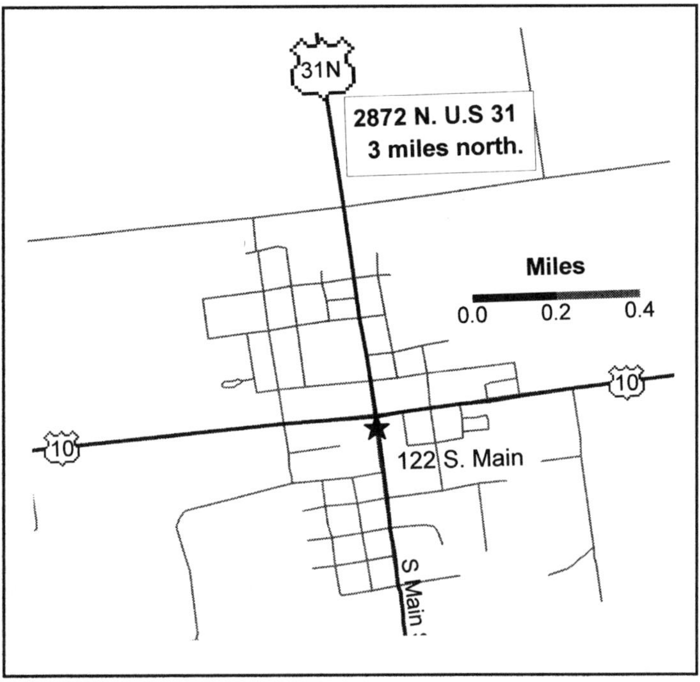

10 Scottville Antiques & More
122 South Main Street, Scottville MI 49454
231-757-3162
Summer: Tues. to Sat. 10 to 5, Sun. 12 to 5
Winter: Wed. to Sun. 12 to 5
Downtown, west side of the street.
Antiques, collectibles, crafts, glassware, lures, jewelry, lightning rods, books.

11 Red Rooster
3503 S. Darr, Scottville MI 49454
231-757-4060
Primitives, quilts, glassware, collectibles, dried flowers.

12 Proposed antique store.
101 N. Main Street., Scottville MI 49454
Where Main Corner Antiques used to be located.

13 Frick's Old Country Store
120 North Main Street, Scottville MI 49454
231-757-4708
By chance, summer only.

14 School House Antiques
2872 North U.S. 31, Scottville MI 49454
231-757-9364
Usually Every Day 10 to 5
Northeast corner Sugar Grove & U.S. 31, 3 miles north of Scottville.
Primitives, country, windmills, etc.

WALHALLA

15 Olde Friends Antiques
6796 East U.S. 10 , Walhalla MI 49458
231-757-3081
April to Dec.: Thurs. to Sun. 11 to 5;
July & Aug. open daily
North side of the highway at the curve, 22 miles east of Ludington.
Glassware, china, books, vintage clothes, furniture..

7.2 Lake County

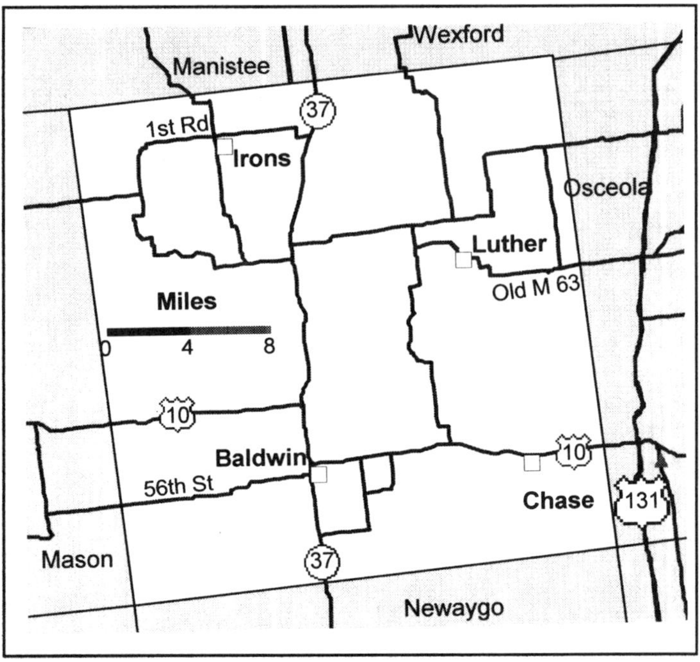

BALDWIN

(Map on the following page.)

1 Paul Bunyan Antiques Mall
9175 South M-37, Baldwin MI 49304
231-745-2637 bobart@net-port.com
Daily April 1 to Oct. 31 Evenings and winter weekends by chance or appointment.
Three miles south of Baldwin, on the west side of Highway M-37.

2 River Bend Trading Post No. 2
876 North Michigan (M-37), Baldwin MI 49304
231-745-3101

3 Katts Meow
879 Mich Avenue, Baldwin MI 49304
231-745-9303

Baldwin:

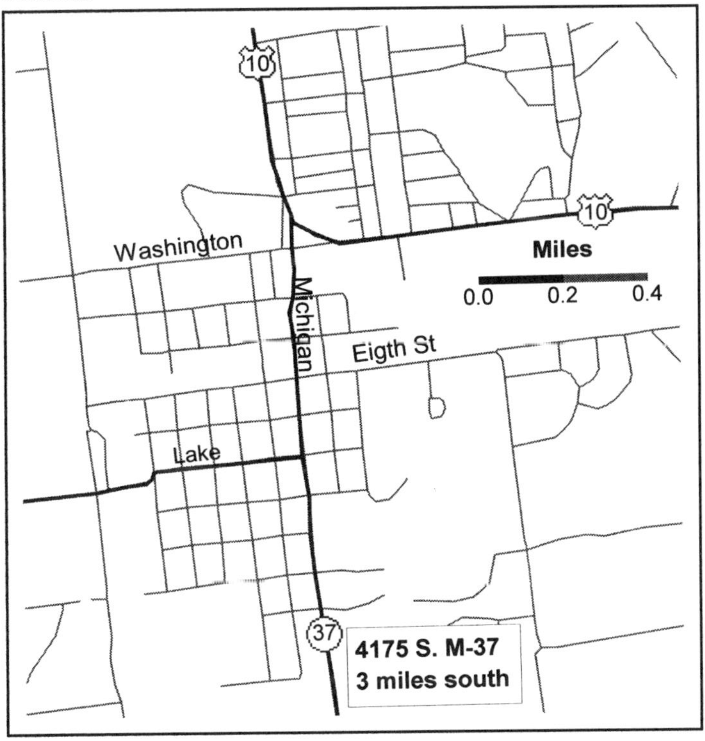

LUTHER

4 Hopeful Antiques
6390 Skookum Road, Luther MI 49656
231-829-3977

IRONS

5 Wheeler Dealer Store
10 1/2 Mile Road, P.O. Box 127, Irons MI 49644
231-266-5521

6 Antiques on the Corner
10486 Brook Road, P.O. Box 254, Irons MI 49644
231-266-6111 April to November

CHASE

7 Chase Depot Antiques & Collectibles
7118 S. Depot Street, Chase MI 49623
231-832-1947

7.3 Osceola County

Osceola and Clare Counties:

EVART

1 LC's Chicken Coop
2100 Haenlein Dr., 1014 North M-66, Evart MI 49631
231-743-2456 Summer by chance.

2 Davis Merchandise Sales
141 N. Main Street, P.O. Box 197, Evart MI 49631
231-734-6891
davismerchandise@hotmail.com
Summer: Mon. to Sat. 9 to 6, Sun. 11 to 3
Winter: call for hours.
From 131 Freeway exit to U.S. 10, reed City. Go east to Evart approximately 13 miles to stoplight, then one block north on Main.
General line of antiques, quality used furniture, antique furniture, collectibles, and lots lots more.

MARION

3 Good Friend's Antiques and Flea Market
15396 M-115, Marion MI 49665
231-743-6173

4 American Traditions Craft & Antique Mall
105 West Main Street, Marion MI 49665
616-743-9929 Crafts, collectibles, antiques.

TUSTIN

5 High Button Shoe
19338 19 Mile Road, Tustin MI 49688
231-829-3308

7.4 Clare County

(Map in previous section.)

CLARE

1 House of Antiques & Collectibles
10472 South Clare Avenue (Old U.S. 27), Clare MI 48617
517-386-3571

2 Vintage Victorian Marketplace
8498 S. Clare Ave. (Old U.S. 27), Clare MI 48617
517-240-2820

HARRISON

3 Guiette's Inc
251 South Clare Avenue, Harrison MI 48625
517-539-9381

4 Antique Marketing Co. (aka Lott's Antiques)
7112 West Temple Drive (M-61), Harrison MI 48625
231-743-6222

7.5 Gladwin County

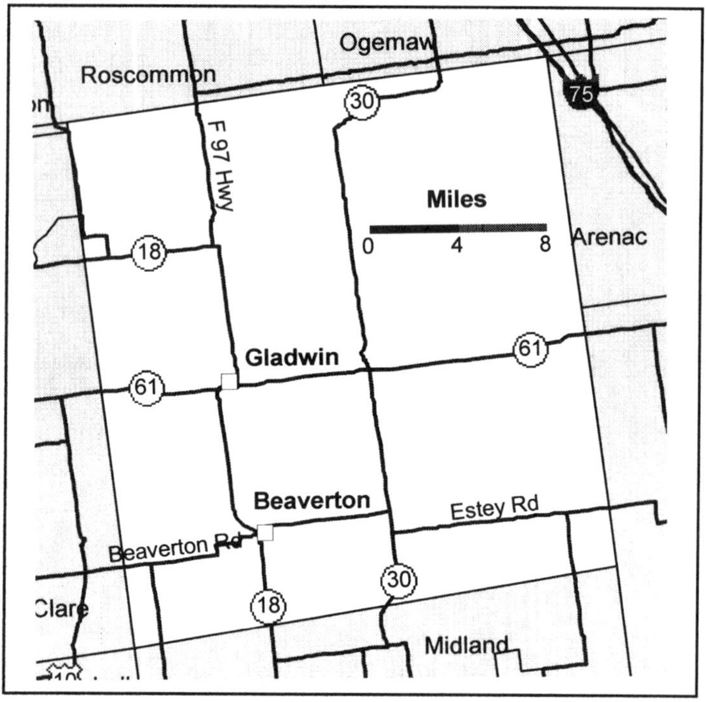

BEAVERTON

1 The Trumpeter
104 West Brown, P.O. Box 46, Beaverton MI 48612
517-435-4719
Open Summer.
Gifts and antiques.

GLADWIN

(Map on the following page.)

2 Passin' Time
225 West Cedar Avenue (the main street), Gladwin MI 48624
517-426-7823
Tue. to Fri. 9 to 5, Sat. 9 to 12
Downtown, south side of street.
Clocks and clock repair. Also furniture restoration and restored antiques.

Gladwin:

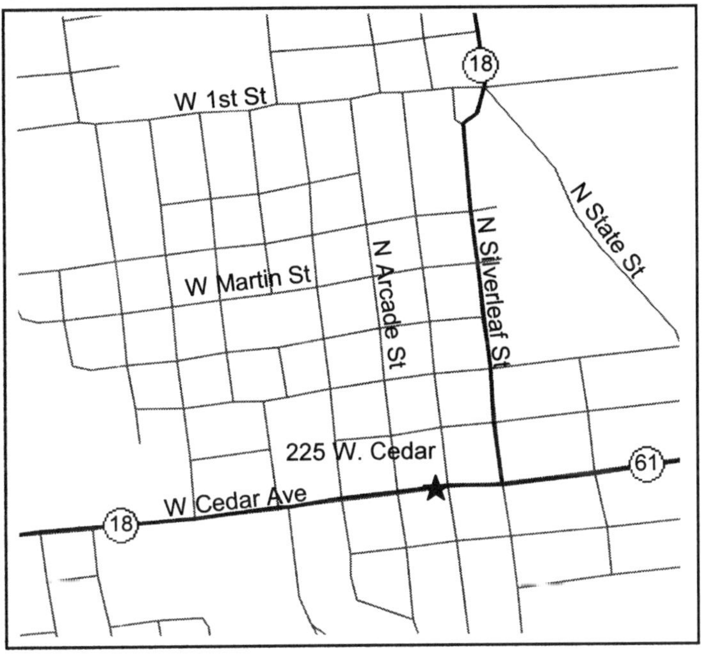

3 Schwager's Antiques
125 Cedar Avenue (M-61), Gladwin MI 48624
517-426-9221

4 Truelove Antiques
123 Cedar Avenue, Gladwin MI 48624

7.6 Arenac County

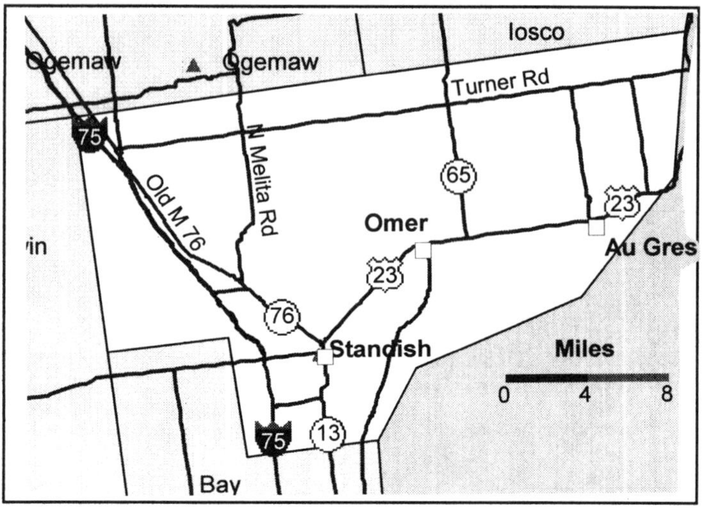

OMER

1 Quilt Patch Antiques
429 East Center (U.S. 23), Omer MI 48749
517-653-2332
May 1 to Nov. 1

AU GRES

(Map on the following page.)

2 Antique Shops
427 West U.S. 23, Au Gres MI 48703
517-876-2100
Tues. to Sat. 10 to 6, Sun. 11 to 3
Downtown
Furniture, primitives, glass, collectibles.

3 The Second Time Around
611 East Michigan Avenue, P.O. Box 35, Au Gres MI 48703
517-876-7413

Au Gres:

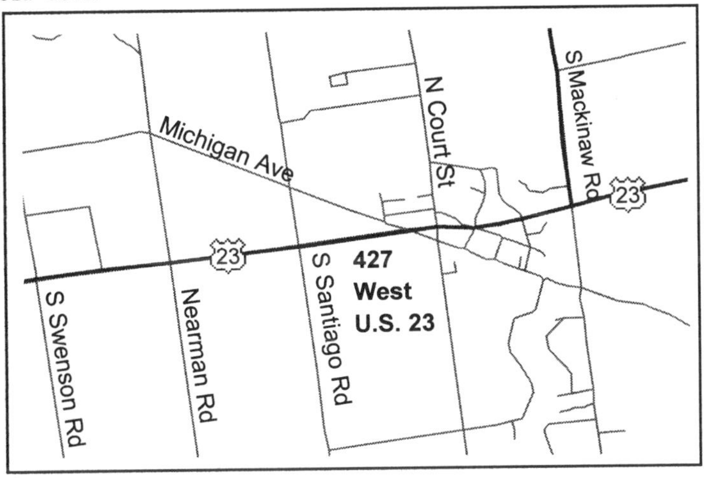

STANDISH

4 The Up North Store
201 South Main, Standish MI 48658
517-846-4633

TIER 8: THE M-55 ROUTE

8.1 Manistee County

MANISTEE

1 Victoria's Attic & Arbor
347 River Street, Manistee MI 49660
231-723-5183 vicattic.11net.com
www.vicattic.11net.com
Mon. to Sat. 10 to 4; Sun. 12 to 3
Highway 31 to River Street; west past theater.
Cottage, garden, country.

2 Antiques & Uniques
351 River Street, Manistee MI 49660
231-398-9339 jbtrucks@jackpine.com
Daily year round 10 to 5, Sun. 12 to 5.
Downtown, south side of the street. Note: River Street is one-way west-bound.
Furniture, prints, lamps, postcards, jewelry, glass, pottery.

Manistee:

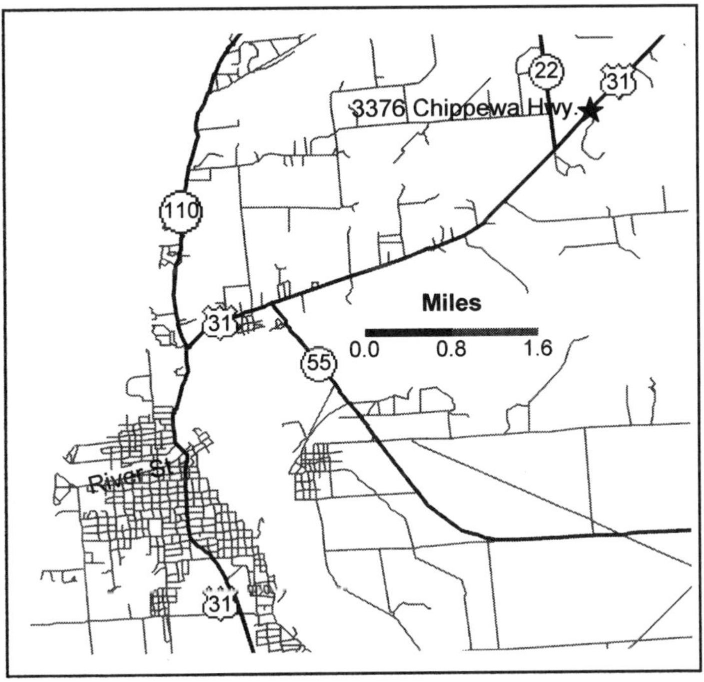

Downtown Manistee:

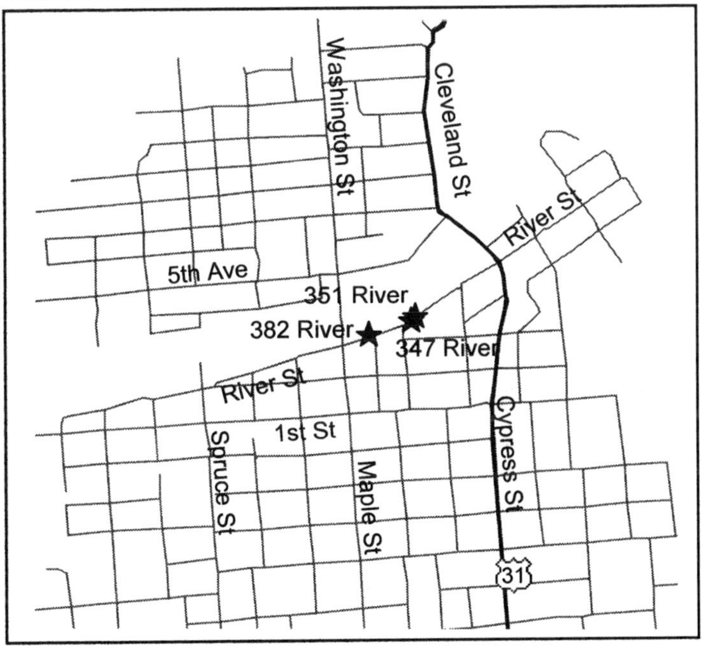

3 River Street Antiques
382 River Street, Manistee MI 49660
231-723-9133 rsantiques@jackpine.com
Open 7days all year; extended hours in the summer.
Summer: Mon. to Thurs.: 10 to 5, Fri. & Sat. 10 to 8, Sun. 12 to 4
Winter: Mon. Thurs. Sat.: 10 to 5; Fri. 10 to 8; Sun. 12 to 4
Downtown Manistee.
Antique mall with several dealers; all types of antiques and collectibles.

4 Little Johns Antiques
2267 Caberfae Highway, Manistee MI 49660
231-723-3347 Open summers.

5 North Country Antiques
3376 Chippewa Highway (U.S. 31 N.), Manistee MI 49660
231-723-5675
Open all year by chance or appointment.
7 miles north of Manistee, house on west side of highway.
General line of antiques; furniture and glass. Also antique restoration.

6 Old School Antiques
8532 Chippewa Highway (U.S. 31 N.), Manistee MI 49660
231-889-4632

7 The Old Farm Store
8011 First Street, Onekama MI 49675
231-889-3733 Art, antiques, Americana.

ONEKAMA

8 Country Corner
5119 Main Street, Onekama MI 49675
231-889-4451
By chance.

BEAR LAKE

9 Ye Olde Junque Shoppe
7718 Lake Street (U.S. 31), P.O. Box 263, Bear Lake MI 49614
231-864-3365
Summer only.

10 Old School Antiques
8532 Chippewa Highway (U.S. 31), Bear Lake MI 49614
231-889-4632

11 Victorian Treasurers
7809 Lake Street (U.S. 31), P.O. Box 211, Bear Lake MI 49614
231-864-3735

Cadillac:

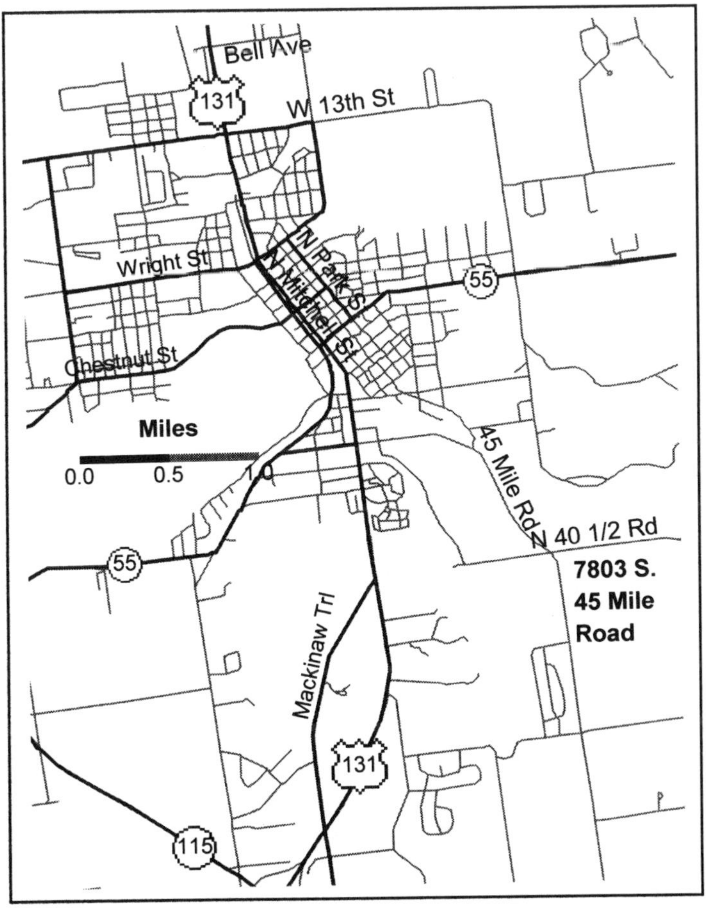

8.2 Wexford County

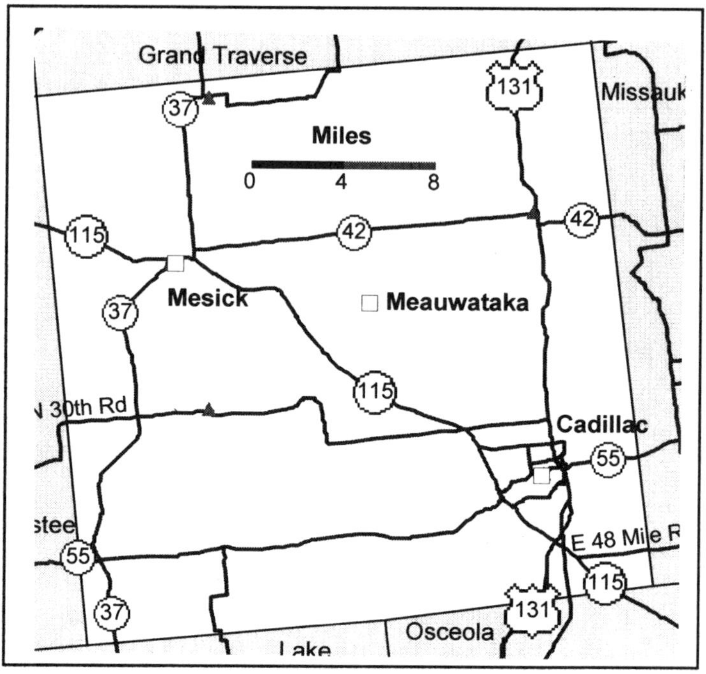

CADILLAC

1 Phyllis' Olde House Antiques
7803 South 45 Mile Road, Cadillac MI 49601
231-775-7502 josie@wmis.net
Sells on e-bay
Year round by chance or appointment, closed Saturdays.
From Cadillac: Two miles east-southeast from US 131 at Citizens South Branch Bank, around the bend; on the east side of the road, one door south of Fox TV.
Shop in home; general line with glassware, china, smalls plus furniture.

2 Downtown Antiques & Collectibles
105 S. Mitchell Street, Cadillac MI 49601
231-876-2399

3 Royer's Antique Mall
211 Bell Avenue, Cadillac MI 49601
231-779-2434
North two miles on U.S. 131, east at Wendy's Restaurant.

Northwest Cadillac:

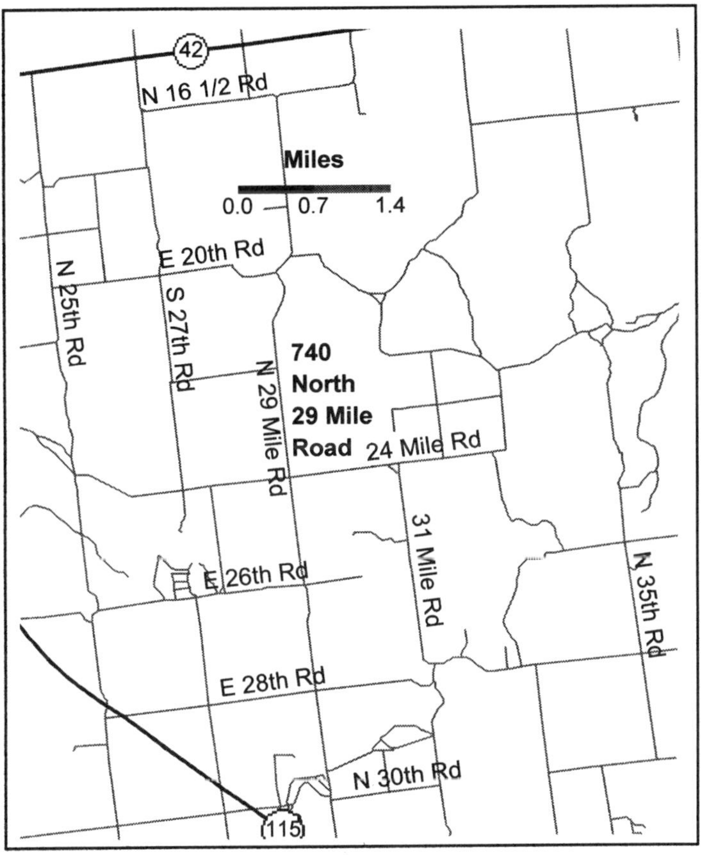

4 Thomason's Antiques
740 North 29 Mile Road, Cadillac MI 49601
231-775-0028
Daily 10 to 6, year-round.
Northwest from U.S. 131 on M-115 to 29 Mile Road, then 3.5 miles north. Quarter mile south of Meauwataka Store. Jewelry, china, general line of quality antiques: glass, pottery, furniture, etc.

MANTON

5 Manton Antiques
212 S. Michigan (U.S. 131), P.O. Box 525, Manton MI 49663
231-824-3783
Shop may be closing by early 2001.

MESICK

6 Hide-Away Antiques and Sugar Bush
9431 N 13 Mile (M-37), P.O. Box 567, Mesick MI 48668
231-885-2900

7 Family Tree Antiques
1599 Old # M-37, Mesick MI 49638
231-389-0079
Open weekends in summer.

Lake City:

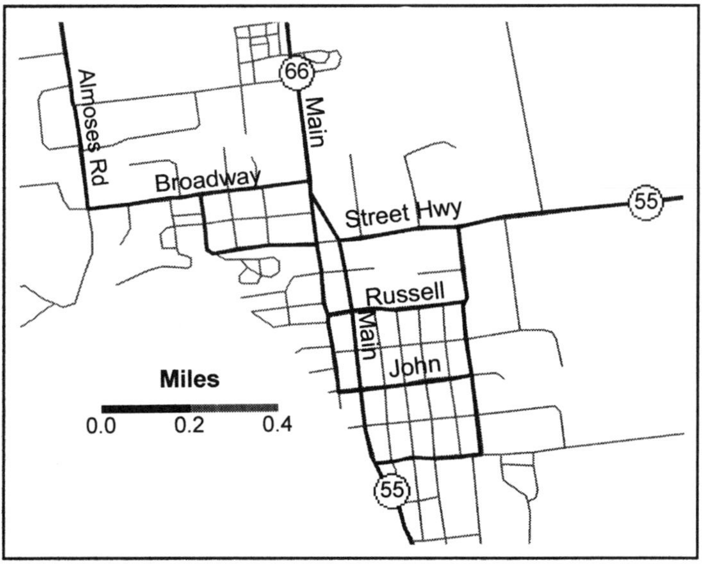

8.3 Missaukee County

Missaukee & Roscommon Counties:

McBAIN

1 Ala Carte Antiques
5921 S. Dickerson, McBain MI 49657
231-825-2820

LAKE CITY

(Map on preceding page.)

2 Larry's Used and Antiques
838 North Morey Road (M-66), Lake City MI 49651
231-839-4210 robinkirt@triton.net
Memorial Day Weekend through Labor Day Weekend
Mon. Tues. Thurs. & Fri. 10 to 5, Sat. & Sun. 12 to 4.
A mile north of town.

8.4 Roscommon County

(Map on preceding page.)

HOUGHTON LAKE

1 A Summer Place
6415 West Houghton Lake Drive (Old Highway 55),
Houghton Lake MI 48629
517-422-6030
May to Dec.

2 Berta's Antiques and Collectible Mall
6970 West Houghton Lake Drive (M-55), P. O. Box 83,
Houghton Lake MI 48629
517-422-5298

3 Maxine's Antiques
7821 Stone School Road, Houghton Lake MI 48629
517-422-5751

PRUDENVILLE

8 The Carousel Shoppe
1460 West Houghton Lake Drive, P.O. Box 860,
Prudenville MI 48651
517-366-5477
Gifts, crafts, antiques.

ROSCOMMON

4 Finders Keepers
1756 East Michigan Hwy. M-18, Roscommon MI 48653
517-275-5650

5 Lake Street Mall
903 Lake Street, P. O. Box 40, Roscommon MI 48653
517-275-0111 lakestreet@voyager.net
Summer: Daily 10 to 6
Winter (Jan. thru May): Closed Tues. & Wed.
One block north of light. Exit 244 south or 239 north off Hwy 75.
Over 45 dealers from throughout the state, mostly antiques & collectibles.

Roscommon:

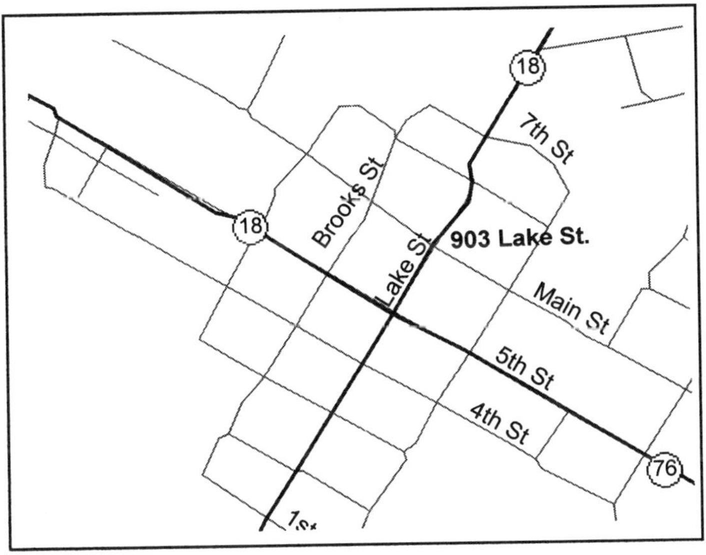

6 Broken Wheel
M-76, Roscommon MI 48653

7 Yorty's Antiques
103 Yorty Drive (West Higgins Lake Drive), Roscommon MI 48653
517-821-9242
Open Summer.

8.5 Ogemaw County

Ogemaw & Iosco Counties:

WEST BRANCH

1 Crockers Attic
3156 West M-55, West Branch MI 48661
517-345-1780 crocker@voyager.net
Mon. to Sat. 10 to 5, Sun. 11 to 4;
Winter: Mon. to Sat. 11 to 4
One mile west of downtown West Branch or one mile east of I-75 Exit 215.
Quaint country store featuring primitive antiques.

2 The Potato Barn Antique Mall
615 West Houghton, West Branch MI 48661
517-343-3333
Tues. to Sat. 10 to 5, Sun. 12 to 5
Downtown, north side of the street, behind the China Inn Restaurant.
General line of antiques and collectibles.

West Branch:

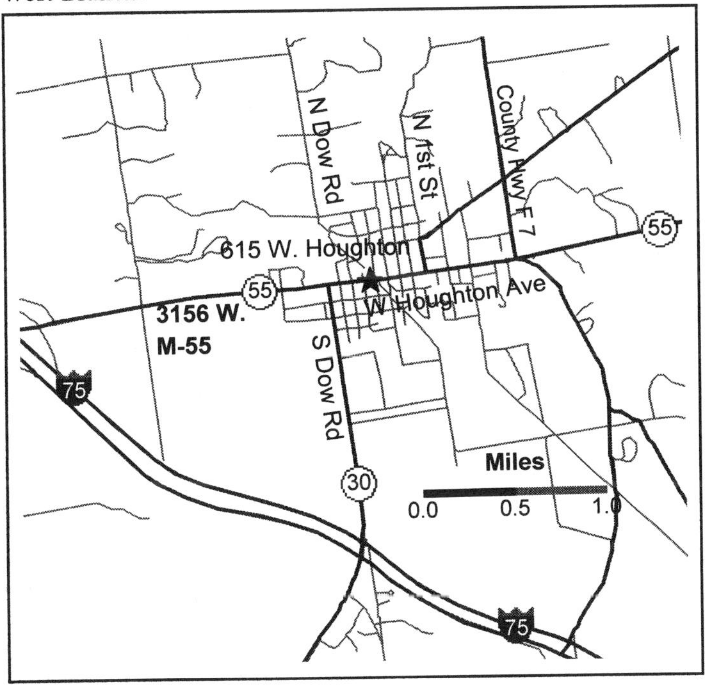

PRESCOTT

3 Hilltop House Antiques
2016 East M-55, Prescott MI 48756
517-345-3540; 517-345-7242

Tawas City:

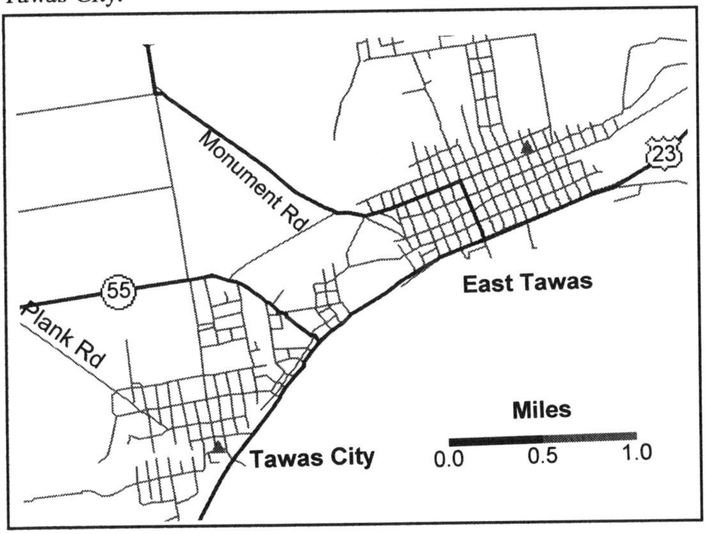

8.6 Iosco County

(Map in preceding section.)

TAWAS CITY

1 Alabaster Corners
2441 South U.S. 23 (Huron Road), P.O. Box 155 ,Tawas City MI 48763
517-362-7777
Every day 10 to 5
Four miles south of Tawas City, west side of highway.
Gifts, collectibles, antiques, Yankee Candles, & year-round Christmas shop. Also storage barns.

2 Uncle Winnies
402 Lake Street (U.S. 23), Tawas City MI 48764
517-362-6644

3 Time After Time Antiques
729 M-55 West, Tawas City MI 48763
517-362-2298
E-mail: eternity@i-star.com
Fri. thru Tues. 10 to 5, Wed. & Thurs. by appointment.
Two miles west of U.S. 23.
Glassware, crystal, furniture, primitives, vintage jewelry, collectibles, and much much more. Visa, Master Card and Discovery Cards honored; gift certificates available. Buy & sell; open all year.

EAST TAWAS

4 McNamara Antique Mall
2083 North U.S. 23, East Tawas MI 48750
517-739-5435 thinkirish@mail.com
Summer: Every day 10 to 4;
Winter: Fri. through Mon. 10 to 4
On U.S. 23 halfway between Tawas and Oscoda.
Antiques, collectibles, primitives. Outdoor yard ornaments.

OSCODA

5 Wooden Nickel Antiques
110 Park, Oscoda MI 48750
517-739-7490 Seasonal hours.

6 Ryland Co. Clocks and Antiques
2091 N. U.S. 23, P.O. Box 308 , Oscoda MI 48750
517-739-0810
Fri. to Sun. 11 to 5, or by chance or appointment.
5.5 miles south of Oscoda, across from Point Road.

7 Hobart's Antique Mall
4219 U.S. 23, Oscoda MI 48730
517-739-4000

8 Powers Antiques
7324 Loud Drive, Oscoda MI 48750
517-739-1840

9 Elsie's Hale Creek Antiques
201 North Washington (M-65), Hale MI 48739
517-728-2538

HALE

10 Mary's Hope Chest
6625 M-65, Hale MI 48739
517-728-2888

TIER 9: THE M-72 ROUTE

9.1 Benzie County

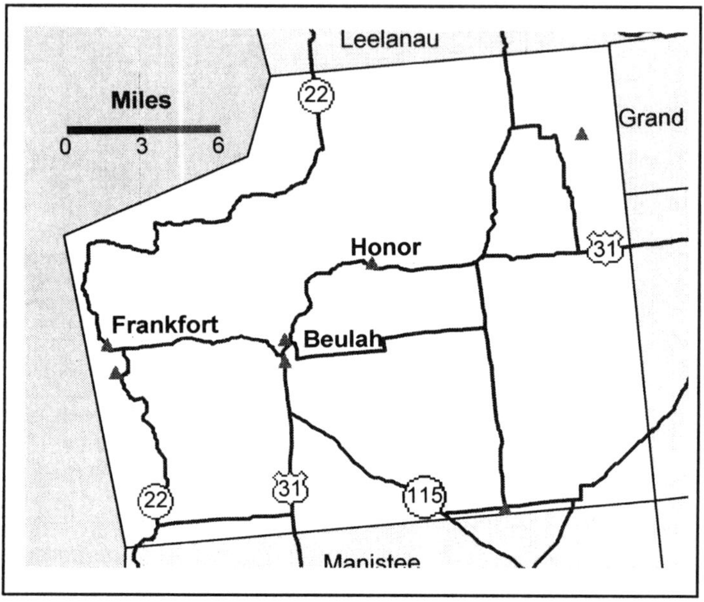

FRANKFORT

1 Frankfort Antique Market
735 Main Street, Frankfort MI 49635
231-352-7707

BEULAH

2 Crystal Lake Antiques
244 South Benzie, P.O. Box 542, Beulah MI 49617
231-882-5081

3 Myers Granary Antique Market
7300 Crystal Avenue, P.O. Box 125, Beulah MI 49617
Phone & Fax: 231-882-4299
myersgranary@coslink.net
May to Oct.: Daily 10 to 6
Downtown Beulah, on the new Trail.
General line of antiques.

Beulah:

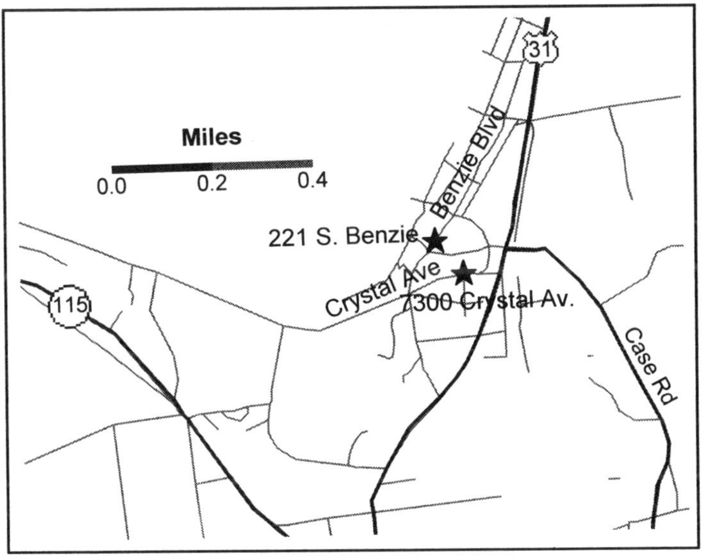

4 Black Horse Antiques
11 North Benzie Boulevard, P.O. Box 451, Beulah MI 49617 231-882-0231

9.2 Leelanau County

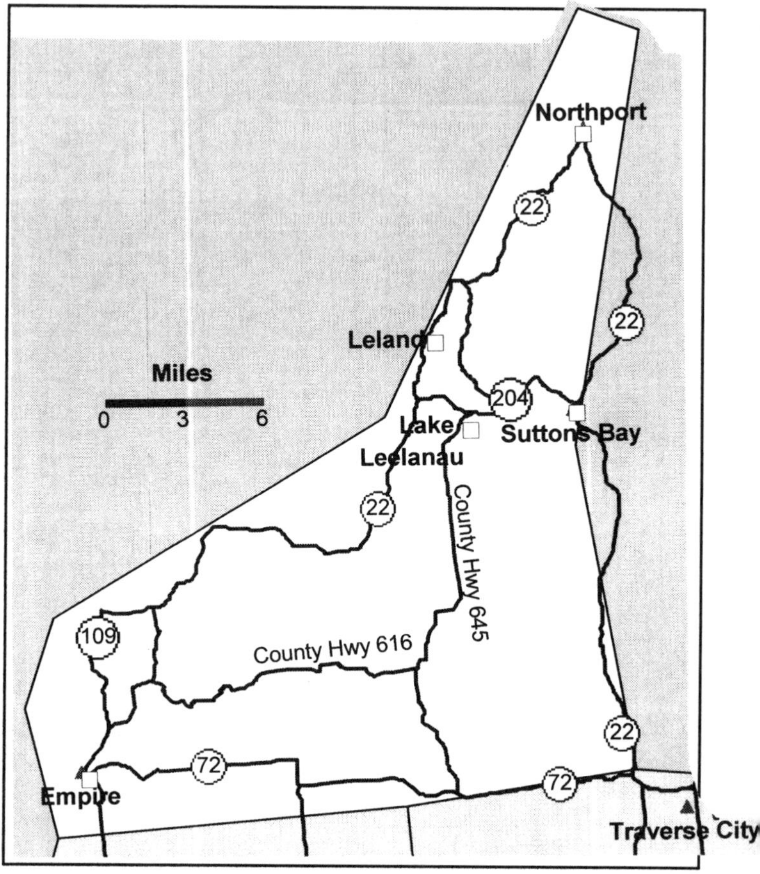

SUTTONS BAY

(Map on preceding page.)

1 Circa Antiques
316 St. Josephs, Suttons Bay MI 49682
231-271-4849

2 Hilltop Corner
5046 Southwest Bay Shore Drive, Suttons Bay MI 49682
231-271-3750

3 Danbury Antiques
305 St. Joseph Avenue, Suttons Bay MI 49682
231-271-3211
May to Oct.: Mon. to Sat. 10 to 6; Sun. 12 to 4; rest of year by chance or appointment.
Downtown **English smalls.**

Suttons Bay:

4 Applegate Collection
405 St. Joseph Avenue, Suttons Bay MI 49682
231-271-5252

5 Up North Antiques
311 North St. Joseph Street, P.O. Box 723, Suttons Bay MI 49682 231-271-5400

6 Sutton's Bay Galleries
102 Jefferson Street, P.O. Box 15, Suttons Bay MI 49682
231-271-4444

LAKE LEELANAU

7 Lake Leelanau Antiques
102 Meinard Street, Lake Leelanau MI 49653
231-256-7951

LELAND

8 The Old Library
103 East River Street, Leland MI 49654
231-256-7428 Seasonal

NORTHPORT

9 Fifth Street Antiques
201 Mill Street (M-201), P.O. Box 161, Northport MI 49670 231-386-5617 Summer only.

10 Cobweb Treasures
393 West Street, P.O. Box 4, Northport MI 49670
231-386-5532 E-Mail: cobweb@traverse.com

9.3 Grand Traverse County

INTERLOCHEN

1 Betsie-Bo's Antiques
6470 Betsie River Road South, Interlochen MI 49643
231-276-9514
May thur Oct.: open by appointment.
One and a quarter miles northeast of Karlin, west side of road, by the bridge.
Dishes, glassware, furniture, books, decorative items. In antique business 25 years.

2 The Miser's Hoard
9955 U.S. 31 South, Interlochen MI 49643
231-276-7642

WILLIAMSBURG

3 Bunk House Antiques
9866 old M-72, Williamsburg MI 49690
231-267-9011

TRAVERSE CITY

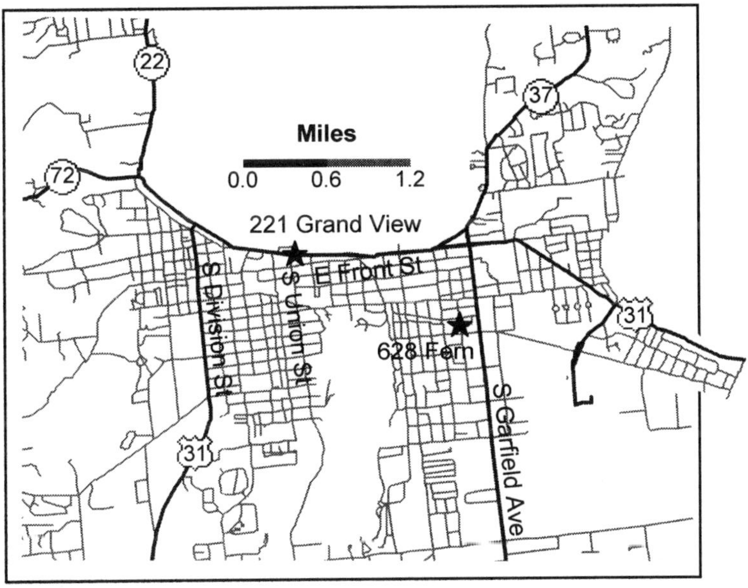

4 Grey Wolf Antiques
20848 Cedar Run Road, Traverse City MI 49650
(231) 275-7471

5 Chum's Corner Antique Mall
4200 US 31 South, Traverse City MI 49684
231-943-4200

6 Rolling Hills Antiques
5085 Barney Road, Traverse City MI 49684
231-947-1063 rollinghills@infinitecom.com
Every day 11 to 6, other times by appointment for serious buyers.
From downtown: West on Front Street, right on Cedar Run, right on Barney Road, top of the hill on left.
Specializing in American furniture from 1800 to 1925, and accessories.

7 Bay West Antiques
221 Grand View Parkway, Traverse City MI 49684
231-947-3211 baywestantiques@aol.com
Every day 10 to 6
Downtown, across from the power plant & Bay, 1/2 block west of Union.
25 dealers; large variety; 1st antique mall in Northern MI.

8 Wilson Antiques
123 South Union Street, Traverse City MI 49684
231-946-4177

9 Fascinations
140 East Front Street, Traverse City MI 49684
231-922-0051

10 The Painted Door Gallery
154 East Front Street, Traverse City MI 49684
231-929-4988
A few antiques for sale.

11 Oberschulte Gallery
544 East Eighth Street, Traverse City MI 49684
231-946-0424

12 Rickman's Antiques
628 Fern Street, Traverse City MI 49684
231-946-6609
Mon. to Fri. 10 to 6; Sat. 12 to 5

13 Antique Company - East Bay
4386 U.S. 31 North, Traverse City MI 49686
231-938-3000 ACoEast@aol.com
Daily: 10 to 6
Winter hours: Jan., Feb., March & April: Fri., Sat. & Sun. 10 to 6
East Bay, just south of Acme, beside the Traverse Bay Woolen Company and Troutsman.
General line of items circa 1880-1950.

14 Cherry Acres Antiques
12396 Peninsula Drive, Traverse City MI 49484
231-223-4813

15 Walt's Antiques
2513 Nelson Rd, Traverse City MI 49686
231-223-4123; or home 231-223-7386
E-mail: feiger@traverse.net
Web page: www.michigantravler.com/antiques
Spring, Summer & Fall: 7 days a week 10 to 6;
Winter: by chance or appointment.
Old Mission Peninsula, eight miles north of Traverse City on M-37, west one half mile on Nelson Road to the barn.
Antique gas pumps, advertising, flow blue, vintage clothing, and other rare and common antiques.

Traverse City North & East Side:

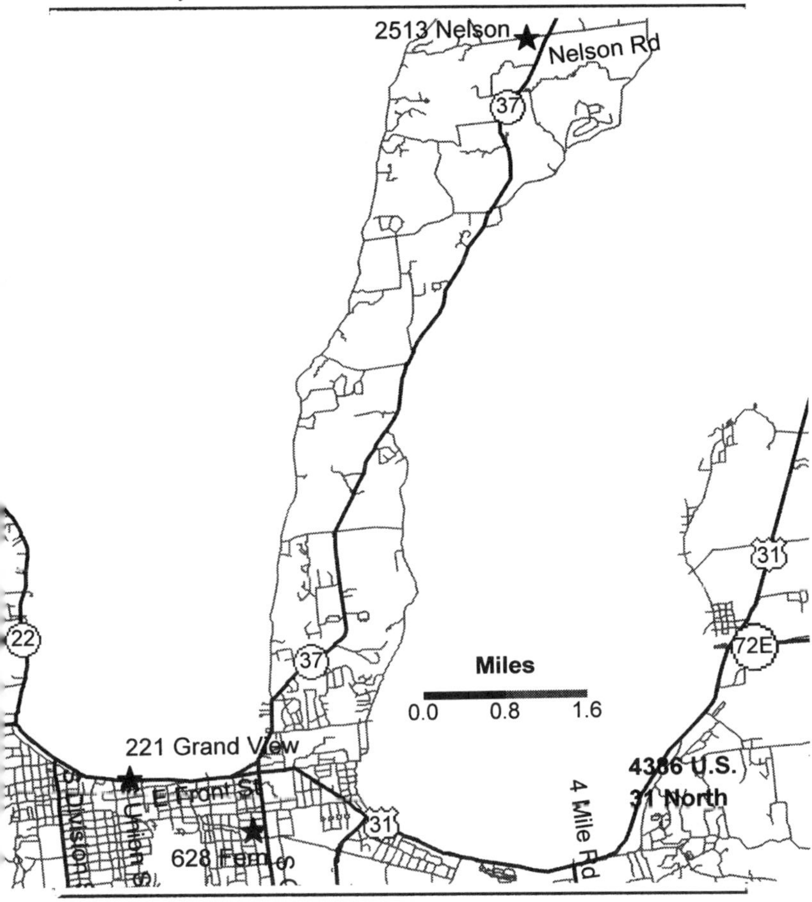

9.4 Kalkaska County

Kaskaska & Crawford Counties:

RAPID CITY

3 Millers Antiques
Downtown Rapid City, P.O. Box 69, Rapid City MI 49676
231-331-6104

4 Doty's Antiques
6898 Crystal Beach Road, Rapid City MI 49676
231-322-2807
Summer: Daily 10 to 4; Sunday by chance.
North side of road, 1 mile west of County Road 597.
Clocks, country furniture, pewter, folkart, stoneware, copper and brass, handwoven rugs, & general line.
Note: Do you want to own an antique shop? This shop may be for sale; come and take a look.

KALKASKA

1 Kalkaska Antiques
324 S. Cedar St. (U.S. 131), P.O. Box 1042, Kalkaska MI 48746 231-258-5500

Mancelona shops also in 10.1: Antrim County.

2 Somewhere in Time Antiques
552 West Bear Lake Road, Kalkaska MI 48746
231-258-5653
Memorial Day to Labor Day: Fri. & Sat. 9 to 4

MANCELONA

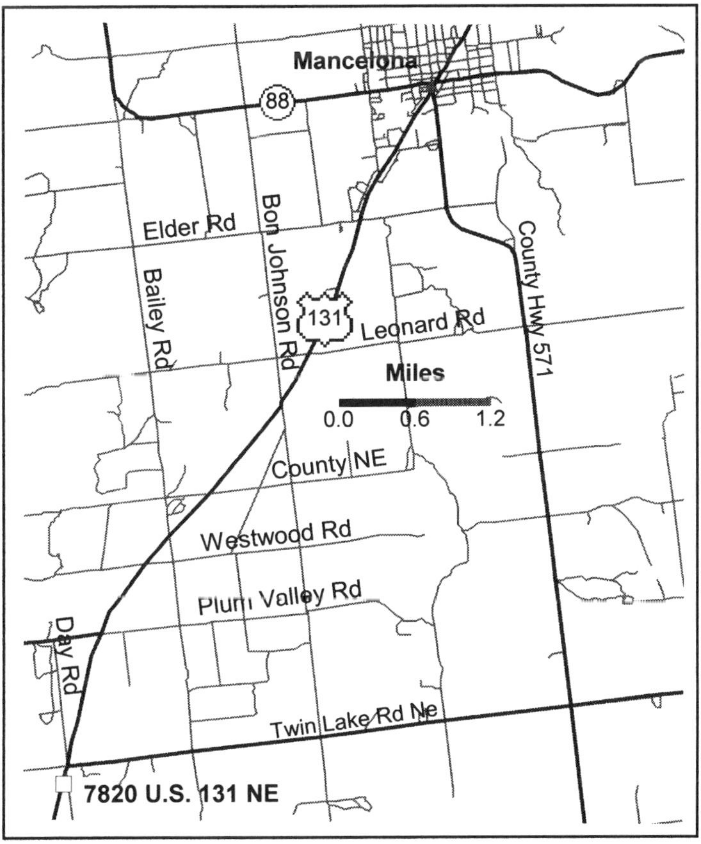

5 K.G. & Co.
7820 U.S. 131 N.E., P.O. Box 616, Mancelona MI 49659
231-258-1100; Fax: 231-258-6729
kgco@gtii.com www.kg-co.com
Oct. to May: Thurs. to Sun. 10 to 5:30, or by chance or appointment;
June to Oct.: Open 6 days 10 to 5 (Thurs. to Tues.), closed Wed. "Watch for the Flags."
Midway between Mancelona and Kalkaska, just south of Twin Lake Road.
Antiques, collectibles, gift items, plus quality furniture refinishing products & repairs.

9.5 Crawford County

(Map in previous section.)

GRAYLING

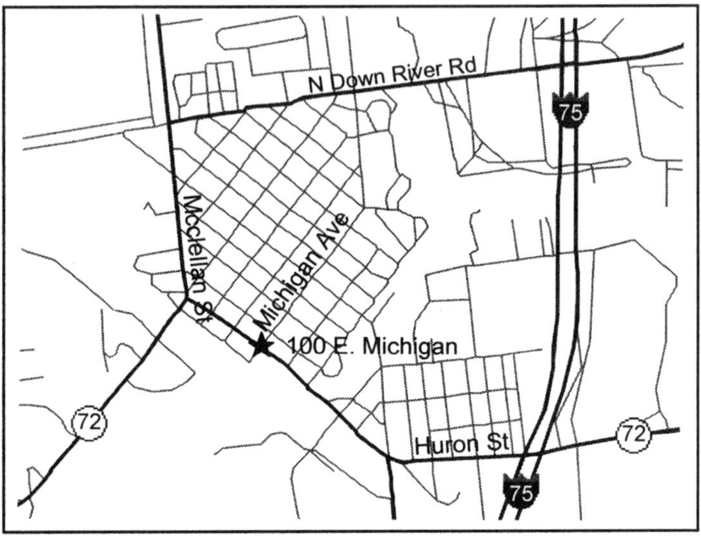

1 Au Sable Antiques & Dulcimer Co.
235 M-72 West, Grayling MI 49738
517-348-5972

2 Annendale Antiques
576 Wesman Drive, Grayling MI 49738
517-348-2130

3 Potbelly Antiques
4729 North Down River Road, Grayling MI 49738
517-348-8578

4 South Branch Antiques
7901 East M-72 , Grayling MI 49738
517-348-2514

5 Heirloom Antique Mall
100 East Michigan Avenue, Grayling MI 49738
517-348-2482
May. to Oct.: Daily 110 to 5, Sun. by chance;
Nov. to April: Tues. to Sat. 10 to 5
Downtown

9.6 Oscoda County

Oscoda & Alcona Counties:

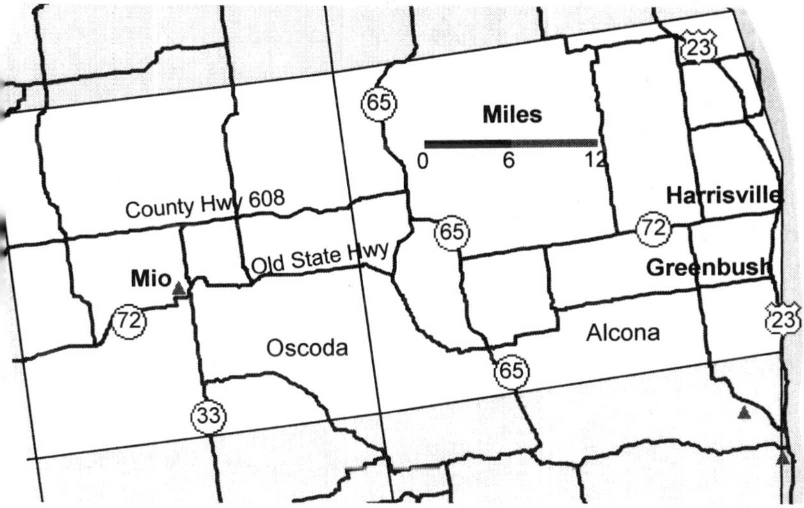

MIO

1 Granny's Antiques
109 East 8th Street, Box 636, Mio MI 48647
517-826-5674

2 The Stables
1665 West Kittle Road, Mio MI 48647
517-826-5454

9.7 Alcoma County

(Map in preceding section.)

GREENBUSH

1 The Cedar Closet
4034 U.S. 23 South, Greenbush MI 48738
517-739-2632 (home phone)
jcrichtontaylor@juno.com
Generally open: Apr. to Nov.: Mon. to Sat. 10 to 4; Dec. and Mar. by appointment.
Little house and large pole barn on the west side of the road, 3.5 miles south of Greenbush.

HARRISVILLE

2 Lake Street Daisy's
115 Lake Street, P.O. Box 607, Harrisville MI 48740
517-724-6229

3 Kenneth Roy Antiques
312 South U.S. 23, Harrisville MI 48742
517-724-5600

4 Ed's Antiques & Collectibles
5414 M-72, Harrisville MI 48742
517-724-5072

Antrim County:

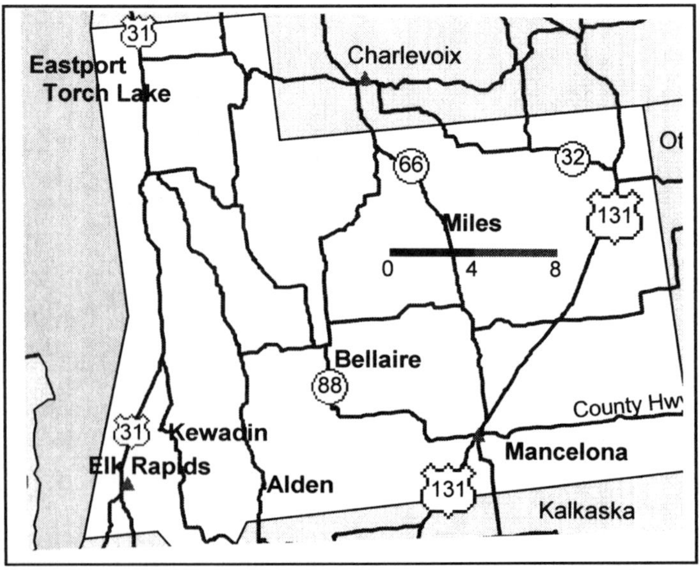

TIER 10: THE M-32 ROUTE

10.1 Antrim County

(Map on preceding page.)

KEWADIN

1 Sentimental Journey Antiques
7224 Cherry Avenue, Kewadin MI 49648
231-264-6955

ALDEN

2 Cottage Antiques
10366 E. Torch Lake Road, Alden MI 49615
231-331-6066

BELLAIRE

3 Poor Mary's Cottage Antiques
408 North Bridge Street, P.O. Box 694, Bellaire MI 49615
231-533-5530
By chance July 4 to Labor Day.

TORCH LAKE VILLAGE

4 School House Antiques
2592 U.S. 31 North, Torch Lake Village MI 49627
231-599-2056
Mid-June to Sept.

ELK RAPIDS

(Map on following page.)

5 A Summer Place Ltd.
125 River Street, Elk Rapids MI 49629
231-264-6556; (off season: 517 631-0509)

·6 Harbor Antiques
151 River Street, P.O. Box 969, Elk Rapids MI 49629
231-264-6850 www.HarborAntiques.com
Mon. to Sat. 10 to 6, Sun. 10 to 4
Downtown
Quality furniture, glassware, pottery, etc.

Antique Mall

ELK RAPIDS, MICHIGAN

151 River Street, Historic Downtown
Elk Rapids, Michigan ~ ~ ~ 616-264-6850

www.HarborAntiques.com
Featuring Garden Courtyard and Gift Shop

Open 7 Days
Street Festival Every Summer Wednesday
Walk to shops, restaurants, & waterfront

50 Plus Dealer Capacity ~ Inquires Welcome

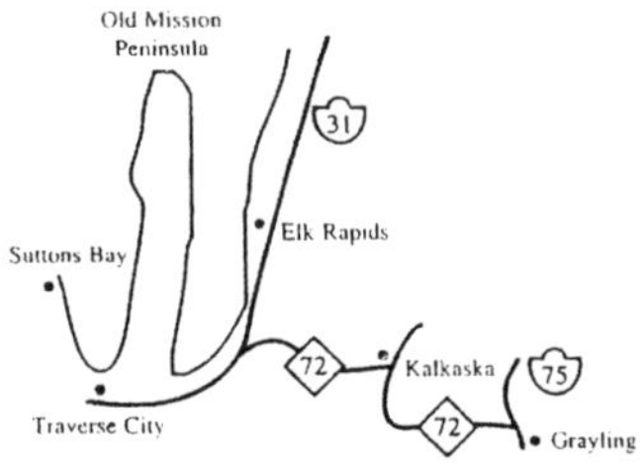

- 15 Minutes North of Traverse City
- 5 Minutes North of Grand Traverse Resort
- 25 Miles South of Charlevoix

Elk Rapids:

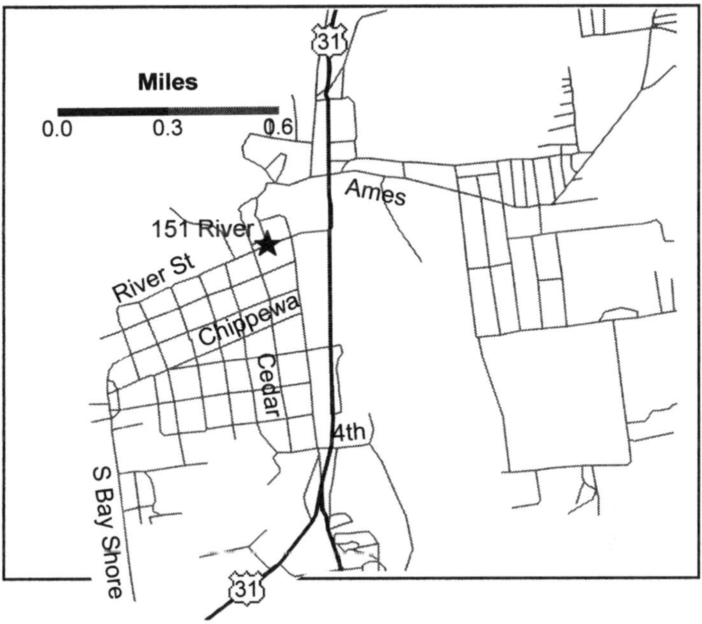

EASTPORT

7 D & J Antiques
6067 North M-88 (U.S. 31 & M-88), Eastport MI 49627
231-599-2710
Seasonal

MANCELONA

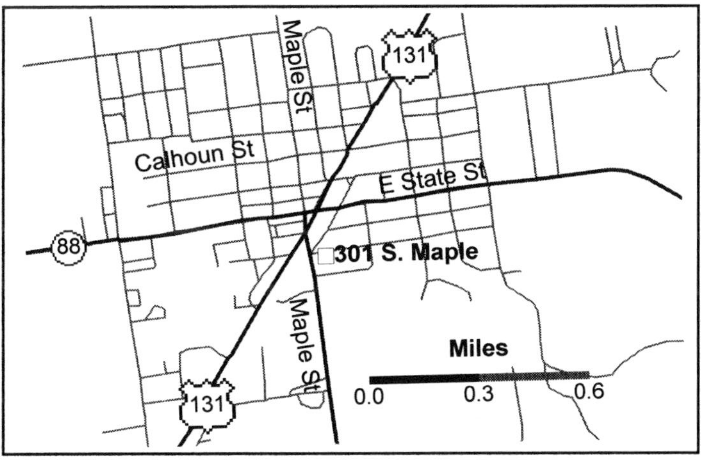

8 Dee's Antiques
301 South Maple, Mancelona MI 49659
231-587-8121
Mon. to Sat.: 11 to 4, Sun. by chance or appointment, closed Tues. Best to call first in winter.
1 block south of U.S. 131, east side of street.
Hand made Victorian lamp shades made by Dee.
Victorian house full of unique antiques.

9 Red Windmill Antiques
3775 Doerr Road, Mancelona MI 49659
231-587-5121
April 1 to Sept. 1 by chance.

10.2 Otsego County

Otsego & Montmorency Counties:

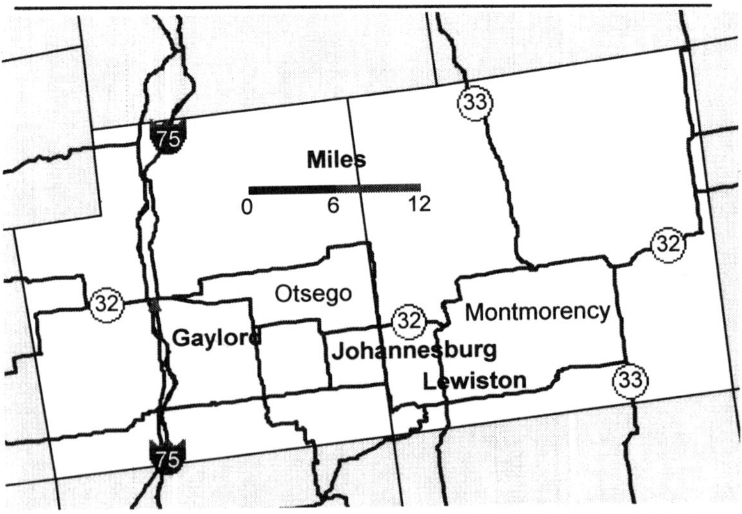

JOHANNESBURG

1 Cozy Corners Antiques
10816 M-32 East, P.O. Box 412, Johannesburg MI 49751
517 732-2225

GAYLORD

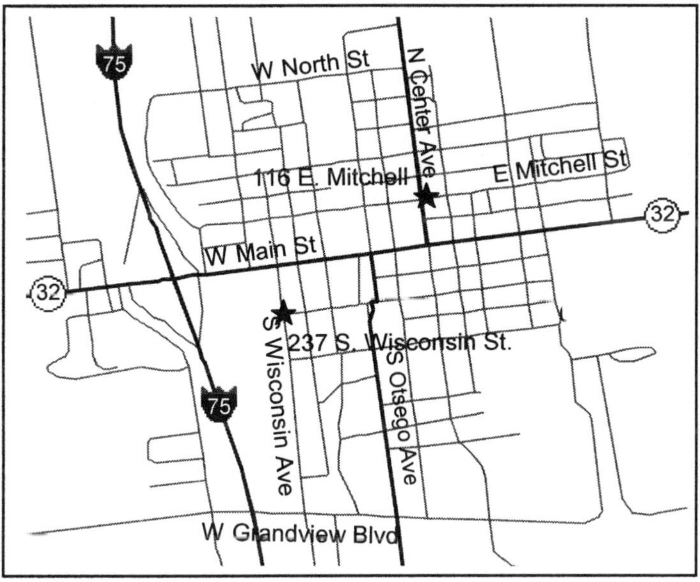

2 Antiques Out of the Blue
237 South Wisconsin Street, Gaylord MI 49735
517 731-6053
Mon. to Sat. 10:30 to 5:30, Sun. 1 to 4
West of downtown, south of Route 32 two blocks; next to Dan's TV.
Flow Blue, antique clocks, handmade baskets, & general line of antiques.

3 Antique Attack
205 North Center Avenue, Gaylord MI 49735
Scheduled to open in late 2000.

4 Architiques
116 East Mitchell Street, Gaylord MI 49735
517-731-5496
architiques@voyager.net
May thru Nov. Thurs. to Sat. 11 to 6, other times by chance or appointment.
Northeast end of downtown. East Mitchell is 2 blocks north of Main Street and one half block east of Center Street (Old 27 North). Red house kitty corner behind the 7-11 and across from the Country Attic.
Architectural accents and furniture, especially primitive, rustic and painted; Also garden and folk art.

5 Duck Creek Antiques
1273 Duck Creek Trail, Gaylord MI 49735
517 732-3972 Fax: 517-732-8932
Sat. 10 to 5, Sun. 12 to 4 most weekends; seasonal: call ahead.
From Gaylord take M-32 east to Wilkinson Road (F-44) turning left. Wilkinson Road to Marquardt Road (F-44) to Sparr Road. Turn right on Sparr Road (F-44). From Sparr Mall continue east 2.3 miles to private "Duck Creek Trail" and turn left (north) only. If the flag is out they are open. About eight miles east of Gaylord.
Country collectibles, primitives, folk art.

10.3 Montmorency County

(Map in preceding section.)

LEWISTON

1 Everlasting Treasures
5541 N. Red Oak Road, Lewiston MI 49756
517-786-7017

2 Antiques Depot Mall
5030 County Road 612, P.O. Box 874, Lewiston MI 49756
517-786-4897

Eastern Gaylord:

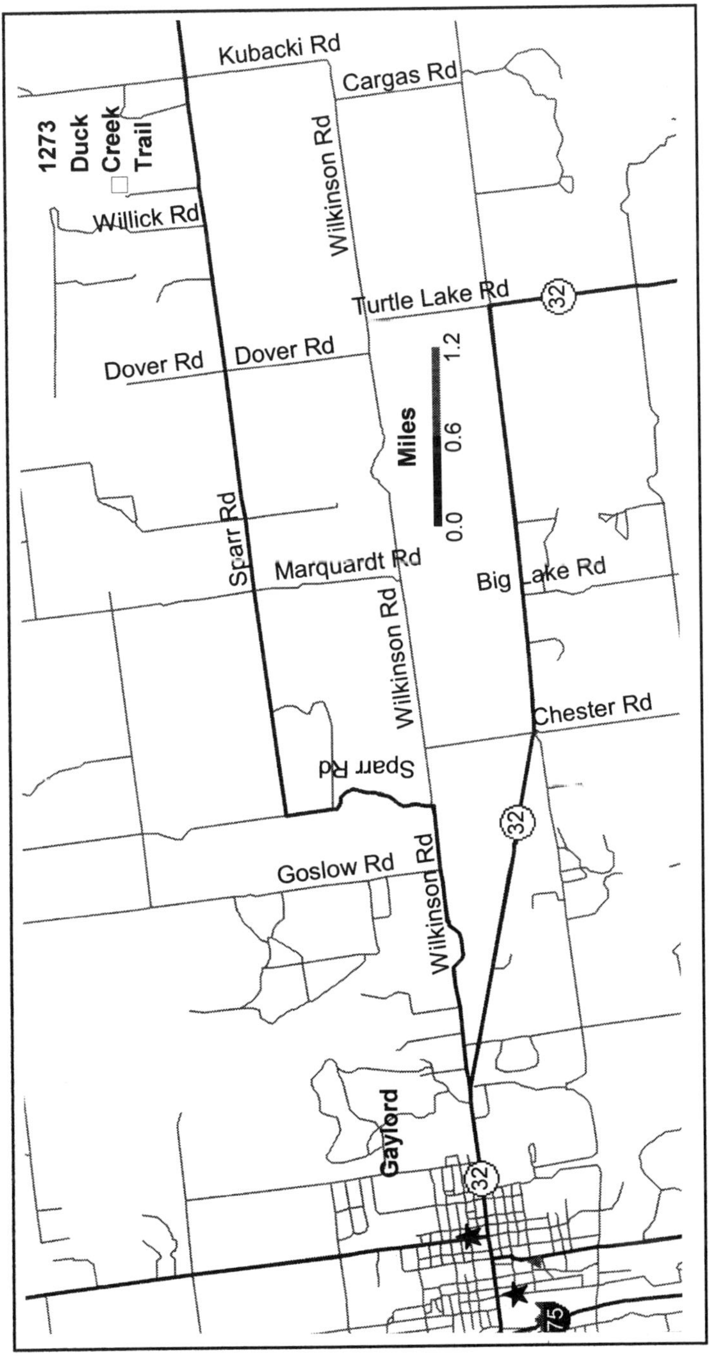

10.4 Alpena County

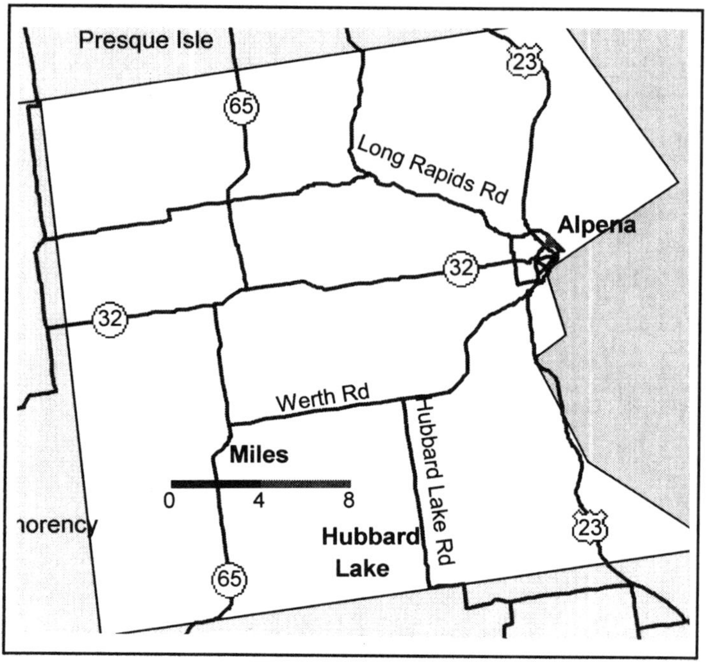

ALPENA

1 John Henrys Coins & Antiques
209 North 2nd Avenue, Alpena MI 49707
517-354-6036

2 Pass Time Antiques
300 block Chism Street, Alpena MI 49707
No telephone listed.

3 Country Cupboard
102 North Second, Alpena MI 49707
517-356-6020 countryc@freeway.net
Mon. to Fri. 10 to 5:30, Sat. 10 to 5
Downtown
Unique old drug store; antiques, collectibles, country gifts.

4 Helen's Antiques & Gifts
127 North 2nd Avenue, Alpena MI 49707
517-356-3298
Glassware, jewelry, furniture, collectibles, gifts, and Beanie Babies.

Alpena:

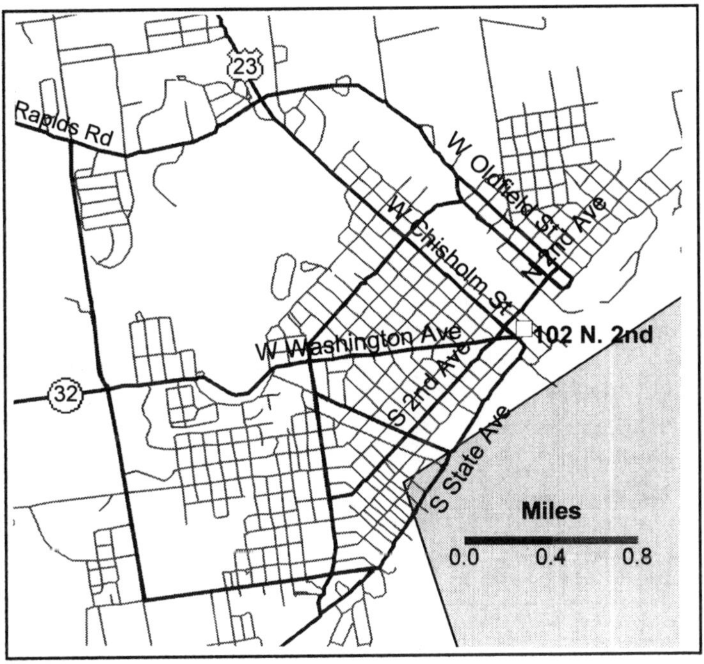

5 Artis Antique Mall
203 North Second, Alpena MI 49707
517-354-3401

6 Artis Books & Antiques
201 North Second
Links to Artis Antique Mall., Alpena MI 49707
517-354-3401

7 Kathy's Bargain Barn
6465 U.S. 23 North, Alpena MI 49707
517-354-3070
Summer only.

HUBBARD LAKE

8 C. Leigh's
13822 Hubbard Lake Road, P.O. Box 95, Hubbard Lake MI 49747
517-727-2362

TIER 11: SOUTH OF MACKINAC

11.1 Charlevoix County

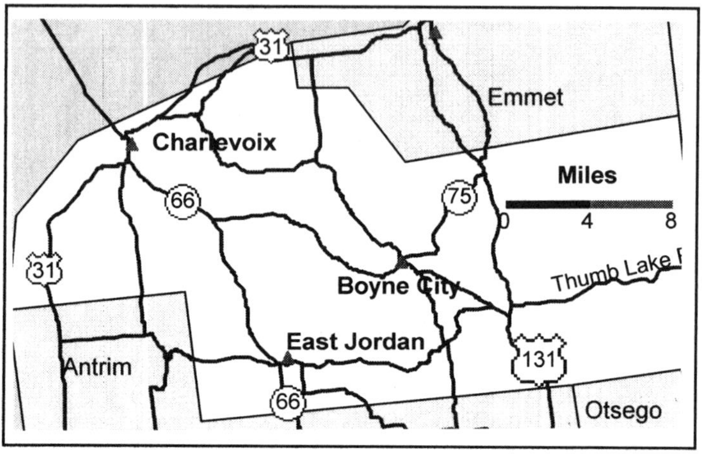

CHARLEVOIX

1 The Sisters Antiques
U.S. 31 South, Charlevoix MI 49720
231-547-6457; 231-547-6914

2 The Garage Sale
755 Petoskey Ave. (U.S. 31 North), Charlevoix MI 49720
231-547-5700

3 North Seas Gallery
330 Bridge Street, Charlevoix MI 49720
231-547-0422; 231-547-2959 Closed Jan. to April.

4 Rose Cottage Antiques
107 Mason Street, Charlevoix MI 49720
231-547-0636, or 231-547-5842

5 Antiques
1209 Bridge Street, Charlevoix MI 49720
(231) 547-3135

6 A Place of Interest Artisans and Antiques
805 Bridge Street, Charlevoix MI 49720
231-547-4501

Charlevoix:

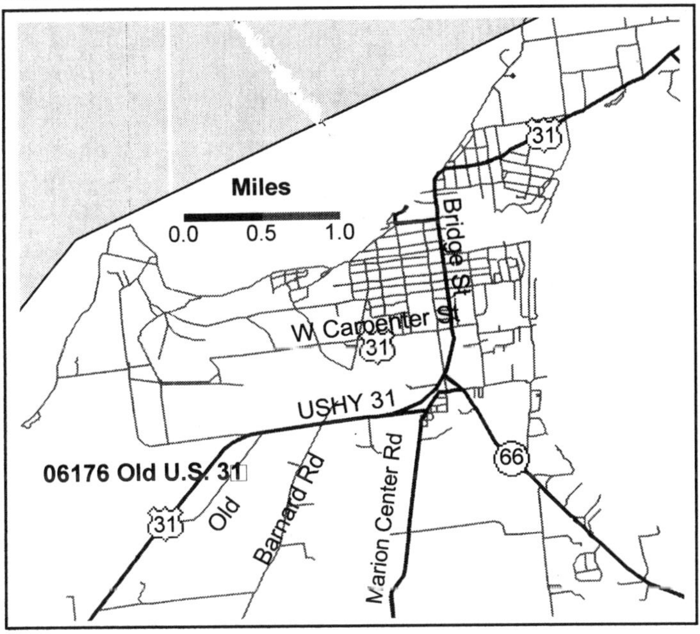

7 Kelly's Antiques
06176 Old U.S. 31 South, Charlevoix MI 49720
231-547-0133
Open most days 8 to 5, Sundays by appointment.
One and a half miles south of Charlevoix, turn onto Old U.S. 31South (from U.S. 31), near Brumm's Studio Showroom or Sister's Antiques.
Specializing in golden oak, European pine, and vintage wicker furniture. Sold "as found" or completely restored to customer specifications. Other services: wicker restoration and spray-painted finishes.

8 Shop of All Crafters
704 Bridge Street, Charlevoix MI 49720
231-547-0257 Mission oak.

EAST JORDAN

9 Busy Bridge Antiques & Gifts
207 Main Street, East Jordan MI 49727
231-536-3511

10 Stonehedge Antiques
02195 M-66 North, East Jordan MI 49720
231-547-5527

11.2 Emmet County

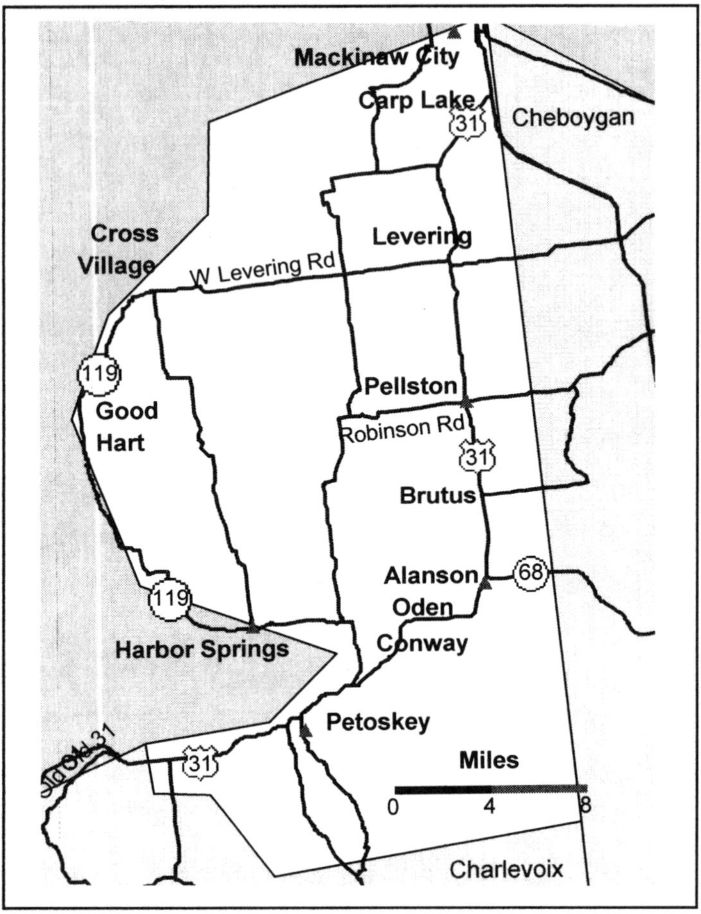

PETOSKEY

1 Amish Way Antiques
08600 Camp Daggett Road, Petoskey MI 49770
231-347-3898

2 Joseph's World Classic Antiques
2680 Charlevoix Avenue (U.S. 31 South), Petoskey MI 49770
231-347-0121
19th & 20th Century decorative arts; a few antiques.

3 Marietta Antique Shop
106 East Mitchell Street (U.S. 31), Petoskey MI 49770
231-347-8369

Petoskey:

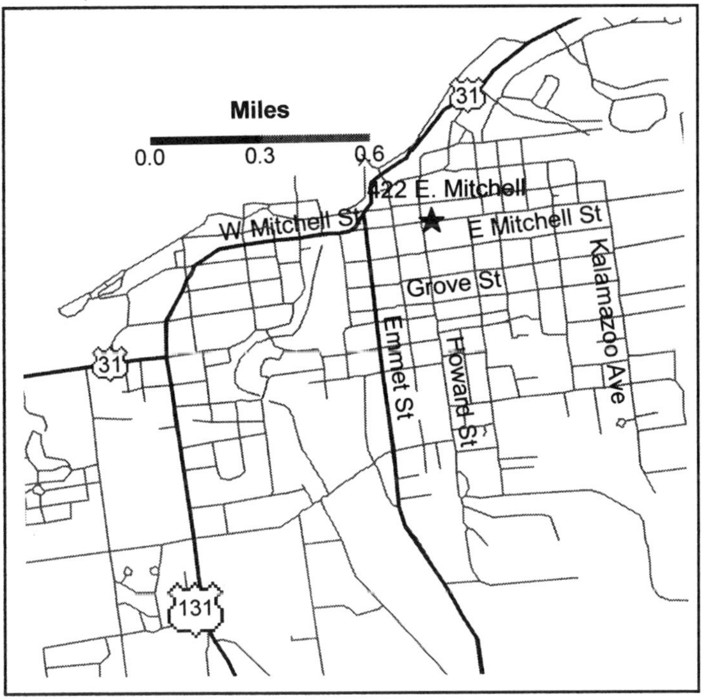

4 J C's Antiques
203-A Howard Street, Petoskey MI 49770
231-348-0840

5 Longton Hall Antiques
410 Rose Street, Petoskey MI 49770
231-347-9672

6 Jedediahs Antiques
422 E. Mitchell Street, Petoskey MI 49770
231-347-1919 jeds@freeway.net
Mon. to Sat. 10 to 5
Downtown, across from Pennsylvania Park.
Featuring dealers from Canada to California carrying a multitude of regional pieces.

7 Joie De Vie Antiques
1901 M-119 (Harbor-Petoskey Road), Petoskey MI 49770
231-347-1400; FAX: 231-347-9029

8 Porters
1844 M-119 (Harbor Petoskey Road), Petoskey MI 49770
231-487-0706 Ralph Loren store with a few antiques.

HARBOR SPRINGS

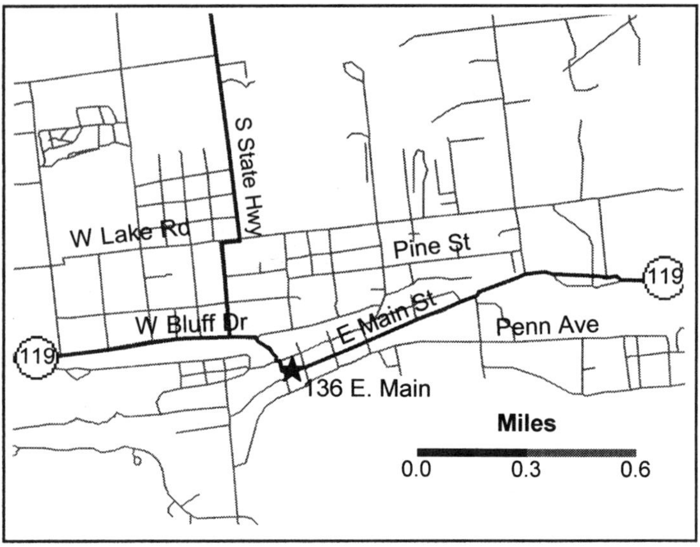

9 Huzza
136 Main Street East, Harbor Springs MI 49740
231-526-2128 huzza@voyager.net
Summer (May - Oct.): Mon. to Sat. 9:30 to 6
Call for winter hours.
Downtown, south side of street.
Antiques, interior design, home accessories, tableware.
Fine apparel & jewelry.

10 Patricia Woods Antiques
120 East Main, Harbor Springs MI 49740
231-526-9691; Fax: 231-526-9692

11 L'Esprit
195 West Main & 220 State Street, Harbor Springs MI 49740
231-526-9888; E-mail: lesprit@lesprit.com
www.lesprit.com;

12 Elliott & Elliott
292 East Third Street, Harbor Springs MI 49740
231-526-2040 Seasonal

13 Bishop's Antiques & Fine Arts Gallery
378 Third Street, Harbor Springs MI 49740
231-526-8075

14 Pooter Olooms
39 State Street,P.O. Box 304, Harbor Springs MI 49740
231-526-6101
Scandinavian country pine, quilts, folk art.

GOOD HART

15 TLC Summer Place
811 North Lakeshore (M-119), P.O. Box 139, Good Hart MI 49723
231-526-7538

16 Good Hart Antiques
M-119, P.O. Box 912, Good Hart MI 49737
231-526-9533 Only open a few months a year.

CROSS VILLAGE

17 The Red House at Cross Village
M-119 & State Road, Cross Village MI 49723
231-526-2343 June 15 to Oct. 15

18 Rose's Antiques & Collectibles
5550 North Lakeshore (M-119), Cross Village MI 49740
231-526-5934
April to Dec.: Usually every day 10 to 5:30.
1.5 miles south of Cross Village.
General line of antiques and collectibles.

CONWAY

19 Desiree's Country Nostalgia
2343 Cook Avenue (West Conway Road), P.O. Box 360 , Conway MI 49722 231-347-8661

ODEN

20 Oden Antiques
Highway 31, Oden MI 49764
231-439-0935

ALANSON

21 Second Hand Man & Crooked River Rustic
7493 U.S. 31, P.O. Box 53, Alanson MI 49706
231-548-5173

22 Hazel's Antiques & Gifts
U.S. 31, Alanson MI 49706

23 Regina's Lakeview Antiques
M-68 West, Alanson MI 49706
231-548-5398

BRUTUS

24 Adams Antiques
3771 U.S. 31, Brutus MI 49716
231-529-6596

25 Graham's Antiques
1812 Gregory Road, Brutus MI 49716
231-539-8275 Mid-May to Mid-Oct.

PELLSTON

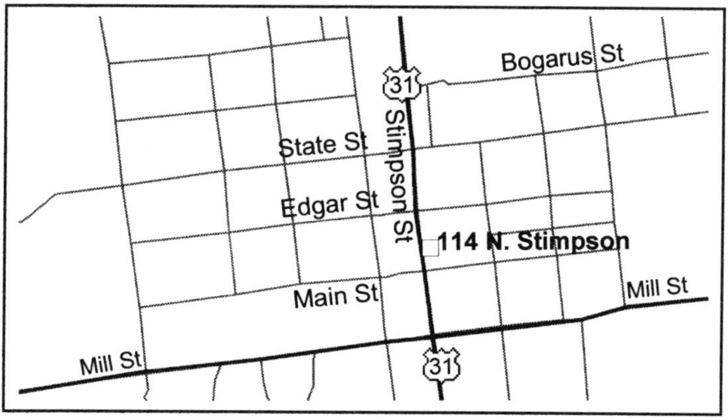

26 Town & Country Antiques
128 Stenson (U.S. 31), Pellston MI 49769
231-539-8340 Used items & some antiques.

27 Antiques, Art & Collectibles
114 North Stimpson (U.S. 31), Pellston MI 49769
231-539-8030
Summer: Daily 10 to 5
Downtown, east side of the highway.

28 Blue Barn Antiques & Collectibles
123 Stimpson (U.S. 31), Pellston MI 49769
231-539-8550; 231-439-0940

LEVERING

29 Levering Antiques & Rustic Furniture
1 Robinson Street, Levering MI 49755
231-537-4972 Old and new rustic furniture.

30 Gaslight Antiques & Collectibles
7116 N. U.S. 31, Levering MI 49755
231-537-2089
June thru August: Mon. to Sat. 11 to 5:30, closed Thurs., Sun. by chance. Closed July 4 weekend for Petoskey Antique Show.
2 miles north of Levering blinker light, east side of road. General line of antiques and collectibles; wicker, lamps, pottery, primitives, 50.s, etc.

CARP LAKE

31 The Maples Resort & Antiques
8982 Paradise Trail (Old U.S. 31), Carp Lake MI 49718
231-537-4814 April to Nov.

11.3 Cheboygan County

(Map in following section.)

INDIAN RIVER

1 Bearly Used Antiques & Treasures
6033 East M-68, Indian River MI 49749
Residence: 231-238-9772 May 15 thru October 15

2 Of Cabbages & Kings Gift Shop
Indian River, P.O. Box 700, MI 49749 M-27 Downtown
231-238-7700

CHEBOYGAN

3 Treasure Hunt Flea Market & Antiques
405 Duncan Avenue, Cheboygan MI 49721
231-627-6080

4 Talk of the Town
329 North Main Street, Cheboygan MI 49721
231-627-9883 Art & antiques.

11.4 Presque Isle County

Chebyogan & Presque Isle Counties:

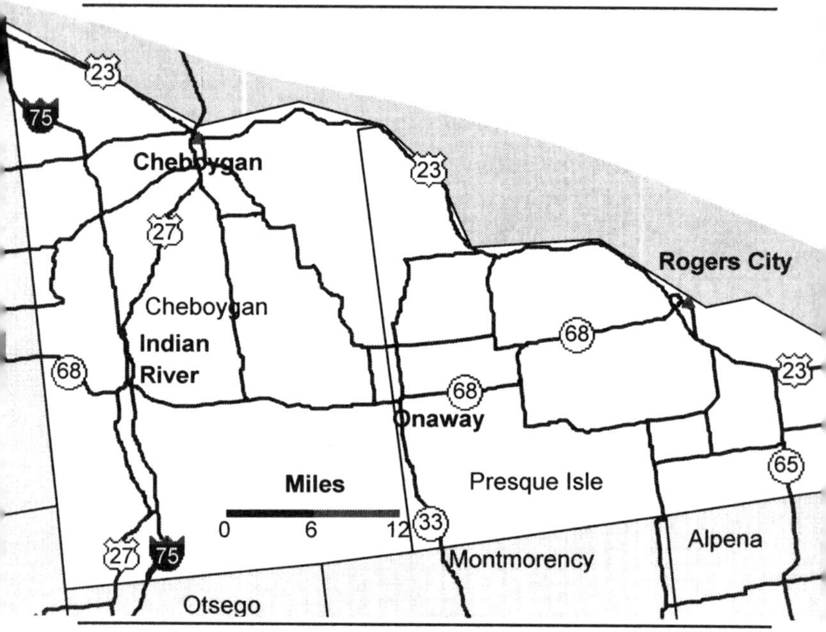

ONAWAY

1 And Yesterday's Trash
Highway M-33, Route 2 Box 80, Hackett Lake Highway, Onaway MI 49765
517-733-6434 Primitives, old logging tools, etc.

2 Antiques & More
20451 State Street, P.O. Box 146, Onaway MI 49765
517-733-4449

ROGERS CITY

3 Big North Antiques
208 East Michigan Avenue, Rogers City MI 49779
517-734-3319

TIER 12: THE UPPER PENINSULA

12.01 Mackinac County

Mackinac, Chippewa & Luce Counties:

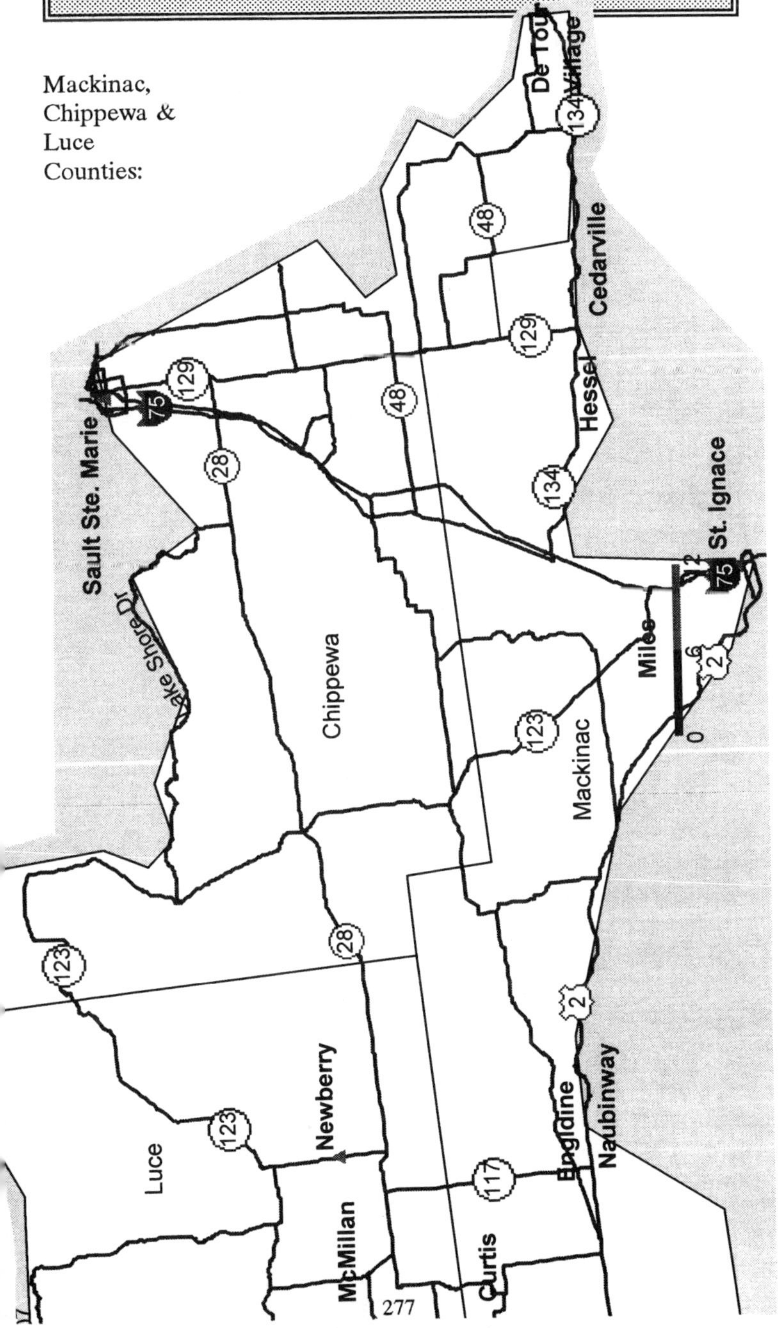

HESSEL

1 Hessel Marketplace
Highway M-134, P.O. Box 160 , Hessel MI 49745
906-484-3002

ST. IGNACE

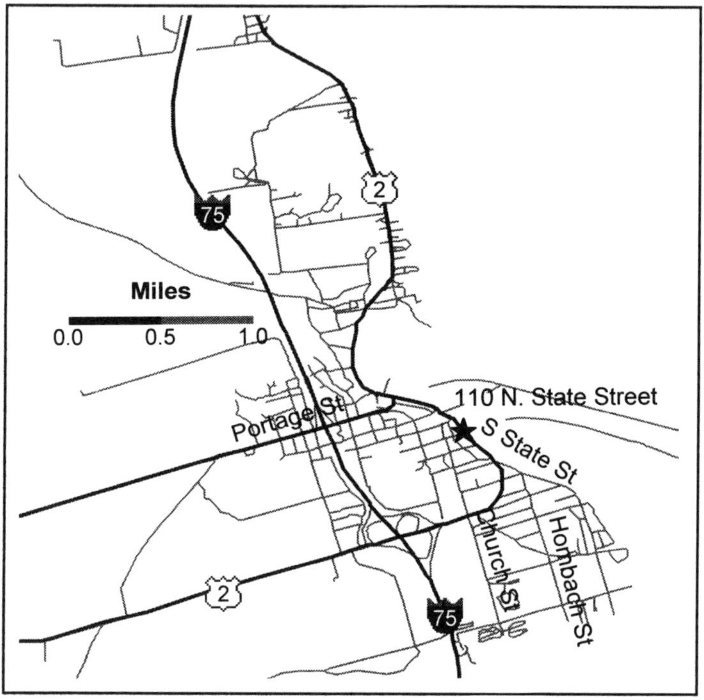

2 The Emporium
110 North State Street, St. Ignace MI 49781
906-643-6565; fax: 906-643-0113
E-mail: KPbrady@up.net; Web page: www.ignace.com
Open year round, Mon. to Sat. 9 to 5. Open Sun. by appointment.
Downtown across from Arnold Ferry.
Specializing in Antique lighting and furniture.

3 Treasures & Trinkets (& The Unique Shop)
334 North State Street, St. Ignace MI 49781
906-643-6622
Gifts, Indian Jewelry, figurines, pewter, glassware.

4 Anchor In Antiques
2122 West U.S. Highway 2, St. Ignace MI 49781
906-643-8112; Res.: 906-643-9917
Emphasis on Great Lakes Nautical Items.

NAUBINWAY

5 Uncle Tom's Antiques
Blake & Main Streets, Naubinway MI 49762
906-477-6259
June, July, Aug. 10 to 5
From U.S. Highway 2: south at the blinker light one block, then east two blocks. Follow the signs.
General line, plus fishing & hunting and rustic & primitive collectibles.

CURTIS

6 Antiques at the Old Boat House
Main St. at the bridge. P.O. Box 218, Curtis MI 49820
906-586-6033
jtgor@portup.com www.exploringthenorth.com
May thru Sept: Daily 10 to 5; winters by appointment.
Eight miles off U.S. 2 on Highway 33.
Antiques and artifacts from around the world. General line of furniture for the home or cottage. Textiles, silver, cast iron, pottery, paintings, and prints. Oriental rugs a specialty.

ENGADINE

7 Da Antique Network
Junction of U.S. 2 & M-117, Engadine MI 49762
906-477-6038
10 to 5 most days.
Dishes, and a general line of antiques.

12.02 Chippewa County

(Map in preceding section.)

DE TOUR VILLAGE

1 Log Cabin Antiques & Collectibles
637 Ontario Street, P.O. Box 503, De Tour Village MI 49725
906-297-2502

2 Red Oaks Antiques and Collectibles
16185 East M-134 #68B , De Tour Village MI 49725
906-297-2404
7 miles west of town.

KINCHELOE

3 Our Town Antiques
5189 West M-80 Suite G, P.O. Box 5170, Kincheloe MI 49788
906-495-3114

PARADISE

4 Wild Works Antiques & Gifts
8239 North M 123, Paradise MI 49768
906-492-3308

SAULT STE. MARIE

(Map on the following page.)

5 La Galerie Gifts
1420 Ashmun Street, Sault Ste. Marie MI 49783
906-635-1044
Closed Jan. Feb. & March.

6 Silver Lining Antiques & Appraisal Service
530 Ashmun Street, Sault Ste. Marie MI 49783
906-632-4929 silverlining@30below.com
Mon. to Sat. 10 to 6, or by appointment.
Heart of downtown, 3 doors down from the Soo Theater. Antique furniture, jewelry, pottery, linens, china, silver, crystal. Household & personal property appraisal specialist, accredited with I.S.A.

Sault Ste. Marie:

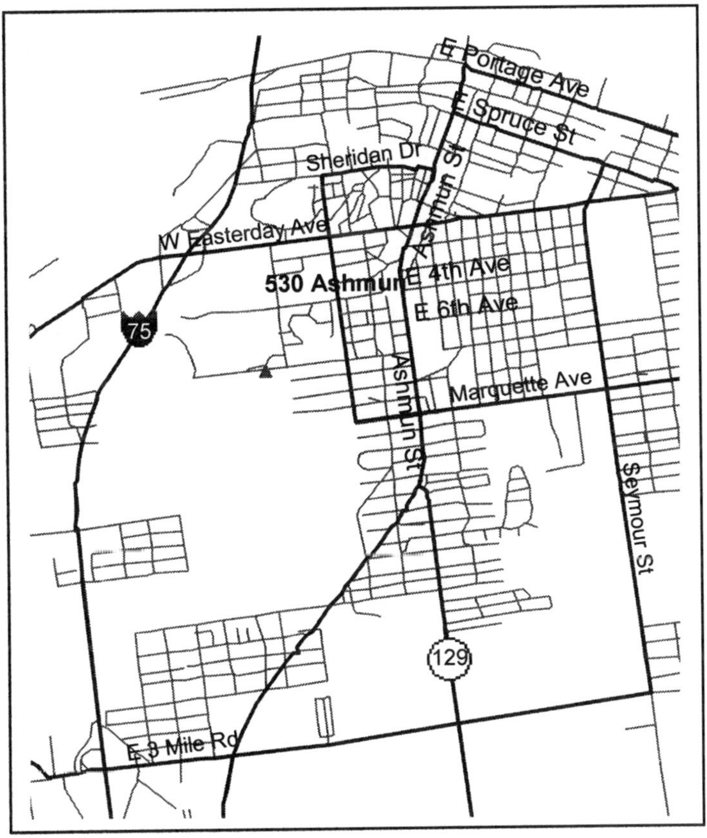

7 Austin Oak & Tobacco Shop
539 Ashmun Street, Sault Ste. Marie MI 49783
906-635-1242

12.03 Luce County

(Map in previous section.)

NEWBERRY

1 Antiques By Donelle
101 East John Street, Newberry MI 49868
906-293-8044; res.: 906-586-9544

2 Falls Hotel Antiques
301 Newberry Ave. (MI Highway 123), Newberry MI 49868

3 Country Gallery
607 Newberry Avenue (MI Route 123), Newberry MI 49868
906-293-8262
Mostly gifts, some antiques. Antique 1940's soda fountain.

4 Doc's Coffee Shop & Antiques
224 Newberry Avenue, Newberry MI 49868
906-293-3254

5 The Cat's Meow
204 Newberry Avenue, Newberry MI 49868
906-293-6369

6 Katie's Antiques
Route 4 Box 1095, Newberry MI 49868
906-293-5766
May 1 to Oct. 31: Open every day 10 to 6; winters by chance or appointment.
From U.S. 2 go north on M-117 13 miles to Red Camp Road, then east (right) to first house on left. Follow the signs.
Gas station collectibles, hunting & fishing, glassware, furniture, crafts.

McMILLAN

7 Farmhouse Antiques
County Road 438, Rte. 3 Box 2279, McMillan MI 49853
906-293-8792

12.04 Schoolcraft County

Schoolcraft, Alger & Delta Counties:

GERMFASK

1 Suzantiques
Highway 77 - Blaney Park, Route 1 Box 59-A, Germfask MI 49836
906-586-3135 suzantiques@portup.com
Year round, random hours.
Two miles north of Highway 2, seven miles south of Germfask, east side of highway.
General line of antiques; buttons, postcards and other paper ephemera.

GULLIVER

2 Best Northern Whats It Shop
US 2, Gulliver MI 49840
906-283-3876

MANISTIQUE

(Map on following page.)

3 Christopher's
211 Oak Street, Manistique MI 49854
906-341-2570
Downtown, just east of the post office.

4 Maple Cottage
227 Maple St., Manistique MI 49854
No telephone.

5 Marble Head Antiques
U.S. 2 East, Route 1 Box 1585, Manistique MI 49854
906-341-8114
Summer only.

6 Hampton's Antiques
1152 West Lakeshore Dr., Manistique MI 49854
906-341-5350
June to Oct.

7 Traders' Point Antique Mall
375 Traders' Point Drive, P.O. Box 491, Manistique MI 49854
906-341-7500 jstark@up.net
906thedock.com
Winter: Tues. to Sat. 11 to 5
Summer: Daily 10 to 5
Just off U.S. 2 west of the Manistique River bridge.
Fishing & hunting items, glassware, pottery, etc.

12.05 Alger County

(Map in previous section.)

AUTRAIN

1 Red Barn Antiques at LaValley's Resort
N-7017 AuTrain-Lake Road Highway 3, P.O. Box 99, Au Train MI 49806
906-892-8455 LaValleys@mail.tds.net
www.exploringthenorth.com/redbarn/antiques
Mon. to Sat. 10 to 6, or by appointment.
Usually open Sat. in July & Aug.
Two miles south of M-28.
General line, specializing in 1940's to 1960's furniture & decorative objects, and Pyrex Fire King, Frankoma, and Munising woodenware.

Manistique:

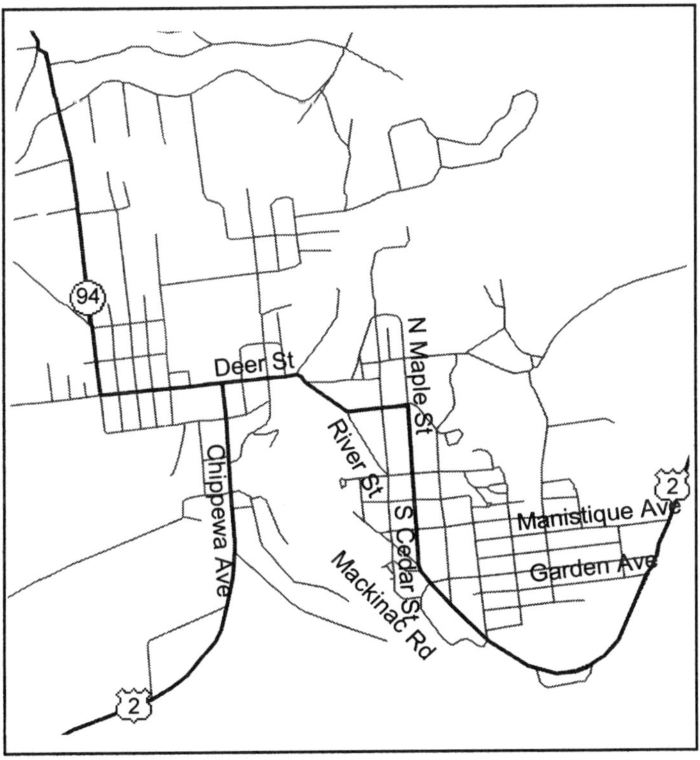

12.06 Delta County

(Map in previous section.)

FAYETTE

1 Fayette Antiques
2251 II Road (County Road 183), Fayette MI 49835
906-644-2620; 906-644-2401
janal@up.net or fayantiq@up.net
June 1 to Oct. 15: Tues. to Sun. 10 to 6
Seven miles south of Fayette State Park.
Antiques & unique things; garden items, primitives, fine dishes, nautical, fishing equipment.

PERKINS

2 Backstage Antiques
5183 East 31st Lane, P.O. Box 115, Perkins MI 49872-0115
906-359-4123
Mon. to Sat. 10 to 4:30
One mile north of Perkins on Highway 35; at the Midtown School go right on 31st Lane.
Buy, sell, trade general line of antiques. Also antique and collectible flags.

GLADSTONE

3 Chicken Coop Antiques
7051 P Road, Gladstone MI 49837
906-786-1150

4 Foxx Den Antiques
7509 U.S. 2 & 41 & M-35, Gladstone MI 49837
906-786-9014

5 Timeless Treasures Past & Present
1017 Delta Avenue, Gladstone MI 49837
906-428-3125
Mon. to Fri. 10 to 6, Sat. 10 to 5
East about six blocks from U.S. 2 on Delta, the main street.
Antiques, collectibles, fork art, crafts, gifts.

KIPLING

6 Keepsake Workshop & Antiques
8905 23.15 Street, Kipling MI 49837
906-428-4275
Open every day by chance or appointment.
Old Highway 2 between Gladstone & Rapid River. Watch for signs.
Quilts, pottery, twig furniture.

ESCANABA

7 The Market Place
500 Ludington Street, Escanaba MI 49829
906-789-1326

8 The Belle Pearl
121 S. 11th Street, P.O. Box 642, Escanaba MI 49829
906-789-0041; 906-786-4919

9 Reminisce Antique Mall
1215 Ludington Street, Escanaba MI 49829
906-786-0772

RAPID RIVER

10 The Oldest Antiques on Earth
(U.P. Treasure Hunters Antique Mall)
7946 U.S. Route 2, P.O. Box 364, Rapid River MI 49878
906-474-5049
E-mail: kencharlebois@uplogon.com
Web page: www.class.idsite.com
Ebay Auction Code Name: YOOPER

11 Country & Company
200 Main Street, P.O. Box 97, Rapid River MI 49878
906-474-6323 Antiques, handcrafted gifts, collectibles.

12 Little Bit of Everything
7885 U.S. Highway 2, P.O. Box 182, Rapid River MI 49878
906-474-6774 Summer only.

13 Northern Exposure Flea Market
Highway 2 East, P.O. Box 424, Rapid River MI 49878
906-474-9998

12.07 Menominee County

Menominee & Dickinson Counties:

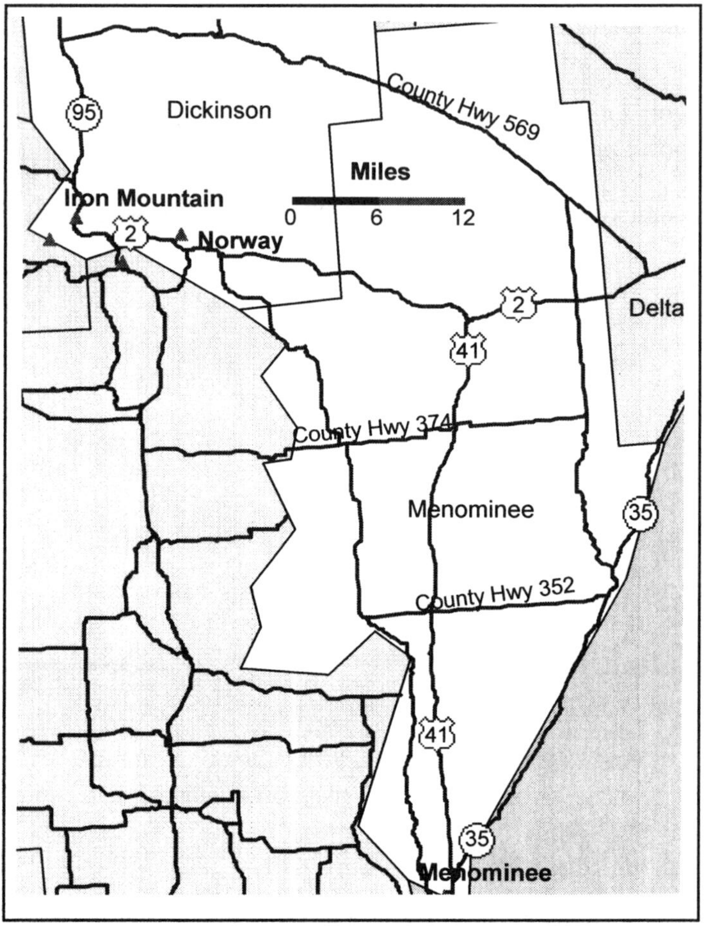

MENOMINEE

1 Timeless Treasures
902 2nd Street, Menominee MI 49858
(906) 864-2412

2 Dusty Attic Antiques
2433 13th Street, Menominee MI 49858
906-863-3183

12.08 Dickinson County

(Map in preceding section.)

IRON MOUNTAIN

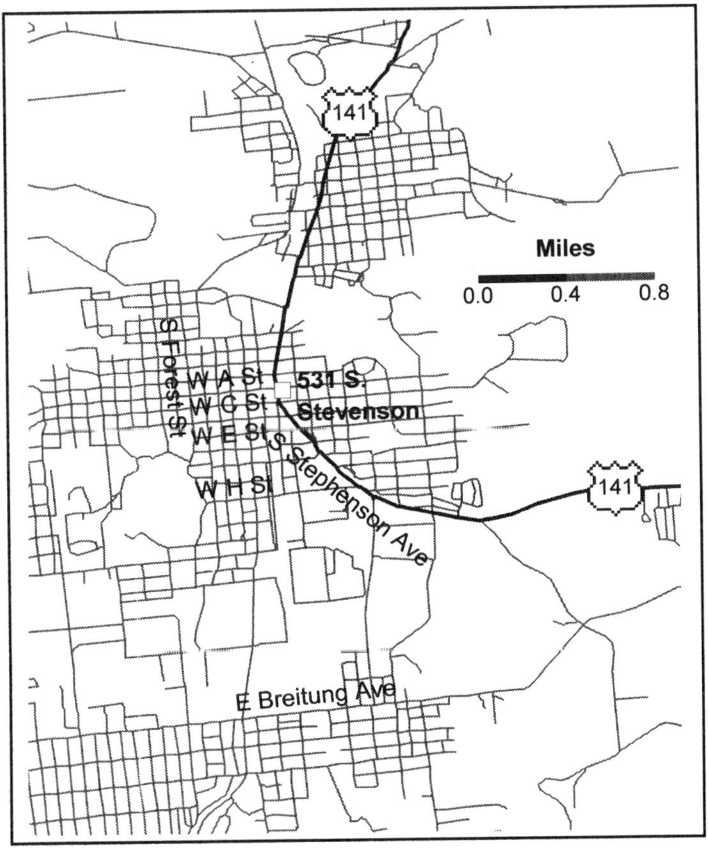

1 Cobweb Antiques
N-3956 North U.S. Highway 2, Iron Mountain MI 49801
906-774-6560

2 Edie's Interiors & Antique Mall
531 South Stephenson (U.S. 2), P.O. Box 745, Iron Mountain MI 49801
906-774-1851
Mon. to Sat. 9 to 5;
Thanksgiving to Christmas also open Sun. 12 to 4
Downtown, at B Street.
General line of antiques. All major credit cards accepted. Parking in the rear.

NORWAY

3 Norway Antique Mall
729 Main Street, Norway MI 49870
906-563-8246
One Block north of U.S. Highway 2; turn at the light.

12.09 Marquette County

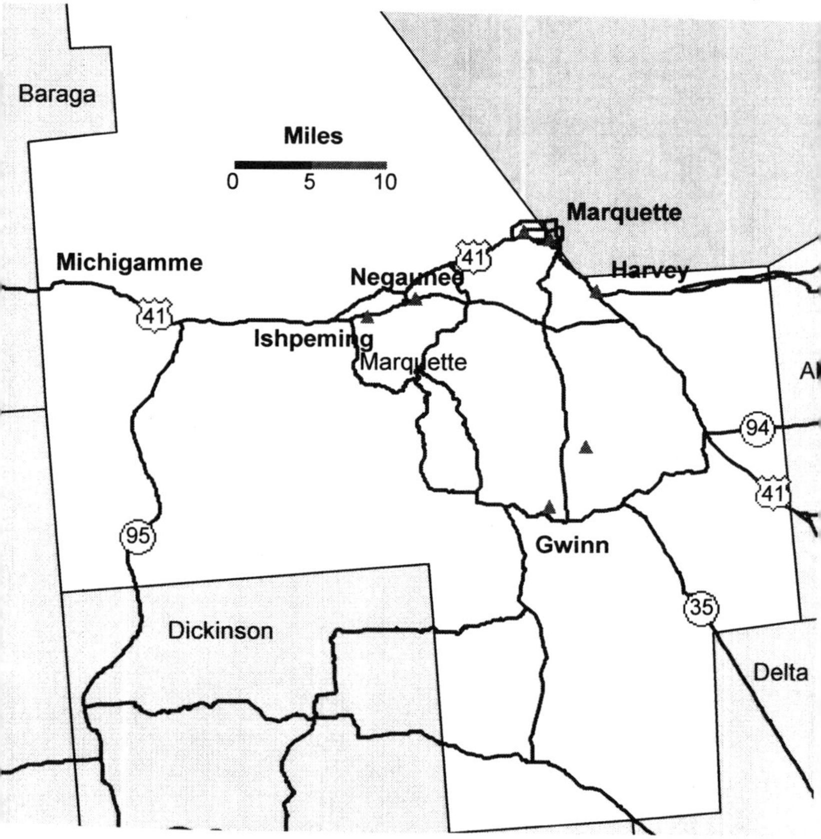

HARVEY

1 Antique Village
2296 U.S. 41 South, Harvey MI 49855
906-249-3040

MARQUETTE

2 The Collector Antiques
214 South Front, Marquette MI 49855
906-228-4134

3 Past and Presents
116 West Spring Street, Marquette MI 49885
906-226-8533

4 Summer Cottage and Recycled Arts
110 West Washington, Marquette MI 49855
906-226-7775
Architectural arts & goods crafted from antiques.

5 Fagan's Antiques
333 West Washington, Marquette MI 49855
906-228-4311

6 Peddler's Hill
325 Erickson Avenue, Marquette MI 49855
906-225-0155

NEGAUNEE

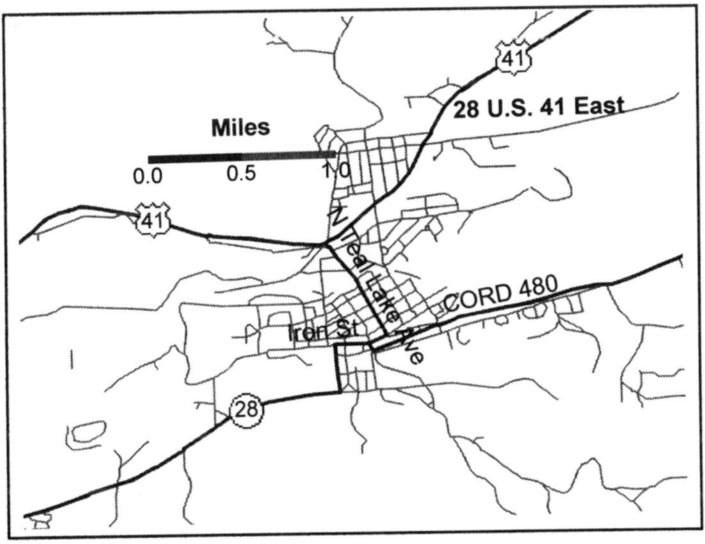

8 Old Bank Building Antiques
331 Iron Street, Negaunee MI 49866
906-475-4777

7 Kate's Collectibles
28 U.S. 41 East, Negaunee MI 49866
906-475-4443 finnaho@aol.com
Mon. to Sat. 10 to 5, Sun. 12 to 5
South side of highway, one mile east of town.
Fine general line of antiques.

9 Midtown Bake Shoppe & Antiques
317 Iron Street, Negaunee MI 49866
906-475-0064 or 906-475-5664 after hours
www.midtown00@bresnanlink.net
Open year-round: Mon. to Fri. 8:30 to 6, Sat. 10 to 5; plus most Sundays.
Downtown Negaunee.
Architectural items, folk art, pottery, primitives, rustic items, art deco, and gourmet cheesecakes and desserts.

10 Upper Level Design & Antiquities
415 Iron Street, Above Teddy's Florist, Negaunee MI 49866
906-475-4464

ISHPEMING

11 Paul's Jewelry & Gifts
209 South Main Street, Ishpeming MI 49849
Some antiques.

12 Just Browsing
206 Cleveland Avenue, Ishpeming MI 29849
906-485-6449

MICHIGAMME

13 Olde Millstream Antiques
Mill & Main Streets, P.O. Box 231, Michigamme MI 49861
906-323-0023
June. to Sept.: Tues. to Sun. 11 to 5; Oct. & Nov. weekends only; closed Dec. to May.
General line of antiques & collectibles.

14 The Red Door
HCR1 Box 2130, U.S. Highway 41, Michigamme MI 49861
906-323-6143

12.10 Iron County

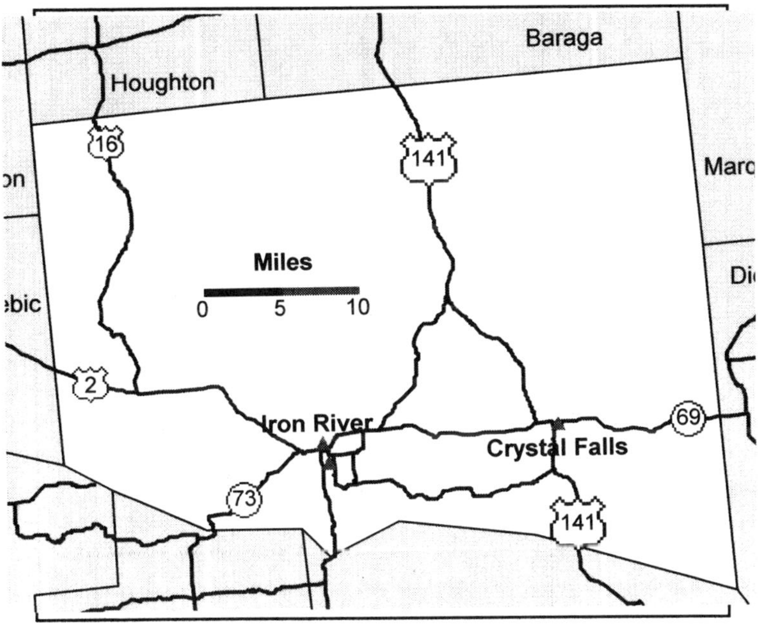

CRYSTAL FALLS

1 Bargain Barn Antiques
1340 West U.S. 2, P.O. Box 3, Crystal Falls MI 49920
906-875-3381

2 Oldies But Goodies
801 Crystal Ave. (U.S. Highway 2 West), Crystal Falls MI 49920 906-875-6294

3 Old Tradition Shop
612 Michigan Avenue, Crystal Falls MI 49920
906-875-4214

4 Junktion Antiques & Collectibles
1339 South U.S. 2, Crystal Falls MI 49920
906-875-4699

IRON RIVER

5 Ethel Joyce Turbessi at the Antique Cottage
545 West Ice Lake Road, Iron River MI 49935
906-265-9753 or 906-265-2756

12.11 Baraga County

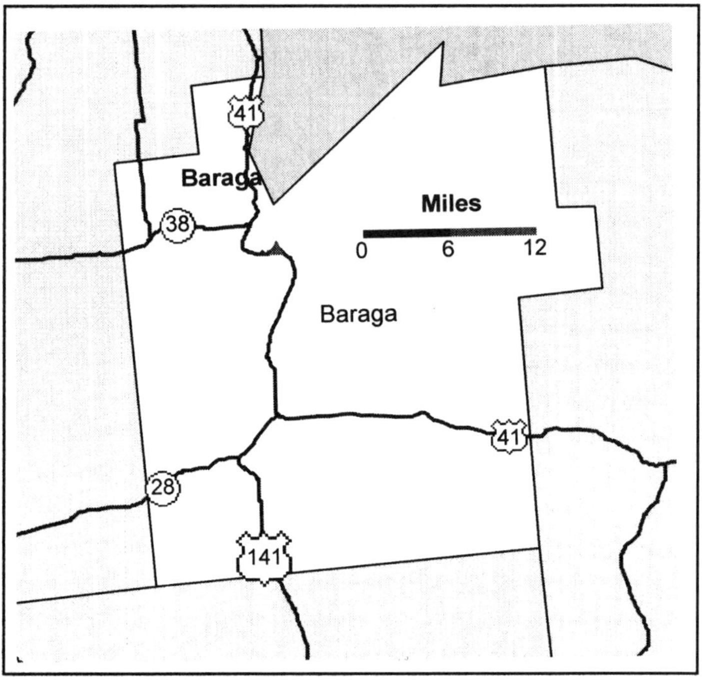

BARAGA

1 The Country Shop
Rte. 1 Box 66, Baraga MI 49908
906-353-7230
By chance.

12.12 Houghton County

(Map on following page.)

CHASSELL

1 Eagle Shop
148 N. Wilson Drive (U.S. 41), Chassell MI 49916
906-523-4423

Houghton County:

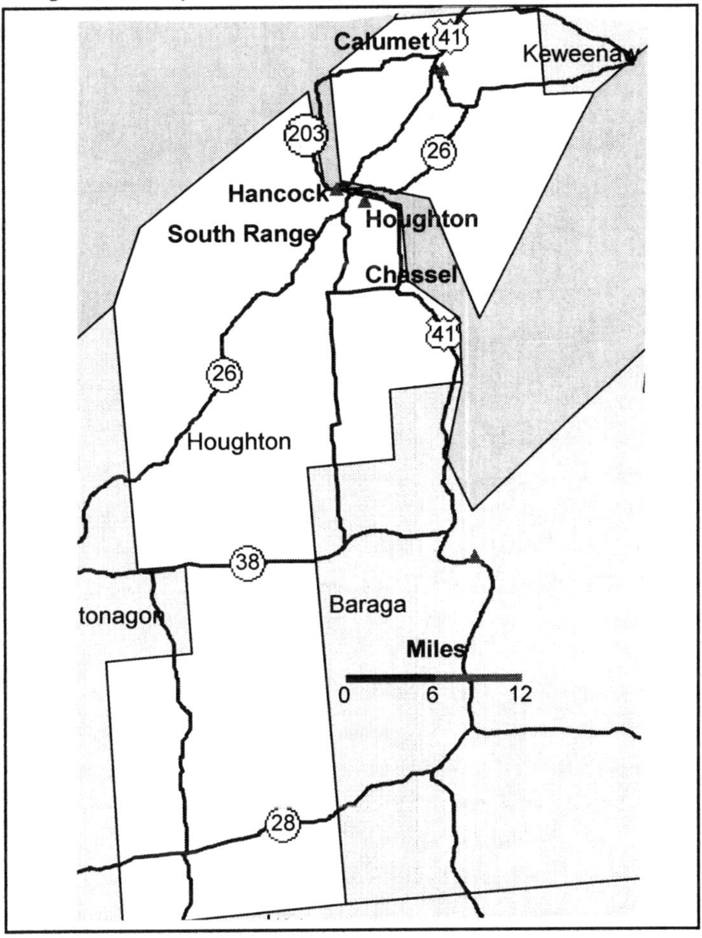

2 Grandma's Antiques
300 Wilson Memorial Drive (U.S. 41), Chassell MI 49916
No telephone listed.

3 Porch Antiques
447 U.S. 41, P.O. Box 174, Chassell MI 49916
906-523-4819

HANCOCK

4 Northwoods Trading Post
120 Quincy, Hancock MI 49930
906-482-5210 Fax: 906-482-5228

HOUGHTON

5 Main Street Antiques
6 Main Street, Houghton MI 49931
906-482-0790; 906-482-4113

SOUTH RANGE

6 Etc. Etc.
42 Tri Mountain Road (M-26), P.O. Box 265, South Range MI 49963
906-482-9171

CALUMET

7 Copper World
101 Fifth Street, Calumet MI 49913
906-337-4016
New and old copper items.

8 Upscale Antiques
215 6th Street, Calumet MI 49913
906-337-5500

9 The Rose & The Thorn
451 Pine, Calumet MI 49913
906-337-1717
Ceramics & gifts 1st floor, some antiques in basement.

10 J. Thiel & Associates
436 6th Street, Calumet MI 49913
906-337-1780

11 Antiquities
1156 Calumet Avenue (Highway 41), Calumet MI 49913
906-337-5573

12.13 Keweenaw County

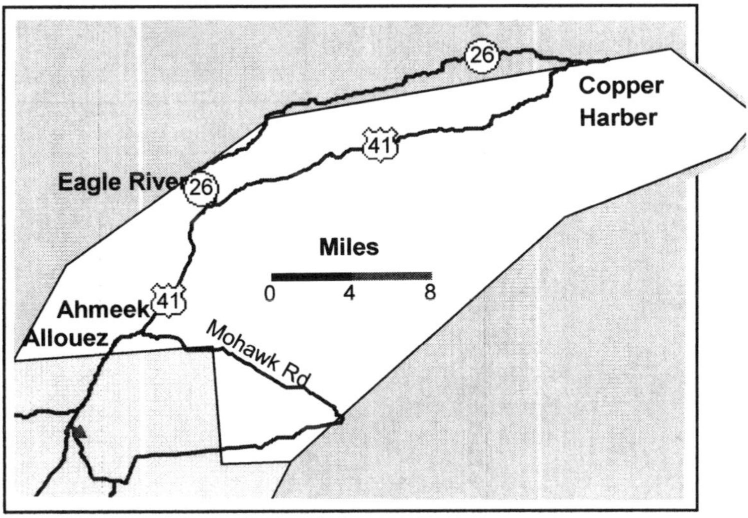

AHMEEK

1 True North Antiques
P.O. Box 141, Ahmeek MI 49901
906-337-1961

ALLOUEZ

2 The Last Place on Earth
U.S. 41, Box 76, Allouez MI 49805
906-337-1014
May 1 to Oct. 15

EAGLE RIVER

3 Leapfrog Collectibles
HCI Box 644, Eagle River MI 49950
906-337-6712

COPPER HARBOR

4 Johnson's
U.S. 41 & MI 26, Copper Harbor MI 49918

5 Harbor Shop
745 MI Highway 26, Copper Harbor MI 49918

12.14 Gogebic County

Gogebic & Ontonagon Counties:

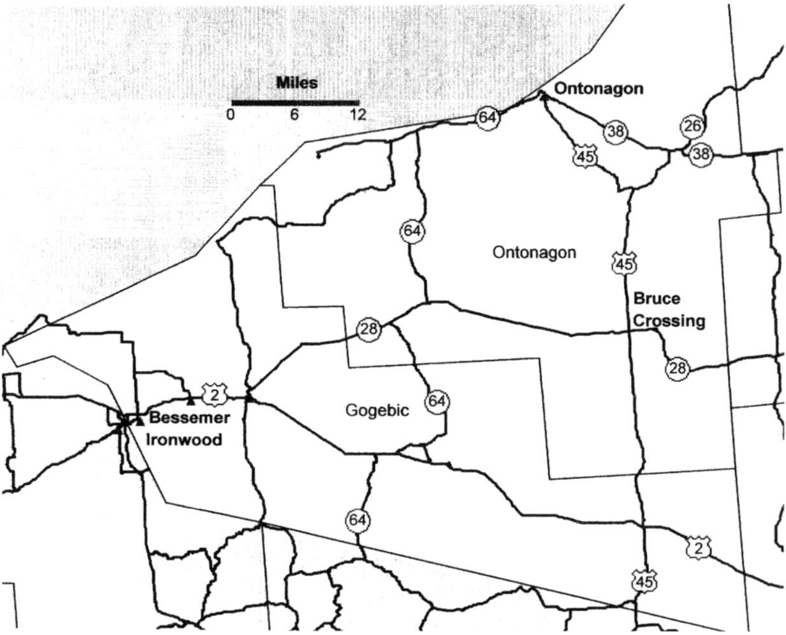

IRONWOOD

1 The Depot Antiques
318 Lake Street, Ironwood MI 49938
906-932-0900

2 Doreen's Antiques
313 Lake Street, Ironwood MI 49938
906-932-4310

3 The Carriage House Antiques
303 South Lowell, Ironwood MI 49938
906-932-0766; 906-932-2710 res.

4 Old Country Store
1445 East Cloverland Drive, Ironwood MI 49938
906-932-2771

Ironwood:

5 Dan's Antique Mall
111 East Aurora St., Ironwood MI 49938
906-932-5002
Daily 10 to 5
Downtown, on U.S. Business 2, the main street.
General line of antiques.

12.15 Ontonagon County

(Map in preceding section.)

BRUCE CROSSING

1 Northern Lights Antiques & Artisans
575 Himanka Hill Road, H.C. 1 Box 21, Bruce Crossing MI 49912 906-827-3933

ONTONAGON

2 Heritage Antique Mall
233 River Street, Ontonagon MI 49953 906-884-4747

INDEX OF DEALER SPECIALTIES

WISCONSIN
• Milwaukee
IOWA
• Chicago
ILLINOIS

SELECTED ANTIQUE SHOWS & MARKETS IN MICHIGAN

ALLEGAN ANTIQUE MARKET:
Allegan County Fairgrounds, Allegan.
Last Sunday of the month, April through September.
www.allegananantiques.com
616-453-8780 or 616-735-3333

ANN ARBOR ANTIQUES MARKET:
5055 Ann Arbor - Saline Road, I-94 Exit 175 then south three miles.
Generally Sunday the third weekend of the month, April through October.
850-984-0122

ANTIQUE SHOW AT THE BARRY EXPO CENTER:
M-37 (Broadmore Avenue) Middleville, twenty minutes south of Grand Rapids' 28th Street.
Spring and Fall Shows in March and November.
616-735-3333

CENTERVILLE ANTIQUE MARKET:
The Fairgrounds, M-86 East.
Second Sunday of the month, June through October, but no show in Sept. First Sunday in May.
www.antiquemarkets.com
773-227-4464

GRAND RAPIDS ROTARY EAST ANTIQUE FAIR & SALE:
East Grand Rapids high School.
Fri. & Sat. early April; (date varies, call for information).
773-227-4464

LUDINGTON AREA ANTIQUES EXPOSITION:
West Shore Community College, 300 N. Stiles Road, Scottsville.
616-845-7414 or 616-845-0460
Summer weekends; Fall Festival; Winter Fun Fest; call for dates.

MICHIGAN ANTIQUE FESTIVALS:
Midland Fairgrounds, U.S. 10 at Eastman Avenue
June, July, and September; call for dates.
517-687-9001